AGRICULTURE, FORAGING AND WILDLIFE RESOURCE USE IN AFRICA

AGRICULTURE, FORAGING AND WILDLIFE RESOURCE USE IN AFRICA

CULTURAL AND POLITICAL DYNAMICS IN THE ZAMBEZI VALLEY

RICHARD HASLER

KEGAN PAUL INTERNATIONAL
LONDON AND NEW YORK

First published in 1996 by
Kegan Paul International
UK: P.O. Box 256, London WC1B 3SW, England
Tel: (0171) 580 5511 Fax: (0171) 436 0899
E-mail: books@keganpau.demon.co.uk
Internet: http://www.demon.co.uk/keganpaul/
USA: 562 West 113th Street, New York, NY 10025, USA
Tel: (212) 666 1000 Fax: (212) 316 3100

Distributed by

John Wiley & Sons Ltd
Southern Cross Trading Estate
1 Oldlands Way, Bognor Regis
West Sussex, PO22 9SA, England
Tel: (01234) 779 777 Fax: (01234) 820 250

Columbia University Press
562 West 113th Street
New York, NY 10025, USA
Tel: (212) 666 1000 Fax: (212) 316 3100

© Richard Hasler 1996

Set in 11 on 12½ pt Baskerville
by Intype, London

Printed in Great Britain by
TJ Press, Padstow, Cornwall

All rights reserved. No part of this book may be reprinted
or reproduced or utilized in any form or by any electronic,
mechanical or other means, now known or hereafter invented,
including photocopying and recording, or in any information
storage or retrieval system, without permission in writing
from the publishers.

British Library Cataloguing in Publication Data

Hasler, Richard
  Agriculture, Foraging and Wildlife
  Resource Use in Africa: Cultural and
  Political Dynamics in the Zambezi Valley
  I. Title
  333.9509679

  ISBN 0-7103-0515-x

Library of Congress Cataloging-in-Publication Data

Hasler, R.
    Agriculture, foraging and wildlife resource use in Africa
  cultural and political dynamics in the Zambezi Valley/Richard
  Hasler.
    220 pp. 19.5 cm.
    Includes bibliographical references (p. 200) and index.
    ISBN 0-7103-0515-X
    1. CAMPFIRE (Program) 2. Wildlife management – Zimbabwe.
  3. Wildlife management – Zambezi River Valley. 4. Commons – Zimbabwe.
  5. Commons – Zambezi River Valley. 6. Agriculture – Zimbabwe.
  7. Agriculture – Zambezi River Valley. I. Title.
  SK575.Z55H36 1995
  333.95.'9'096891 – dc20   95-14863

DEDICATED TO THE MEMORY OF
THE LATE MR. MTAMAWO

Contents

Preface		xi
Acknowledgements		xiii
1	Introduction	1
2	An Introduction to Chapoto Ward (Kanyemba)	40
3	Agriculture and Foraging in Competition with Wildlife	66
4	The Cultural and Political Dynamics of Wildlife Resource Use in Chapoto Ward	111
5	Coping with Wildlife	129
6	Gardeners of Elephants: Competing Bundles of Rights to Wildlife	155
7	Conclusion	186
References		200
Index		207

Illustrations

Maps

Map 1	Zimbabwe	2
Map 2	Chapoto Ward	35
Map 3	Local scenes in Chapoto ward	46

Figures

2.1 Abbreviated genealogy of the spirit world and chieftainship of the VaChiKunda of Chapoto Ward 62

4.1 Diagrammatic summary of the political and cultural dynamics of wildlife resource use in Chapoto Ward 112

Plates   *between pages 146 and 147*

1. Mvura *dimba* on the banks of Mwanzamtanda River
2. Close-up of *dimba* cultivation showing round holes in which maize is grown
3. Close-up of *masawo*, an important edible fruit from the bush
4. A well-maintained homestead belonging to a VaChiKunda cotton-grower
5. A Mvura dwelling-place, showing pyramid-like chicken coop (right foreground) and thorn-bush fence (behind boy) to keep out animals
6. Mr. Samson Dumba, a VaChiKunda cotton-grower, posing with gun
7. Mvura 'portable granary' (*chibande*) made from woven bark, and a clay pot inside a grass enclosure

8. The late Mr. Mtamawo (Mvura) with part of his family
9. A *dara*, a raised sleeping-platform for guarding field at night
10. Ingenious suspended chicken coop, with spiked deterrents for predators and thorns underneath
11. Mr. Bandera with bark rope tied to tins to startle animals
12. A buffalo, the safari hunter's dangerous prize
13. Spirit medium (in black hat) with cooking oil outside chief's store during a drought relief distribution of maize
14. A safari operator (left) with two Spanish clients determined to hunt buffalo

Preface

Zimbabwe is undertaking an experiment in the sustainable use of wildlife for the benefit of local communities. The Communal Areas Management Program for Indigenous Resources (CAMPFIRE) aims to devolve control and benefits from hitherto state-controlled wildlife through locally based wildlife utilization common property regimes.

This study is the documentation and analysis of anthropological fieldwork spent among the VaChiKunda and Mvura of Chapoto ward. The focus of the research is the cultural and political dynamics associated with wildlife resource use relevant to the CAMPFIRE program. Chapoto ward is a test case for the program, because it has ecological characteristics which suggest that wildlife utilization could become a sustainable alternative means of land usage.

Conflicting and ambiguous rights and vested interests in natural resources emanating from ward, district, national and global levels result in multiple jurisdictions concerning use, ownership, access to or control of wildlife. This militates against the success of locally based common property wildlife utilization regimes as envisaged by CAMPFIRE. The cultural and political dynamics of wildlife resource use, which buttress these vested interests and ambiguous rights, include historical factors, global factors, national policy, system of local government, ethnicity, chieftainship, indigenous knowledge, marriage arrangements, micropolitics, ancestral belief systems, settlement patterns, household cluster economics and decision-making, and competing land-use strategies including foraging, hunting, and cotton and maize production.

The social heterogeneity of Chapoto ward and the differentiation of vested interests and rights in resources makes us question the analytic potential of common property theory for sustainable wildlife utilization. The CAMPFIRE emphasis on locally based communal property regimes may be misplaced because of the multiple levels and jurisdictions involved. Local bundles of rights in wildlife include those associated with the safari operator, Department of National Parks and Wild Life Management, local government, district council, ancestral spirits, chief, illegal hunters, foragers, agriculturalists, the wildlife committee, and others. It is argued that a multi-tiered co-management regime may be analytically more appropriate in dealing with the complexity of levels and jurisdictions involved. Such a regime would entail clarification and articulation of these various rights. In this regard, appropriate institutional arrangements for managing wildlife at local level are suggested.

Acknowledgements

This study was conducted while I was employed as a Research Fellow in the Center for Applied Social Sciences (CASS) at the University of Zimbabwe. The Research Fellowship was funded by a joint Ford Foundation/IDRC grant as part of a broader project in socio-economic issues important for natural resource management in Zimbabwe's communal areas. I received additional support in the form of a Rockefeller Sub-Saharan Africa Dissertation Internship Award. I would like to express my sincere thanks for this generous support.

My job in CASS was a component of a larger research endeavor concerning the identification, evaluation, monitoring and implementation of the Communal Areas Management Program for Indigenous Resources (CAMPFIRE). Four agencies were involved in this collaborative research agenda. Ecological and economic research was mainly conducted by the World Wide Fund for Nature (WWF) and the Department of National Parks and Wild Life Management (DNPWLM). Socio-economic research was mainly conducted by CASS, and implementational issues were mainly addressed by the Zimbabwe Trust (ZimTrust) and DNPWLM.

Sincere thanks go to the chairperson of my doctoral committee, Professor William Derman of the Anthropology Department, Michigan State University and to my director, Professor Marshall Murphree of CASS, University of Zimbabwe. I am indebted to Professor Murphree for identifying the ward as a suitable research site and offering assistance, support and feedback. I would like to thank Professor Derman for visiting me while I was in the field and for assisting in the development of the study in all its stages by facilitating, and where necessary, challenging my ideas and helping me to overcome obstacles to the completion of this work. I also would like to acknowledge the support of my other committee members, namely, Professor Charles Cleland, Professor John Hinnant of the Anthropology Department and Professor David Campbell of the Geography Department, all at Michigan State University. Sincere thanks to you all.

Thanks also to Dr. Calvin Nhira, Research Fellow, CASS, University of Zimbabwe, who introduced me to the ward in October 1989. I would like to acknowledge that both Calvin Nhira and Dr. Charles Cutshall, who was then a senior lecturer in CASS, had conducted important survey research in the ward prior to this fieldwork. In addition, Mr. Alistair Buchan, a research fellow with the WWF, conducted an ecological resource survey while I was in the field. I am indebted to all these colleagues, whose work I have drawn on, for laying the groundwork for this study.

Thank you to the former District Administrator for Guruve district, Mr. T. Maveneke, for giving permission to do the research. Thanks also to Chief Chapoto and to the ward councillor, Mr. Zekiel Kanyemba, for allowing me to reside in the ward. I am particularly indebted to my chief research assistants, Mr. Matthew Chidota Kaputi and Mr. Prosper Kuyeri. Together we walked and talked many hours of Zambezi time in sweltering heat.

I am also indebted to all those people in the ward who facilitated my stay, including Headman Mr. Mugonapanja and his family, Mr. Dumba and his family, who always offered me food and drink, Mr. Charuma, the headmaster, Mr. Marisa, the nurse, and the many others who spent time with me and/or my assistants discussing issues. I would also like to thank the late Mr. Mtamawo and Mr. Eria, Mr. Isaac, Mr. Kaberi and Mr. Chiyambo for their time. There are so many others that I should mention but space does not allow me to mention them by name. Thank you to all Chapoto ward residents.

I am indebted to Mr. Drummond and Mr. Mavi of the Botanical Gardens in Harare for the identification of all the plants listed in the study. I take full responsibility for any errors as the specimens that I brought were not the best.

Last but not least I would like to thank my wife, Andrea Rother, who participated by conducting research amongst women and who edited the study. Both her intellectual and practical contributions in the field and during write-up enabled the book to take form. She shared in the adventures, the revelations and the excitement of fieldwork. Not least of her achievements was the manner in which she was able to cater for our infant daughter in the sometimes rugged conditions associated with the Zambezi Valley.

CHAPTER 1
Introduction

The important context of culture, history, economics and politics is the broad backdrop against which a Zimbabwean natural resource management program entitled the Communal Areas Management Program For Indigenous Resources (CAMPFIRE) is being played out. This program fosters a sense of proprietorship for the sustainable use of wildlife resources at the local level. It is part of a government-sponsored attempt at decentralization of the responsibility and benefits of wildlife through locally based wildlife utilization communal property regimes. The Chapoto ward (also known as Kanyemba) material discussed in this case-study is central to the success or failure of CAMPFIRE, because along with its implementational dimensions, it raises a set of problems in the application of common property analysis. The broader political and economic context within which CAMPFIRE is embedded, as well as the unique qualities of the ward under investigation, are both intimately intertwined in the establishment of the multiple jurisdictions concerning the use and control of the wildlife resource. An appreciation of the circumstances under which these rights are expressed (and accommodated) is vital for understanding what kind of property regime is appropriate for wildlife.

The focus of this study is on how people in a remote and isolated part of the Zimbabwean Zambezi Valley (see Maps 1–3) organize themselves and are organized in relation to wildlife and other natural resources. This focus raises the general question of the efficacy of communal property regimes in situations where there is a heterogenous mix of interests and structures involved in the control, use and management of resources.

An important dimension of the study is how rights to the use and control of resources have changed over time, especially in the last 100 years. This includes a discussion of the inhabitants' socio-cultural means of maintenance, as well as the methods of organiz-

AGRICULTURE, FORAGING AND WILDLIFE RESOURCE USE IN AFRICA

Zimbabwe

Map 1   Map of Zimbabwe
Source: J. Herbst *State Politics in Zimbabwe* (Harare: University of Zimbabwe Press, 1990).

ing themselves in relation to the environment and to political and economic forces. Dynamic processes of social organization, whose key elements are centred in the domains of culture, politics and economics, provide the raw material of the study. Knowledge of these dynamics is vital for an understanding of natural resource use in the area, because this enables understanding of the vested interests in resources and the diverse property rights associated with competing land-use strategies.

Before describing and analysing the case-study material, we need to reflect why our focus is on the management and use of wildlife resources, rather than on other resources. We also need to scrutinize assumptions ensconced in wildlife utilization programes such as CAMPFIRE. A discussion of these issues precedes and supports the theoretical framework to this study which centers on a discussion of common property theory.

The scrutiny of CAMPFIRE in this study is not meant to cripple the program but to strengthen it. It should be stated from the outset that the researcher generally supports the idea of the local utilization of wildlife resources. The case-study has enabled the researcher to evaluate the program, based on the Chapoto ward experience between 1989 and 1991. This learning process provokes thought about the program and challenges some of its assumptions.

From the outset it must be stated that the focus on wildlife is in a sense artificial, as a discussion of this resource is intricately intertwined with the use and control of other resources. Such resources include water, soil, mineral and oil deposits, forests and grasslands. At present in Zimbabwe, different agencies are responsible for different resources. Thus, though wildlife includes both fauna and flora, the Department of National Parks and Wild Life Management (DNPWLM) has responsibility for the national parks and wildlife estates. The Forestry Commission is responsible for designated forest areas. Though the DNPWLM is attempting to decentralize aspects of their control and use of the wildlife resource, other potentially valuable resources, such as oil deposits or uranium or water resources, fall under the jurisdiction of other central authorities, and local communities have little authority in these matters. The implication of this is that all sorts of contradictions in terms of property rights and access may emerge in the future, if, for instance, control of one resource is successfully decentralized whilst other interdependent resources are controlled from the center.

The category 'wildlife' is, itself, problematic in that the term is imbued with specific cultural connotations and values. It may be argued that in Europe both the concept and the category were historically associated with the privileged classes (Gilbert and Dodds 1987: 2). The notion of wildlife and national parks in the African context has been historically associated with colonialism. Latterly, tourist game viewing provides an example of a specific cultural value attached to wildlife. It is important to note that such values are not universal and that both the concept and the category of 'wildlife' may be instrumentalized by vested interests in the resource. Let us now consider the central assumptions concerning sustainability and rationality which support the CAMPFIRE project.

Sustainability

The key word for describing the kinds of resource management hoped for in the future is 'sustainable' (World Watch 1990: 12). The word is applied loosely and the idea itself is debatable. Broadly, the term can be used to describe the homeostasis of a system despite major disturbances or it can be used to prescribe a goal for how a system can reach a state of equilibrium through time. Contradictions between ecological, social and economic sustainability pose problems for analysts. Despite these different usages, the term is often used in general to describe a state in contrast to the present unsatisfactory and unbalanced state of environmental affairs on a global level. There is a danger that this term prescribes a utopian and unrealistic situation in which the world arrives at a point of sustainability and thereby ceases to be in dynamic flux and tension, which, one could argue, has characterized the exploitation and evolution of global resources (particularly wildlife) throughout history.

It is argued that the goal of 'sustainability' of resources should be qualified by the concerns of human welfare (Redclift 1987). As Chambers has said, 'the environment and development are means, not ends in themselves. The environment and development are for people not people for environment and development' (1986: 7). A large proportion of the world's population is not concerned about the sustainability of many global resources, such as the ozone layer or the rhino, except insofar as these are perceived to impinge on their immediate livelihoods. In a world that is rapidly changing, many societies are concerned about short-term maintenance through crises such as wars, droughts and famines. In such cases, they and their children may not be around to witness the possibility of a sustainable world in the future. This is not to say that such people in crisis situations do not think of the future, but rather to say that sustainable practices may often be adhered to because they enable survival. Unsustainable practices, which lead, for example, to deforestation, overgrazing, and soil erosion, may indeed also be adopted because they enable short-term goals. The notion of 'sustainable practices' raises a question of reference: sustainable for whom and in connection with what? Are such practices ecologically, socially or economically sustainable or unsustainable? What contradictions arise between different domains of sustainability? For instance, many ecologically sustainable practices (such as reforestation) may not be socially sustainable. Leonard argues that the real conflict is 'often less between what is good for the environment and what is good for the poor than between what is good for the poor of today and the poor of tomorrow' (1989: 4–5). Simultaneously he states that 'in many marginal rural areas growing numbers of poor people inevitably have to degrade the environment a little more each day just to make ends meet' (ibid. 5).[1] Hence the need for 'sustainable development'.

Arnold claims that 'sustainable development is not yet a theory or even an approach but more an evolving vision representing the coming together of a variety of different concerns, disciplines and political pressures' (1989: 21). Its essence is captured in G. H. Brundtland's report (1987) entitled *Our Common Future: From One Earth to One World*, which suggests that sustainable development should 'ensure that it meet the needs of the present without compromising the ability of future generations to meet their own needs' (ibid. 21). The problem is often conceived in economic terms 'minimizing regrets rather than maximizing output' (Goodland 1988: 8) or 'the total stock of all forms of wealth that must not be depleted' (Pearce 1989: 17).

As Redclift points out, 'economists like Pearce argue that it is possible to consider the environment within the governing economic paradigm and that the field of bio-economics has already made substantial progress' while 'the alternative view [in economics] entails the abandonment of a unitary economic paradigm' (1987: 37). This view is expressed by Noorgaard (1985), who has

---

1. Leonard proposes a number of strategies which address poverty and environmental degradation simultaneously (1989: 33).

suggested that 'neo-classical economics is incapable of fully incorporating environmental considerations into its methodology without what amounts to a paradigm shift' away from 'the atomistic-mechanical world view' of neo-classical economics (Redclift 1987: 38). Instead of being interested in the economist's central question about how scarce goods can best be allocated, Noorgaard is interested in determining whether resources are scarce from how they are allocated.

Despite such discussions about appropriate paradigms, the central ideas behind the concept of sustainable development appear to be culturally bound within the domain of rationalist western economic theory. As Redclift has pointed out, 'economists are interested in scarcity as the underlying reality behind human choice. Environmentalists are concerned that economic growth is the reality which makes human choice less and less possible under conditions of scarcity' (ibid.).

The domain of rationalist western economic theory assumes that individuals will maximize their economic benefits. A broader application of this is held by CAMPFIRE, which assumes that economic benefits in the form of community projects and/or household dividends will tend to foster individuals and communities as proprietors of the ecological resource base. A central problem is that the assumptions that are part of western economic theory are not always accurate for other cultural settings. Assumptions about maximizing economic benefits need to be tested in the culture and life-style of the people concerned. From the point of view of my research context, foragers and agriculturalists differed widely on what constitutes maximizing of benefits. For example, some of the more marginalized semi-foragers in my research context value their own traditional medicine above western medicine and cannot afford to send their children to school. Proposed community projects, suggested by more affluent agriculturalists, for upgrading the clinic or school, therefore did not appeal to them.

In Chambers' view,

> sustainable development is a 'first' concept, the poor are largely concerned with their immediate livelihoods; it is the enlightened rich who give priority to sustainability... The perspective of the poor is at variance with that of most economists and biologists, placing the immediate satisfaction of needs and the avoidance of risk before sustainability or higher productivity. (1986: 35)

'Sustainable development' certainly appears to be the terminology of managers and is not as yet the terminology of the managed. In regard to wildlife utilization in my research context, it is a concept that has arisen from the top and is filtering down rather than being one that has emerged unsolicited at the grass roots.

Chambers' (1986) 'sustainable livelihood thinking' is an example of an attempt to incorporate the perspective of the poor in the deliberations about the environment and development, by focusing on the relevance of these for people's better livelihood. An important question raised about this by Redclift is: 'for sustainable development to become a reality it is necessary for the livelihoods of the poor to be given priority, but how can this priority be pursued at the local level while the effects of international development systematically marginalizes them?' (1987: 36).

'Rationality'

Rationality refers to the conditions of reason (Habermas 1984) which are the contexts in which reasoning takes place. The background context of communicative action, what Habermas refers to as the 'lifeworld', is a set of ideas and concepts which are not amenable to the empirical analytical sciences but should be approached hermeneutically (i.e. through studying the interpretations of the subjective meaning actors give to social reality). According to Habermas, reflection upon the conditions of reason in the reconstruction of theory, history and the analysis of society can lead to a kind of intellectual emancipation. Amongst other things, a discussion of rationality is important in applied work because scientific ideas upon which people act are the product of a certain time and culture, and reflect the political and economic forces which predominate. Scientific ideas often do not address the subjective world of actors in which communication takes place. Furthermore, as Freeman has pointed out in his critique of conventional natural resource management science,

> The stark reality is that, over time, nearly all current scientific knowledge will be replaced by new knowledge; the later knowledge being found in turn to be imperfect. Not only are current scientific facts not the truth, science is unable to say what form the truth if discovered will take. The clearest induction from the history of science is that

science is always mistaken ... so then we have no reasonable alternative but to suppose that much or all of what we vaunt as scientific knowledge is itself presumably wrong. (1989: 92).

This is not mentioned as a form of attack on programs such as CAMPFIRE, but rather to point out the necessity of humility and self-criticism within disciplines, which an analysis of rationality may offer.

An important trend that follows the goal of 'sustainability' is the idea that people should be actively involved in conserving, protecting and exploiting resources in a rational manner. The underlying assumption here is that rational resource management techniques are identifiable through interdisciplinary research programs designed to this end. The problem is that the conditions of reason of program designers and planners may differ radically in themselves depending on discipline (e.g. ecology and anthropology), theoretical framework (e.g. stressing 'systems' versus stressing 'process' and/or 'conflict') and methodology (e.g. soft versus hard approaches). These reasoning processes are seldom those embraced by the various segments that constitute what academics refer to as 'local people'. There appears to be little or no homogeneity of rationalities among local people or planners when it comes to discussing the environment. Thompson, for instance, in reference to the cultural construction of nature and the natural destruction of culture, discusses 'the clash of plural rationalities each using impeccable logic to derive different conclusions (solution definitions) from different premises (problem definitions)' (Thompson 1986: 2). For instance, different ecological zones in the African context may partially account for differences in marriage arrangements (e.g. bridewealth and brideservice) influenced by the presence or absence of cattle, which in turn is influenced by the presence or absence of trypanosomiasis. These marriage arrangements in turn may strongly influence attitudes towards livestock which in turn may influence the contexts and conditions of reasoning about the benefits and liabilities of wildlife (the host animals for tsetse fly).

When embarking upon the present research, it was clear that colleagues and participants who advocated CAMPFIRE, including myself, went through an entirely different thought process from local people. Residents stated that wildlife should be wiped out in their area, so that tsetse fly could be eradicated and they could use cattle to plough their fields. They would then not have to spend so much time on crop protection from crop-raiding animals. Wildlife ecologists in Zimbabwe have usefully pointed out the economic and ecological rationale of managing wildlife as a renewable resource on marginal land where cattle ranching and dry-land cropping alone are likely to have very poor yields (Taylor and Martin 1983; Child 1984; Martin 1986), but local communities do not respond to economic and ecological argumentation in a vacuum. As has been pointed out, local people may be concerned about a number of contextual, political or cultural factors which may color their perceptions as to the best courses of action.

It is this picture of the local context which anthropologists study and which may helpfully locate the larger plans envisaged by resource managers and ecologists amongst the perceptions, culture, history and political and economic arrangements of the people affected. It is well know that cattle do not merely have economic or ecological significance in isolation from the social meanings attached to them. For instance, cattle may be a source of prestige, a means of providing bridewealth, or a means of ploughing one's fields. Large African mammalian wildlife, alienated through protectionism, also has positive and negative social meanings. Wildlife may be perceived as a menace, a threat to one's existence, destroying one's crops, raiding one's livestock, or killing and injuring one's friends and relatives. Wildlife may also pervasively influence such decisions as the design of granaries, the design of sleeping platforms in one's field, where one can safely store one's produce and what time the children leave for school in the morning. On the other hand, wildlife also has both material and symbolic positive value. For example, its relevance in terms of ancestral belief systems, or the secret and illegal hunting opportunities offered.

Theoretical Orientations Regarding the Study of People and Wildlife

It may be argued that very little work has been done specifically on the anthropological aspects of 'wildlife management' as it is conceived in western thought. However, the notion of holism in the anthropological method refutes this idea. Ethnographies are accounts of ways of life. The use, management, symbolism and cultural significance of animals and plants are integrated into countless chapters in ethnographies focusing on issues other than wildlife management. Therefore, anthropology is no stranger to the subject and the anthropological lens has enlightened many a wildlife manager (Gilbert and Dodds 1987).

Marks 1984, *The Imperial Lion*, provides a cultural ecological analysis of an indigenous hunting system amongst the Valley Bisa in Zambia. It is not concerned only with this analysis, as it also shows how localized wildlife resources in Africa have been exploited by outsiders (e.g. urban dwellers, the north). The lineage-based management systems of the Valley Bisa are the subject of an earlier study (Marks 1976), entitled *Large Mammals and a Brave People: Subsistence Hunters in Zambia*. Marks points out that the lineage-based system was sanctioned by ritual process and collective controls. He claims that as long as such rural societies remain relatively isolated, with low human densities and technologies adequate to meet local demand, 'their environmental resources were usually adequate' (Marks 1984: 104). However, with the relaxation of previous restraints, collectivist controls over resources were subverted rapidly and opportunities for private gain subverted the 'traditional wildlife resource processes'. The impact of commerce and state-sponsored initiatives contributed to the situation where 'wildlife is increasingly mined [i.e. depleted] rather than harvested'.

Marks' work straddles two theoretical orientations that are significant for the present study. The first orientation is that of micro-level systems' analysis. Valley Bisa hunting constituted a system which had feedback mechanisms maintaining the status quo. This systems' orientation features in the writing of many cultural ecologists (see, for instance, Rappaport 1984). It often includes the idea that traditional societies, and particularly 'hunter-gatherers', have developed cultural institutions and practices designed to allow them to achieve equilibrium with their environment. The second orientation is the broader political and economic processes within which the micro-level system changes or breaks down. In terms of this orientation, tragedies of the commons (Hardin 1968) are said to be characteristic of 'state systems in which desire for profit or individual aggrandizement motivate uncontrolled exploitation' (McCay and Acheson 1987: 93).

In reference to the first orientation, despite the many insights provided by those cultural ecologists who stressed equilibrium, homeostasis and conservation in traditional society, the notion that traditional societies are somehow innately equilibrious, homeostatic and conservationist can be problematic. Apart from the difficulties of identifying what constitutes 'traditional' society in a changing world, 'equilibrium' models in anthropology (and specifically cultural ecology) have been severely and consistently criticized for being ahistorical, ignoring wider political and economic issues, tautological, normative, and failing to deal with conflict or change.

Marks attempts to redress the inadequacies of the first orientation by including political and economic factors in the wider world. In this regard it is appropriate to refer to the work of Abel and Blaikie (1986) who, for purposes of this study, represent the field of political ecology. They present an analysis of the Luangwa National Parks in the context and history of the Zambian political economy. In doing so they identify social groups who compete for the use of wildlife resources. These include subsistence hunters, commercial poachers, wildlife conservationists, tourists, politicians, the bureaucratic bourgeoisie and safari hunters. Their work reinforces the view that it is not adequate to look at local communities in isolation from the historical and contextual factors which impinge on their ways of life. National parks are edifices of what is now considered to be inappropriate management strategies from the colonial past (see Graham 1973) and many people, including some of those discussed in this study, have been dispossessed of their land and resources, when the latter were declared protected areas by the state.

Abel and Blaikie point out, in connection with national parks, that the 'use of natural resources at a particular place and time is the outcome of conflicting groups of people with different aims. Usually there is no absolute dominance by one group so there are commonly a number of different ways of using resources at the same place and time' (1986: 1). They also make an important point that official definitions and statements concerning resources are often seen as 'no more than normative statements by one particular interest group' (ibid.).

In comparing the approaches from cultural ecology and political ecology, as voiced by Abel and Blaikie, an apt illustration of such normative definitions might be that ward boundaries (as defined by the Zimbabwean state) may conflict with cultural land boundaries (defined by ancestral spirits through their mediums). Neo-functionalist, equilibrium-oriented cultural ecologists may be interested in assessing the role of the territorial/ancestor cults in the management of resources from a micro-system perspective.

(Vayda and McCay 1977). As Marks, and Abel and Blaikie point out in their work, it is not sufficient to do this, because one must also consider the wider political and economic influences (e.g. colonialism, land dispossession) and particularly the various vested interests in the resource. In terms of this study these would include the vested interests in national parks and protected areas.

If one is of the opinion that traditional forms of common property resource management may have potential roles to play in natural resource management programmes such as CAMPFIRE, such potentials must be seen in the wider political context. Though much of the writing on the conservation and management of wildlife resources in the past has seen itself as being apolitical, it has not been recognized that it is intricately intertwined with the resolution of conflict over scarce resources and the vested interests in common property (see below for more on this). The resolution of this conflict requires an interdisciplinary and historical approach. This has been recognized by many ecologists and biologists (Parker 1978; Martin 1986; Bell 1988; Western 1982) who no longer simply attribute conflict of vested interests to mismanagement of the parks, but are now looking at the wider issues in the political economy which influence their work. Wildlife managers are realizing that the conventional methods of management are not working successfully and they are searching for creative ways of solving the many problems and issues that arise out of the interaction of humans and wildlife. This is the thrust of the practical initiatives emanating from wildlife biologists and ecologists. One such idea is that local people who live with all the problems associated with wildlife should directly benefit from these resources. If both responsibility and benefits from the wildlife resources accrue to the smallest accountable units, it is thought that this will enhance the sustainability of the resource whilst simultaneously providing much-needed benefits for local communities. Both theoretically and practically, the assumptions in this have yet to be rigorously tested. One major problem in much of the writing on the subject is that the exact mechanisms by which local communities are to benefit are seldom spelt out.

Common Property Theory and Bundles of Rights to Wildlife

The rights and jurisdictions involved in the use and management of wildlife need to be understood more broadly as property rights.

Property rights are a concern of such natural resource programs aimed at achieving sustainable development. Of special relevance is the question of the commons and common property resource management (McCay and Acheson 1987).

Definitions and Justificatory Theories

A review of common property literature needs to begin by briefly contextualizing the common property debate through looking at how scholars have conceived of property historically and how they have defended or opposed the property institutions of their time. This debate will lead us into a discussion of property issues relating to the current environmental and wildlife crises.

Macpherson (1978) makes the important point that the meaning of property is continually changing. As the meaning changes there is dispute over what it is and what it should be. Conceptions of property and property institutions respond to political, economic, cultural and ecological factors and this process of change involves moral controversy. Historically, there has been a need for justificatory theories of property, because these theories provide societies with the belief that their property arrangements are morally defensible. As Macpherson says,

> property is a right in the sense of an enforceable claim; . . . while its enforceability is what makes it a legal right, the enforceability itself depends on a society's belief that it is a moral right, property is not thought to be a right because it is an enforceable claim: it is an enforceable claim because it is thought to be a human right. This is simply another way of saying that any institution of property requires a justifying theory. (1978: 6)

Conceptions of property and property regimes, therefore, reflect moral and intellectual discourses associated with particular times. For instance, at the end of the seventeenth century, Locke for the first time argued for 'an individual right of unlimited appropriation' (ibid. 15). In Locke's view limited government was necessary to protect unlimited appropriation. His justification of property rights, according to Macpherson, is implied in the constitutions of the first modern capitalist states.

> He that is nourished under the Acorns he picked up under an Oak, or the Apples he gathered from the Trees in the Wood, has certainly appropriated them to himself... That *labour* put a distinction between them and common. That added something to them more than Nature, the common Mother of all, had done; and so they became his private right. And will any one say he had no right to those Acorns or Apples he thus appropriated, because he had not the consent of all Mankind to make them his? Was it a Robbery thus to assume to himself what belonged to all in Common? If such a consent as that was necessary, Man had starved, notwithstanding the Plenty God had given him. We see in *Commons*, which remain so by Compact, that 'tis the taking any part of what is common, and removing it out of the state Nature leaves it in, which *begins the Property*; without which the Common is of no use. And the taking of this or that part, does not depend on the express consent of all the Commoners. Thus the Grass my Horse has bit; the Turfs my servant has cut: and the Ore I have digg'd in any place where I have a right to them in common with others, become my *property*, without the assignation or consent of any body. The *labour* that was mine, removing them out of that common state they were in, hath *fixed* my *Property* in them. (Quoted in Macpherson 1978: 18)

Perhaps if labor only referred to personal labor and not to the labor of others, and if the commons was unlimited, Locke would have had a stronger moral position.

The importance of justificatory theories for property rights in the context of the political climate of the time is made evident in the writing of Rousseau. Towards the middle of the eighteenth century, Rousseau claimed that Locke's 'natural right' approach was totally unjustified because it deprived most men of any property at all. Rousseau's ideas on equality, life, liberty and property were greatly influential in the French Revolution. Unequal private property, in Rousseau's view, enslaved some men to others. Rousseau construed the evolution of property rights within his, now outmoded, unilineal evolutionary conception of the 'advance' from 'savagery' to 'civilization'. Despite the biases and limitations of his schema, Rousseau conceived that rights are not ahistorical nor static and therefore not 'natural'.

INTRODUCTION

Unlike Rousseau, Bentham, the English jurist, came forward with a new theory supporting modern unequal property rights. Bentham was also writing in the revolutionary eighteenth century, but adopted a mainstream position in regard to property. Discarding Locke's case for the natural right to unlimited appropriation, Bentham claimed that unequal property rights were utilitarian or functional since they led to the greatest happiness of the greatest number. His analysis is a cost-benefit one involving subsistence, abundance, equality, and security. In his view,

> if all property were equally divided, at fixed periods, the sure and certain consequence would be, that presently there would be no property to divide. All would shortly be destroyed. Those whom it was intended to favor, would not suffer less from the division than those at whose expense it was made. If the lot of the industrious were not better than the lot of the idle, there would be no longer any motives for industry. (Quoted in Macpherson 1989: 43)

In opposition to such views, which were considered as buttressing the dehumanizing influence of industrial capitalism, Marx, writing during the latter part of the nineteenth century, argued that the property relations of capitalism required the reduction of human beings to commodities. Like Rousseau, he presented the institutions of property in a historical and evolutionary framework. He sums up the moral imperative of his analysis thus:

> The distinguishing feature of communism is not the abolition of property generally, but the abolition of bourgeois property. But modern bourgeois private property is the final and most complete expression of the system of producing and appropriating products, that is based on class antagonism, on the exploitation of the many by the few. In this sense the theory of the Communists may be summed up in the single sentence: Abolition of private property...

Continuing in this vein Marx says,

> ... when, therefore, capital is converted in common property, into the property of all members of the society, per-

sonal property is not thereby transformed into social property. It is only the social character of the property that is changed. It loses its class character. (Quoted in Macpherson 1978: 65)

Marx's forceful, seemingly unambiguous analysis of property relations, is a gloss over the mechanisms by which common property can become the property of all members of the society. Pragmatically, common property involves rights of access and exclusion. Social differentiation, including class differences, is an intricate part of the mechanisms by which access and exclusion is established.

In contrast to Marx, Mill, another nineteenth-century (English) philosopher, weighs up the implications of different property regimes (private property versus communism) and argues that the inequity of the existing system was not because there was anything intrinsically wrong with private property, but merely because of accidental historical features which could be rectified. His liberal position therefore basically defended the status quo of nineteenth-century property relations.

In a different view from either of the above, the American jurist Cohen presents a critical analysis of property as sovereignty. In his early twentieth-century view, property is a right not a thing. It is a relationship between persons in reference to things, but sumultaneously it is a relationship of power between persons. Property is a power to impose one's will on others. In examining the various justifications of property, he concludes that since property means power over others the state therefore has a right to set limits or to impose duties in terms of the general welfare.

Following Cohen, Macpherson endorses the view that property is simply an 'institution which creates and maintains certain relations between people' (ibid. 1). Property is a right, an enforceable claim and not 'things'. Property, according to Macpherson, cannot logically be confined to private property. Common property, in his usage, refers to individual rights to use a common resource or service.

> Common property is created by the guarantee to each individual that he will not be excluded from the use or benefit of something; private property is created by the guarantee that an individual can exclude others from the use or benefit of something. (ibid. 5)

An analysis of the above theoretical positions and justificatory theories in regard to property not only indicates that there have long been mainstream and critical positions, but it also indicates that early theorists were mainly concerned with defending or criticizing western conceptions of private property. The current global environmental crisis has made theorists re-evaluate their conceptions of property in the search for appropriate property institutions which deal sustainably with the environment. In doing so they have drawn on opposing justificatory theories about property.

The Strength of Anthropological Approaches Versus the 'Tragedy of the Commons'

The famous anthropologist and lawyer, Maine, writing 40 years earlier (1884) than Cohen, had first coined the phrase 'bundles of rights' in attempting to describe the complex rights of usufruct that occur in different cultural conceptions of tenure. Western conceptions of property rights are bound within a distinct set of cultural values and constraints. Other cultural systems of tenure can teach theorists new approaches which do not center on the efficacy or non-efficacy of western private property (like many of the scholars quoted above have done), but rather on the modes of access to resources and the culturally defined mechanisms of ownership and usufruct. Bundles of rights refer to the manner in which multiple jurisdictions concerning use, access or ownership in land and resources can be accommodated. For instance, in many African societies, women may have rights to use land held by their husbands. Husbands, in turn, may also have to accommodate the rights of traditional or spiritual leaders or the state (or other institutions, such as kinship, political or religious organization) in the same land. In considering the concept of bundles of rights of use, it is clear that both the cultural and the political dynamics of a particular social context need to be understood in order to understand property rights.

In contrast to this approach, Hardin's (1968) 'tragedy of the commons' model is implicitly a justification of western conceptions of private property. Hardin, a biologist and human ecologist, asserted that all resources owned in common will become overexploited and thus depleted, because rational individuals take for themselves as much as possible of the resource before other users do likewise. Since everyone owns the resources, no one has a sense of proprietorship for them. Hardin's individualism echoes Locke's individualistic gathering of apples and acorns from an otherwise useless commons. He tends to ignore or play down cultural and political organization by emphasizing the notion of marginal utility borrowed from rationalist western neo-classical economic theory. An assumption in this economic theory is that individuals will always try to maximize individual value. Hardin based his argument on Lloyd's nineteenth-century text which supported a Malthusian view of population problems (see McCay and Acheson 1987: 2). According to McCay and Acheson,

> Lloyd offered an analogy between the pastoral commons of old England and the labor market, and between a calf and a human child. Rights to enter both the pastoral commons and the labor market are freely obtainable – common rights – and thus pastures are inevitably overstocked and their resources depleted, and labor markets are oversaturated, causing the low wages and miseries of the laboring classes. (ibid. 2)

Hardin's model is enshrined at the beginning of modern common property theory. Much of the anthropological literature contributing to this debate (e.g. McCay and Acheson 1990) is a reaction or rejection of Hardin's work by pointing out the complex processes inherent in common property regimes, which he overlooks in his model. Fortmann and Bruce indicate that Hardin's model is the best-known one which posits a connection between tenure and the condition of the ecosystem: 'Hardin wrote of tenure as if it could be isolated from the associated system of land use and the encompassing social system' (1988: 4).

The present socio-environmental crisis, the cost of unsound and short-sighted resource management, together with industrial growth and increased populations, has prompted a new evaluation and contextualization of property rights. The justificatory theories of earlier scholars discussed above (Locke, Bentham, Mill, Rousseau, Marx) can be seen to fall simplistically into two camps: those who argue for the efficacy of private property and those who argue for more state control of property. In the current environmental crisis, jointly used air, water, stratosphere and other resources all have implications for the value and status of property. This has prompted a new review of theoretical positions which may have major policy implications in terms of the management of natural resources (see foreword in Berkes 1989). Despite Lloyd and Hardin's model, which is a part of a justificatory theory for the efficacy of private property rights in terms of sustaining natural resources, relatively new theories and evidence indicate that largely overlooked 'common property regimes' create rules about the use of common resources, which may be of use in a world searching for sustainability.

The Question of the Commons (McCay and Acheson 1987: xiv) reviews and evaluates the theory of the tragedy of the commons, by bringing a wide selection of case-study material about fisherman, hunters and mixed farmers from widely different settings (see material by Bauer, Berkes, Brightman, Carrier, Vondal, ibid). This endeavor is part of a broader anthropological goal to document and analyze cultural ecology, social organization, decision-making, cultural institutions, and values and beliefs. As McCay and Acheson point out, the discussion of the commons 'reawakens and contributes to classical concerns in the social sciences that go beyond natural resource management and environmental problems' (ibid. xv). Two main concerns which they mention are, the question of individual behavior and social welfare, and the broader question of how individual and social systems interact. In other words, it is a discussion of the relationship between structure and agency (Giddens 1979).

McCay and Acheson contend that common property resources are 'embedded in historically specific social contexts' (ibid. 7). They show that complex features of socio-economic systems and variable systems of rights, duties, functions and obligations are involved in common property resource management. This awareness refines and refurbishes existing theory. For instance, they and others (Ciriacy-Wantrup and Bishop 1975: 714) point out that Hardin's model makes the assumption that commons situations are always open-access situations. Common property, they argue, should instead be seen as a social institution which, like other social institutions, is subject to a set of norms, values and beliefs which sanction individual behaviour.

Comparable common property institutions have been documented by several of the anthropologists and scholars named above. Berkes and Farvar, in an endeavor to refine common property theory, have typologized property rights regimes relevant to common property resources. These are: open access, state property, communal property and private property.

Open access
Described by Berkes and Farvar as 'free for all; resource use rights are neither exclusive nor transferable, these rights are owned in common but are open access to everyone [and therefore property to no one]' (Berkes 1989: 10). This is arguably not a property rights regime at all because people are thought to use the resources opportunistically but not manage them (Murphree 1991: 4). Furthermore, such opportunistic free use of resources may seldom occur, as there are frequently cultural or political sanctions, or practical restrictions such as lack of equipment or transport which effect who has access to resources. An example might be the historical hunting of Zimbabwean wildlife in remote unpoliced areas.

State property
Defined by Berkes and Farvar as 'ownership and management control... held by the nation-state or crown; public resources to which use rights and access rights have not been specified' (ibid. 10). An example might be the historical protection of wildlife in Zimbabwe by the state.

Communal property
'Use rights for the resource are controlled by an identifiable group and are not privately owned or managed by governments; there exist rules concerning who may use the resource, who is excluded from the resource, and how the resource should be used; community based resource management systems: common property' (ibid. 10). An example might be that this is what is implicitly hoped for under the CAMPFIRE program.

Private property
Where the claim rests with the individual or the corporation (Berkes 1989: 24). An example might be the rights of a Zimbabwean safari operator[2] in his concession for the duration of the lease. However, these rights are also subject to other sets of rights (see below).

---

2. In Zimbabwe, safari operators may lease hunting concession areas for the consumptive use of wildlife. These areas may be on state, communal or private land. Such lease agreements usually entail a hunting quota which is set down by DNPWLM. Operators may sell their quota as hunting safaris to overseas clients. Clients have the right to hunt animals and acquire trophies in terms of the hunting concession agreement and the agreement between the operator and client.

As illustrated by the example of Zimbabwean wildlife, the authors point out that many resources are used in overlapping mixtures of these ideal types and they state that instead of 'emphasizing the ownership status of a resource, it may be more useful to examine the diversity of relationships involving property and access conditions under which a resource is held' (ibid. 38). This statement supports the analysis of multiple jurisdictions concerning wildlife emphasized in this study. In regard to this complexity, they classify four different combinations of property regimes and ownership types. These are:

1. *Open access* – commonly owned resources in which tragedies of the commons are likely to happen.
2. *Limited access* – commonly owned resources in which resources are managed as:
    (a) communal property; or
    (b) state property; or
    (c) joint jurisdiction/co-management regimes.
    [The last is the category of property which we will be dealing with in this study.]
3. *Privatized resources* – held under limited access conditions;
4. *Privatized resources* – held under open access conditions in which rules of exclusion have broken down (ibid. 38).

According to Gibbs and Bromley, who define common property regimes in terms of the communal property definition, such regimes ensure (through rules of access) that the resources on which people depend will be available sustainably (ibid. 43). They claim that the distinguishing features of a well-functioning common property regime will be:

1. a minimum of disputes and limited effort necessary to maintain compliance (efficiency);
2. a capacity to cope with progressive changes through adaptation (stability);
3. a capacity to accommodate surprise or sudden shocks (resilience);
4. a shared perception of fairness among the members with respect to inputs and outcomes (equitability). (ibid. 26).

It is argued by both Berkes (1989) and McCay and Acheson (1987) that traditional resource management practices may often include the components of such common property regimes. They claim that such practices, often tested and adapted through time, have been the chief way in which human beings have obtained access to resources in a sustainable fashion. So often in the past these practices have been overlooked or underestimated in terms of development projects and plans. Recently these common property practices have been promoted as a means for 'institutional innovation towards sustainable development' (Berkes 1989: 19).[3]

In ending this section, we briefly recap and draw a tentative theoretical conclusion. We have noted that, historically, western scholars tend to identify property either in terms of it being private or in terms of it belonging to the state. From this perspective, common property is those resources which are not amenable to private appropriation, nor collectively owned by a group, but are open access, freely available resources such as western conceptions of marine resources (Berkes 1989: 7). This is the way Hardin thinks about common property. In contrast to this use of common property is the idea that common property should be restricted to communally owned resources where rules exist about access to the resource (see Gibbs and Bromley: ibid). Both concepts of common property are subject to property rights regimes within which the resource is used. It is, therefore, important to distinguish between the common property resource and the property rights regime under which the resource is used (Berkes 1989: 9).

The idea of bundles of rights, of rights nested within other rights, seems to have significance for the meaning of common property and for the way in which property regimes interact. From this perspective common property is best seen as not restricted to communal property nor open access, since various property regimes may be involved in claiming differential access to the same resource. As Berkes observes, many resources are held in overlap-

---

3. Such resource management systems and common property regimes are associated with a number of resources including water, pasture, rangeland, forests, wildlife, fisheries and agriculture. Examples include: the *Subak* system of irrigating rice studied by Geertz (1972) in Bali; the common of pasture system studied by Cox (1985) and Dahlman (1980) in England; the *agdal* system of range/pasture studied by Giles *et al.* (1986) in Morocco; the Japanese *iriaichi* system of using forests and meadows (Mkean 1986); Japanese coastal fishing (*irai*) studied by Ruddle (Berkes 1989); the *jhum swidden* agriculture practiced in North East India (Atal 1984) and the *nitihuschii* hunting territories of the Cree (Berkes 1989). Many comparable systems have therefore been identified, but many also have been identified as breaking down or adapting because of socio-political changes (see McCay and Acheson 1987).

ping resource regime categories (ibid. 26). As described in this study, a resource like wildlife is held under multiple jurisdictions emanating from an array of property regimes. There is still, however, a sense among planners that common property only refers to situations where communal property arrangements exist.

Wildlife Utilization in Africa and Common Property Theory

According to Berkes, wildlife is considered a common property resource because it has two characteristics: control of access to these resources is problematic and, secondly, users may subtract from the welfare of other users (ibid. 7). Though the property regimes which deal with this resource fall across the spectrum of regimes identified above by Berkes (i.e. open access, state, private and communal property), the emphasis of development planners dealing with wildlife utilization in Africa has often been on communal property regimes and community-based management systems. The state and private interests in the common property are sometimes analytically underestimated, as illustrated in the following paragraphs.

Lawry points out that effective policies for managing common resources are urgently needed for Sub-Saharan Africa, where most rangelands and forests are used communally, and he questions the effectiveness of policies which rely solely on local-level common property arrangements, which he appears to conceive in terms of Berkes' (1990) definition of communal property. He argues that 'such policies are built on theoretical foundations which do not consider significant constraints on the emergence of local collective action' (Lawry 1990: 404). He claims that establishing local common property arrangements may be associated with a number of difficulties. Lawry cites the changing nature of village economies and social relations, and growing pressure on local resources, as factors which make it difficult for common property regimes which existed under former social conditions to function under contemporary circumstances (ibid. 406). Other critiques claim that 'obtrusive state action' is responsible for the breakdown of local common property management systems (Bromley and Cernea 1989). Lawry argues that this breakdown is a result of modernization, and national economic and political integration. These factors have reduced incentives for individuals to participate in such regimes, have undercut the economic viability of common property institutions, and have reduced political legitimacy of local management authorities. Economic incentives are often not sufficient and for many users the returns will be negative or marginal.

A second problem is that of authority. Lawry claims that interests are often heterogeneous and strong support for the desired resource use is not forthcoming. He argues that in Africa local authority is giving way to state authority and that traditional authority, such as that of chiefs, is losing or has lost its legitimacy. He claims that natural resources used in Africa are both private and individual and that 'villages' are part of larger economies which bring other political and economic forces to bear on situations where rules exist about who has access to resources (in his terms this is a minimum definition of common property). This integration into the larger economies results in the political marginalization and dependency of villages. Simultaneously, while there is a breakdown of local management systems, direct state management has not worked either. States lack information about resource use practices. States often ignore local inputs and initiatives and policing activities are often arbitrary. Thus, neither state nor local control of resources can work by themselves.

Lawry proposes a system of 'co-management' of resources which addresses the weaknesses of both state and community control (see Berkes[1] classification of limited access and commonly owned resources). He states that government action can help create the conditions of local action by assigning 'group rights to a specific territory', giving technical guidance, and providing the economic environment for co-operation (Lawry 1990: 421). His ideas are particularly useful in helping to resolve the current tension which exists between state property regimes and community level property regimes. Though not always consciously advocating co-management, many natural resource programs are in fact creating such regimes.

In Africa, where colonial state intervention has often alienated resources from people whose tenure systems involve aspects of communal use of resources, several countries have developed wildlife natural resource management programs or adapted resource management techniques which build on assumptions in common property theory in the attempt to develop co-management models. The key assumptions are:

1. Leonard proposes a number of strategies which address poverty and environmental degradation simultaneously (1989: 33).

1. that participation of local 'communities' in decision-making and control concerning resources is important for the sustainability (or conservation) of such resources (participation, decentralization);
2. that the benefits arising from such resources should accrue to the 'communities' who manage them (devolution of benefits);
3. that a system of rights of access and exclusion, building on existing property regimes (mainly centered on political structures, processes and institutions reinforced by cultural beliefs and institutions) may be the foundation for institutional development of such common property regimes (defined rights); and
4. that multiple levels of participation are important in the making of common property because of the historical legacy of state control of the resource and the various private and entrepreneurial vested interests in the resource, as well as the participation by the incipient or established communal resource management regime at the local level. In other words, common property regimes can and perhaps should be multifaceted and multi-tiered. Planners are less explicit about this assumption. See conclusion (pp. 186–99) for more on this (multi-jurisdictional regime).

In terms of wildlife utilization, we will briefly consider the attempts toward the making or remaking of common property in five countries. We will bear in mind the above assumptions in considering the programs concerned.

In regard to Zambia, Cumming (1990) reports that Game Management Areas (GMA) (160,488 sq. km. or 21.3 per cent of Zambia), which are mostly next to National Parks (63,590 sq. k. or 7.9 per cent of Zambia), are sparsely settled subsistence farming areas where wildlife is planned to be a major form of land use. Three wildlife management initiatives in GMAs include: the National Parks and Wildlife Service Administrative Design (ADMADE) project, the Luangwa Integrated Rural Development Project (LIRDP) and the Wetlands Project. All of these Zambian projects work with the four assumptions mentioned above. They base their proposed common property management regimes on traditional authority (chiefdoms) buttressed by government agencies. All try to include the participation of local political structures in the attempt to involve local people in decision-making and the benefits associated with the resource, whilst simultaneously initiating co-operation between the state, private interests, and local people.

These projects endeavor to reinforce a system of rights of access and exclusion by reviving traditional authority over resources in conjunction with government institutions. They operate at or involve many bureaucratic levels and are subject to what Bell refers to as 'Murphree's Law', which is that 'each level of an organization strives to wrest power and the control of funds away from the levels above it, and strives to resist the devolution of power and control of funds to levels below it' (Bell 1990: 4).

Bell (1990) states that LIRDP consists of steering (national), executive (provincial), technical, and local leaders' committees (chiefs, ward chairmen, and one woman's representative per chieftainship), plus a revolving fund. ADMADE is operated through the National Parks and Wildlife Services and centers on wildlife management authorities in each GMA. This authority is chaired by the district governor and includes district-level civil servants as well as local representatives, such as chiefs and ward chairmen. The LIRDP summary report for 1989 states that

> the major factors contributing to the success of the wildlife management programme have been the active participation and support of the local leadership, the establishment of direct revenue collection from wildlife utilization and the non-confrontational approach to law enforcement (Bell 1990: 7).

Naturally, support and participation of local leadership in itself does not constitute a well-functioning common property regime as envisaged by Gibbs and Bromley above. As McCay and Acheson stated, property regimes are embedded in specific social contexts. Local leadership's relations between natural resources, the diverse people they govern, and the process of establishing their rights of access to resources amongst competing state and private rights is a crucial dynamic deserving close attention of planners.

In Kenya, the Maasai Mara and Amboseli District Council Game Reserves were specifically established to involve local communities in conservation. Conceived and established 30 years ago, they provide important lessons in terms of common property management. In Amboseli, a development plan was established (Western and Thresher 1973) which was adopted within the traditional political and cultural framework associated with the Maasai, in conjunction with the existing administrative structures of the Kenyan state. This plan worked towards the integration of livestock and wildlife economies to reduce conflict between these land-use strategies. Revenues were to accrue from tourist development, such as the establishment of tourist lodges, which would involve the payment of wildlife utilization fees to Maasai group ranch holders next to the park. These ranches were to accommodate migratory wildlife herds, be involved in leasing out hunting and tourist concessions, develop water resources for their cattle herds, and establish a communal center. The Maasai had historically resisted the establishment of the reserves as they felt it was an attempt to appropriate their land. Despite the success of changing conservative attitudes to wildlife utilization, in the late seventies the plan met with a number of obstacles which included the Kenyan government ban on hunting, depriving ranches of significant revenue, and the flagging tourist market. A significant problem was that resource benefits were being co-opted and mismanaged at national and district levels by the councils, departments and ministries involved in wildlife management (Douglas-Hamilton 1992). In regard to a similar plan in the Mara, administered by the Narok district council, Hamilton points out that revenue generation for Maasai landholders is the critical issue. Despite the 444 million Kenyan Shillings generated in the area during 1987, only 10 per cent remained in the district and less than 1 per cent went to local group ranches (Douglas-Hamilton 1988). Inequity of revenue sharing and the co-opting of local resources by local, district and national élites is therefore a crucial problem in common property management. The Kenyan case employs the assumption about participation and devolution of benefits to local communities through both culturally based and state institutions, but underlines the need to clarify local communities' rights of access to these benefits in such a multi-jurisdictional context.

In Tanzania, projects have recently started in attempting to involve local communities in the management of wildlife resources. Baldus (1989) discusses village participation in the Selous Conservation Area and other projects underway in the Loliondo and Ngorongoro Conservation Area. The International Union for Conservation of Nature and Natural Resources (IUCN), in collaboration with the International Trade Centre (ITC) and the appropriate Tanzanian ministries have been actively studying wildlife utilization options. Two professed goals in their 1988 report indicate that they are searching for common property arrangements. First, they mention 'the need to involve local communities in the conservation of the resource should be recognized in view of escalating people and wildlife conflicts in the country' and, secondly, they mention the need to 'integrate local communities into formal, controlled wildlife utilization, so as to provide a higher return to local communities and thus reduce the existing conflict between people and wildlife' (ITC, IUCN 1988: 38).

In Namibia pastoral herdsmen in Damaraland have been involved as an auxiliary game guard service and would like to 'resuscitate their wildlife populations and use them sustainably' (Cumming 1990: 4). According to Cumming, attempts to involve these communities in wildlife utilization and eco-tourism have started. Potential also exists in Bushmanland, Kaokoland, Owamboland, Kavango and Caprivi. They point out in their project paper for the Namibian ministry responsible that

> the key legal and policy issues to be addressed are probably those of custodial rights and the distribution of benefits. Because the interactions between land, common property issues, benefits, traditional customs and state responsibility for resource conservation are complex, a consultative, participatory and flexible approach will be needed. (ibid: 14)

In Botswana, citizens' hunting schemes involving draws have not achieved a sense of local proprietorship for the resource. The government is now developing community-based wildlife management utilization schemes. In yet another report on the identification of wildlife utilization projects, Cumming and Taylor (1989) state that the terms of reference for their proposed pilot projects are as follows:

> [they] will be of direct material and economic benefit to those communities living in the Wildlife Management Areas or Districts in which Wildlife Management Areas are situated, of benefit to the citizens of Botswana generally, economically viable and thus capable of promoting rural employment and income generation, structured in such a way as to involve the district residents and local authorities in project development, implementation and decision-making, capable of being replicated so that other communities can also benefit. (1989: 54)

This brief overview indicates that there is considerable interest in the co-management of common property through wildlife utilization regimes in southern and eastern Africa. Such initiatives stress community-based common property regimes, but, in fact, usually describe co-management of multi-jurisdictional wildlife with state, private and community interests being exerted simultaneously.

Common property theorists (Berkes 1989; McCay and Acheson 1987) have called for further in-depth case-studies to unravel the complex social contexts within which common property may be held. This study is an attempt to unravel the range of social issues important for understanding wildlife resource use, in a Zimbabwean social context. In doing so the mechanisms of access, participation, benefit and decision-making are looked at largely from a perspective of cultural and political practice at the local level in relation to the CAMPFIRE program. Having considered other African experiences in wildlife utilization, which employ similar assumptions about common property issues, we now address the CAMPFIRE program itself.

CAMPFIRE

The CAMPFIRE program is specifically concerned with the decentralization of management of wildlife resources to the community level and has attracted growing international recognition as a unique experiment in common property resource management (Peterson 1991; Muir 1992). In arid or semi-arid areas, dry-land cropping and/or extensive cattle-grazing pose problems for both the environment (deforestation, soil depletion) and people (low yields, lack of economic development). Wildlife resource utilization, often in combination with these other forms of land use, has been gaining currency as a sustainable, ecologically sound and economically beneficial land-use strategy.

In terms of research, CAMPFIRE has adopted a multi-disciplinary collaborative approach by incorporating research from wildlife managers, ecologists, social scientists, technicians, economists, and legal experts. It has also adopted a multi-institutional approach to implementation by working laterally within and between government departments, Non-Governmental Organizations (NGOs) and the private sector, and by working vertically through ward, district and national institutions.

The rationale behind this government-sanctioned and

ZANU(PF) (governing party)-endorsed program, is that wildlife (and other) resources in the communal areas of Zimbabwe will become more sustainable if local people are responsible for and receive the benefits from these resources. At present, benefits include rural development projects such as the building of schools and clinics and household dividends funded from safari operation revenues. CAMPFIRE's goal, therefore, is sustainable development through resource utilization at ward, village and district levels. One objective of this voluntary program is increased institutional management capacity and empowerment at these levels, since participation of the local community is crucial for meaningful development. Conservation of natural resources is not seen as an end in itself, instead, CAMPFIRE argues, conservation can come about through resource utilization.

During the Rhodesian era, communal areas were known as the Tribal Trust Lands or Native Reserves. Many of these impoverished areas are situated in the less-agriculturally productive lowveld areas of the country where there is low rainfall and poor soils. In these lowveld areas are often also found the main tracts of the national parks estates. In contrast, the commercial farming areas occupy the most fertile land up on the escarpment.

Since colonial times wildlife resources have been legally protected, controlled and administered by DNPWLM under what was then the Minister of Natural Resources. Changes in legislation, particularly the Parks and Wild Life Act 1975, have enabled the emergence of decentralized 'appropriate authorities' for wildlife, which can use wildlife as an economic resource in areas outside the wildlife estate. A group of commercial farmers were the first to have attempted managing wildlife for profit under this new legislation and their endeavor has become extremely successful. Seven years later, amended legislation enabled CAMPFIRE to develop in communal areas. According to Thomas (1991), the 1982 amendment to the Parks and Wild Life Act made provision for the Minister of Environment and Tourism to designate appropriate authority status upon district councils which gave them both the statutory authority and the responsibility for wildlife on lands under their control. Such authority was not divorced from the overreaching custodianship of the resource at national level by the DNPWLM, who continued to set quotas and retained the right to revoke or amend the authority if it was abused. Furthermore, in theory if not in practice, the authority was to be conditional upon the devolution of benefits and responsibility for wildlife to lower institutional levels. Murphree (1992) explains that, since district councils themselves are not the producers or managers of the resource, a conflict of interests is created between this institution and the people whom it represents.

CAMPFIRE uses and modifies mechanisms and institutions deployed by the existing system of local government as its institutional framework. District councils are local government authorities, which also have certain statutory rights over land and natural resources within their district. Their powers include the generation and expenditure of revenues from the land and natural resources under their control, within the constraints placed upon them by overlapping pieces of legislation such as the Parks and Wild Life Act, the Forest Act, the Communal Land Forest Act, the Communal Land Act and the Mines and Minerals Act (Murphree 1991). District councils are legally in a position to enter into joint ventures or other undertakings for the benefit of their constituents. The role and jurisdiction of district councils is further qualified by the fact that they are intimately involved with the Ministry of Local Government, Rural and Urban Development. The district administrator is the senior local government official at district level. He is also the chief executive officer of the district council and he is the chairman of the district development committee, which is composed of government ministries and departments but does not have any democratic representation from lower-level institutions. As this committee is responsible for co-ordinating the district development plan, there is a strong tendency towards top-down planning of development in most districts (Thomas 1991: 21).

Local government is centered on two main institutions, the district administration (formerly the district commissioner's office) and the district council. District council is an elected body drawn from an entire district. A district is made up of a number of wards[4] usually defined in terms of the number of voters. Each ward is made up of villages. A 1984 government directive (Thomas 1991) suggested that six villages should make up a ward. Within each village a Village Development Committee (VIDCO) is elected to represent the problems and needs of the village and to communicate district and ward decisions to households within the village. VIDCO chairmen, secretaries and selected governing political party

---

4. In more remote, less-populated areas, wards may coincide with chieftainships. In the colonial and Rhodesian periods, district commissioners used an administrative system of indirect rule through local chiefs and headmen.

officials (from ZANU(PF) Women's League and Youth Brigade), together with a ward councillor, form what is known as a Ward Development Committee (WADCO). The ward councillor is the chairman of the WADCO and represents it at district level. Ward councilors represent their ward's interests at council meetings and convey council decisions to the WADCOs and VIDCOs whom they represent. The council has an elected chairman and government appointed executive officers, who run the day-to-day affairs of the council. The district administrator, as chief executive officer of council and as chairman of the district development committee, plays a powerful and pivotal role in district affairs and decision-making.

In a somewhat similar fashion to local government institutions, CAMPFIRE has established the election of ward- and village-level wildlife committees whose representatives sit on a district wildlife committee. The district wildlife committee, which is a sub-committee of the district council, includes the ward councilors, representatives from ward wildlife committees, and the executive officers and chairman of the district council. In my research context it also included the district administrator or his representatives.

The district wildlife committee is, in theory, accountable to both the top (DNPWLM, other ministries) and the bottom (ward and village wildlife committees). The committee's responsibilities include: distribution of the revenues from the resource, negotiating on how the resource should be used or distributed (e.g. safari operators, joint ventures, subsistence hunting), and negotiating with various governmental organizations and NGOs involved in the program. Some matters addressed during my research were: safari operator leases, possible joint ventures with other entrepreneurs, collection and distribution of revenues, problem-animal control, implementing poaching control, and the maintenance of any capital equipment such as fencing.

It should be noted that an earlier attempt at incorporating local participation from communal lands in the management of wildlife resources in 1978, entitled 'Project Windfall' (Wildlife Industries New Development for All) (Martin 1978), failed for a number of reasons, some of which may be important factors in the success or failure of CAMPFIRE. One reason for the failure of Project Windfall was lack of accountability for the resource. The goal was that revenue and other benefits, such as meat from culls, were to be given to communities bordering national parks through their district councils, but the communities themselves were not involved in managing wildlife nor were they accountable for them. A second reason for failure was that financial and other benefits did not always find their way to local 'communities', so the connection between revenues and wildlife was not apparent to local people. People in Chapoto ward still remember the disappointments associated with foiled attempts to get money sent back to the ward under Project Windfall. The funds, when and if they were released from central treasury, were simply absorbed by the district council in Guruve which had too big a constituency to be concerned about remote Chapoto. Most of the wards in the district did not have the quantities of game found in the more remote wards, yet it is alleged by people in Chapoto that these non-producer wards attracted most of the development in the district. The aim of the CAMPFIRE program is to devolve responsibility and benefits of wildlife to the lowest levels in the producer wards and villages, that is those wards and villages which have significant quantities of wildlife.

One of the first steps taken in this process of devolvement was to identify appropriate authorities to accrue revenues and administer wildlife management at the district level. There is at present no legal mechanism by which wards themselves can act as appropriate authorities for wildlife and they have to work under the auspices of the district councils. At the time of writing, the number of district councils which had volunteered to participate in the CAMPFIRE program outnumbered the number of wards which were actively participating and benefiting from the program. Having the locus of administrative, political and economic vested interest (i.e. the appropriate authority status) at the district level may contradict the aim of the CAMPFIRE program and is at the heart of a number of problems identified in this case-study. Amongst other reasons for not identifying appropriate authorities at ward or village level was that these levels were deemed not to have the organizational capacity to run such an enterprise. It was also because district council and district administration together form a strong political force in these outlying districts.

Chapoto ward is a significant test case for the viability of CAMPFIRE because it borders on two large tracts of uninhabited land set aside for the consumptive use[5] of wildlife resources known as

---

5. Chapoto ward has an extremely valuable asset in its section of Zambezi river frontage. At the present time revenues are mainly accrued from safari operations, but photographic safaris, walking safaris, canoe safaris and other non-consumptive uses of resources may, in the long run, bring in even more revenue than hunting.

safari areas, and therefore has an abundance of diverse wildlife populations (see Map 2). However, it must be emphasized that CAMPFIRE is in its very early stages in the ward and it is still not clear whether it will be successful there.

Chapoto ward falls under Guruve district and the Guruve district council was one of the first councils to have the status of 'appropriate authority' conferred upon it (November 1988). Effectively, 'appropriate authority' means that the district council, within the limitations and controls (notably the setting of hunting quotas) placed upon it by the DNPWLM, has the responsibility to manage and use wildlife within the district. This is accomplished through the various ward and district wildlife committees formed for this purpose. Currently, revenue from wildlife is mainly obtained from safari operations. Commercial safari operators have to negotiate with councils for leases of hunting concessions in the district. Alternatively, district council may opt for other revenue-generating schemes, including running their own safari operations or entering joint venture contracts with the commercial tourist trade.

For comparative purposes, it is important to remember that in Zimbabwe there is currently a diversity of representative CAMPFIRE experiences being carried out in different districts. Peterson (1991) has documented the experiences of five district-level programs. Though a thorough description of the ecological and social characteristics of these other programs falls beyond the scope of this study, it is worth briefly outlining the administrative characteristics of these programs in order to compare what is happening in Chapoto ward, Guruve district.

Nyaminyami (situated near Lake Kariba) district opted to manage its wildlife potential through a district trust. The trust is composed of elected and appointed officials including ward councillors, chiefs, representatives from government ministries and NGOs. According to Peterson, the trust emphasizes economic development at district rather than ward level. Participation by ward spokesmen and linkages to the ward level through the district council are weak.

In contrast to Nyaminyami, the Guruve district runs its wildlife program through its council. The council established the Guruve district wildlife committee which includes district-level officials as well as councillors and chairmen from the five wards claiming to have wildlife, but in fact only three of these (Kanyurira, Chisunga and Chapoto) have significant quantities. In Kanyurira, the district council opted to run its own safari operation, while in Chapoto

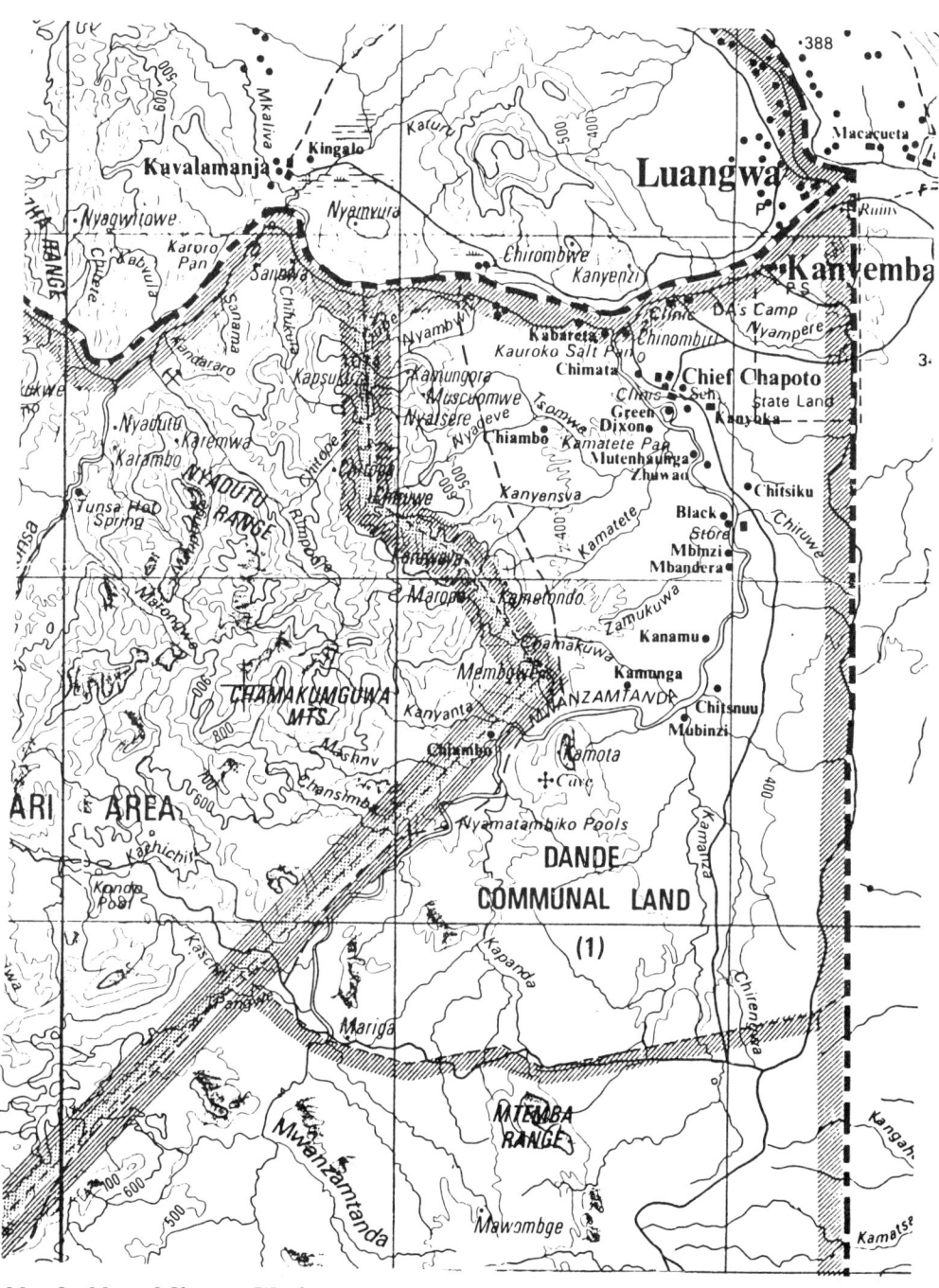

Map 2 Map of Chapoto Ward
Source: Western Dande (Harare: Department of the Surveyor General, 1978).

and Chisunga the concession is leased. Though Kanyurira has handed out household dividends, sub-district-level participation in the other two producer wards was negligible.

A third example of a CAMPFIRE potential is in Gokwe district. Here there is a chronic problem of in-migration and a general lack of support for the CAMPFIRE idea. In contrast to other districts, this district council, while not rejecting CAMPFIRE, has not provided leadership concerning wildlife as an alternative land-use strategy. According to Peterson, people seem more interested in increased cattle production (after the planned eradication of tsetse fly), increased cotton production, and employment in a new coal-mine (1991: 52). All these activities clash with wildlife resource use.

Bulalima Mangwe and Tsholotsho districts have started the first multi-district project, with a joint wildlife committee, but face serious difficulties in planning the identification and fencing of a wildlife area, and, to date, not enough benefits have accrued to those wards experiencing the most wildlife damage (ibid. 57).

Last but not least, Beitbridge district has been able to make considerable progress without the donor assistance which other districts received. This district council has led the way by actively initiating their own program at ward and village levels. Beitbridge is the first district to allocate revenues to both ward and village levels. Since 87 per cent of district revenues from wildlife are from a single VIDCO, the district wildlife committee opted to distribute funds at the village level and allow village residents to decide on what to do with them. District council revenues from the 1990 season totalled Z$50,235, of which Z$45,000 was allocated to the wards and villages where animals had been shot. Of this total, Z$43,930 accrued from Chikwarakwara VIDCO and Z$40,000 was actually allocated. Each household in this VIDCO was allocated Z$400, of which Z$200 was set aside for community projects.

Perceptions and Discourse Associated with CAMPFIRE

It is appropriate in discussing the meanings attached to the pragmatic implementation of CAMPFIRE to mention the ways in which the program is seen from both the bottom and the top. These perceptions are important because they are evidence that people think about wildlife quite differently depending on context.

In 1989 the International Convention on Trade in Endangered

Species (CITES) held debates concerning the banning of the ivory trade and the placement of the African elephant on Appendix One. Zimbabwe used the examples of the Guruve and Nyaminyami districts, the two districts which then had appropriate authority status under CAMPFIRE to illustrate that the economic value of wildlife for local people acted as an incentive to manage it well, and that therefore controlled trade in elephant products should be allowed. It was argued that banning the trade in ivory would only make matters worse as trade would be forced underground, as has happened in the case of the black rhino. Similarly, in the 1994 debates, Zimbabwe and other Southern African countries argued that their relatively high populations of elephant were a result of good management of renewable and economically valuable resources. Again, CAMPFIRE was used to illustrate that local people were becoming involved in the successful management of these resources primarily because the economic benefits potentially outweighed the crop damage and threat to life and property posed by such animals. Since elephants are the major earner of revenue under CAMPFIRE, no trade would mean that economic benefits to local people would be curtailed, leaving them little incentive to tolerate them. It was argued that the ivory trade ban was a bad strategy.

The argument hinges on three related assumptions. One assumption is that involving local people in the economic benefits and management of wildlife will tend to make the resource more sustainable. A concomitant assumption is that local people will actively participate in decision-making and benefits, as they will become the proprietors of the resource. They will do this despite the many jurisdictions and vested interests in wildlife emanating from other levels such as CITES debates, DNPWLM custodianship, district-level appropriate authority and private sector interest. A third and related assumption is that economic benefits targeted for local communities through district councils will actually reach 'the local community', which, as we will see in Chapoto ward, is not as simple as it may appear, since there are a series of different interests and political structures at the local (and other) level(s) which are competing for these resources. Not all of the people in the ward will necessarily benefit and some may actually have further restraints imposed on their way of life.

Rationalizations like those above about sustainability being brought about by economic benefits are rationalizations of planners and administrators, ecologists, social scientists and wildlife planners – the outsiders. Local people have a series of other rationalizations about wildlife, including the notion that some animals may be spiritual beings, some may be useful in providing powerful herbs, some are merely a menace to life and property, some are edible and some are not. However, these values do not always concur with those of outsiders and neither do they necessarily concur with the values of other groups of local people.

Attitudes towards wildlife emanating from the top and the bottom attest to this. Most local people see little or no aesthetic value in large mammalian wildlife, especially crop-raiding animals which usually attract tourists (e.g. elephants, buffalo, kudu). Apart from the fact that these are a source of meat, they are merely regarded by the majority of people as a threat to their existence (Cutshall 1990).

Most outsiders think this form of wildlife is very valuable for a wide range of reasons stretching from the economic to the aesthetic. An important set of assumptions in the CAMPFIRE program is that those who reap the economic benefits from this wildlife are more likely to be positive towards wildlife in some way, and that this will foster a sense of proprietorship for this resource.

Despite the inception of CAMPFIRE during the research period, wildlife in Chapoto ward was largely publicly regarded as a liability with no benefits for those who compete with animals for a meager sustenance. The hopes expressed for wildlife utilization in Zimbabwe, however, emphasize that rural communities will be the ones who suffer the most from the recent ban on the ivory trade.

At this admittedly early stage of the idea that wildlife utilization might be conducted by rural communities on a sustainable basis, in my research context in the years of 1989 and 1990 and the first part of 1991, the locus of administrative and political control of the resource, and the effective control of the distribution of revenues, lay largely in the hands of outsiders. This has been the case for at least the last 100 years, and probably for a lot longer before that. However, political mileage has been accrued by claiming that rural communities such as Chapoto are going to benefit from and control their own resources.[6] Despite the views maintained in the wildlife lobby media which tend to reify the CAMPFIRE program, the record on the ground in my research site was not as impressive as it sometimes appears on paper.

6. ZANU(PF), for instance, endorsed the CAMPFIRE program in its 1990 manifesto.

INTRODUCTION

The 'wildlife lobby' includes what Murphree describes as sentimental conservationists, safari operator interests, and those who believe that, ecologically and economically, wildlife is the most rational of land-use strategies in many marginal areas (Murphree 1988: 6). Only one ward in Guruve district (Kanyurira) had, at the time of the study, had any significant locally perceived benefit from wildlife resources. Yet part of the wildlife lobby argument for local participation in the management of the resource is that this is a useful strategy in the rhino war, where a daily tally is kept of 'poachers' killed compared to rhinos killed.[7] *Zimbabwe Wildlife* reports that

> Zimbabwean conservationists favour the introduction of limited sport hunting (of rhino) on several counts, of which the most important is that of enabling rural communities to benefit from rhino populations in their areas, and hence to provide a significant incentive to abandon poaching or assisting foreign poachers (17 March 1990).

In the context of Chapoto ward this statement makes little sense since during the bulk of the research period the majority of local people did not participate in the deliberations on the wildlife resource despite the hope of participation expressed by planners. The discourse of conservationists, lobbyists and planners does not always mirror what is going on at the local level at this stage of the program.

For some of the marginalized ex-foraging groups that I was observing in Chapoto ward, 'sustainability' often meant 'where will we obtain our next meal?' and 'wildlife utilization' meant digging out worms from the bark of a tree, collecting tubers and berries, or, to the more courageous who could risk their own safety for the temporary relief of their children's malnutrition, setting the dreaded snare.

---

7. In mid-July 1990 the ratio was 'more than three poachers killed for every rhino lost' (*The Herald*, Harare, 18 July 1990).

CHAPTER 2
An Introduction to Chapoto Ward (Kanyemba)

Methodology

In Chapoto ward, as in many other areas in Zimbabwe, there is a feeling that both the individual and the community are subject to the whims of power and authority elsewhere. This has been the case for at least 100 years and probably a great deal longer. Today, despite the democratic façade provided through the formal political organization consisting of VIDCOs, WADCOs, and other committees, people feel relatively powerless in the face of what is seen as monolithic and whimsical officialdom. This, I believe, is not only true of government departments, but also of NGOs and other outsiders who in general rely on bureaucratic processes and formal procedures. These procedures are, in my opinion, often seen as puzzling if not intimidating and they have a momentum and significance which extend into the dim areas of the unknown. This is important to realize in one's methodology, because it may influence what research instruments one might use. What is appropriate: formal questionnaires, open-ended conversations, direct questioning, observation, etc.?

The central method used in the study was that of extended observation.[1] It is realized that 'participant observation', the cornerstone of the anthropological method, can be a pretence on the part of the observer. In the context of Chapoto ward, there were many situations where the degree to which I was a participant is highly questionable. I did not join in hacking at elephant carcasses for meat. I did not set snares. I collected fruit and tubers, but not out of hunger. I was not grossly intimidated by the safari operators

---

1. I am grateful to Prof. Murphree for having clarified this issue. I do not mean to attribute my choice of methodology solely to the powerlessness of Chapoto ward. It is basically a disciplinary preference.

personnel nor by the game scouts. I did not grow cotton, maize or other crops, neither did I have access to a piece of land for cultivation. I did not marry into the community, consult the spirit medium on a regular basis, nor did I work for anyone there. I was the only person in the community who had a vehicle. There were many activities in which I did not or could not participate.

On the other hand, I certainly did participate in numerous activities. At night, if woken by the sound of a buffalo grazing nearby, or by the rhythmical drumming on tins of my neighbors, I too would do as they did and tap lightly on my metal bucket. Amongst other things, I participated in sleepless nights if my neighbors were worried by leopards. I participated in the gossip and the daily run of events. I attended meetings. I visited homesteads. I consulted the spirit medium. I observed the distribution of meat from kills. I walked the 25 kilometers from one end of the habitation to the other frequently. I observed the wide range of activities and ways of doing things that constitute a way of life, and I also walked with people in the forest on collecting trips. I talked to people. In short, I lived in the community, usually for a month at a time. Sometimes I would go down for a shorter period of time (usually not less than 10 days) if, for instance, I needed to attend a meeting or to meet people. I did not restrict my studies to the ward itself and later in my research schedule I spent time meeting and talking to people at the safari operators' camp, the DNPWLM camps in the protected areas, as well as following up leads and enquiries in Harare.

I lived in and visited the community from October 1989 to October 1990 as my initial data-gathering exercise. This covered a full agricultural season. During that time I spent approximately eight months in the field. Later in 1991, I returned to the field on a number of occasions to maintain contact with the ward. I employed three local research assistants, two men and one woman who came from the area. My wife and child were also very significant methodologically speaking. People said it was quite clear that I was not a safari operator, as safari operators do not bring their wives 'on patrol'. My research assistants acted (amongst others) as key informants, and I set them various tasks. Initially, I simply walked with them all over the ward. After discussing the range of issues that anthropologists are interested in, and after they realized that I was a bona fide researcher, we developed good relationships over time. Concomitantly, we developed our mutual interest and understanding of CAMPFIRE through exchange of ideas. Having been employed as a Research Fellow in the Centre for Applied Social Sciences (CASS) at the University of Zimbabwe, I had a briefing to carry out socio-economic research relevant to the CAMPFIRE program. This included the monitoring, evaluation and facilitation of the program. The dialogue with my research assistants gradually extended to the community and, amongst other things, I was asked to speak at ward meetings on this issue and was instrumental in bringing the Kanyurira wildlife committee down to Chapoto to discuss these issues.[2] In general, this made many people inclined to be more open to me, though, of course, one only shares one's secrets with one's loyal friends and trusted relatives.

It was often pointed out to me by my research assistants whenever they conducted open-ended interviews on kinship, brideservice, household decision-making, etc., that the range of issues concerning hunting was a secret and they themselves had had people terminate the conversation when it went in that direction. Thus, it is important to understand that the 'secret' is not merely a secret kept from outsiders; it is also a secret amongst trusted insiders to be kept from those who are not loyal. To complicate matters, however, the 'secret' has a public and a private face. The public secret is that everyone knows that everyone else is potentially hunting. The private secret is that, although people may know I am a hunter, I will only share the meat and the information with a select few. The secret protects me from having to share with many people and the limited spread of information protects me from being reported by my enemies or the indiscretions of drunkards or the jealousies of my neighbors. By saying this I do not want to give the impression that the residents of Chapoto ward engage on a grand scale in illegal hunting, I certainly found very little evidence of this. What I do mean to state is that such issues are highly sensitive.

A central methodological issue for me was the sensitive nature of issues to do with wildlife. The resource was essentially alienated from the local people and tight controls had been placed on illegal

---

2. I also was instrumental in arranging a meeting between the local safari operator, the councillor of the ward and the secretary of the wildlife committee. This was extraordinary, as the safari operator, who had flown down from Harare, refused to speak to the councillor or any local people because he had expected the district administrator to be present and he did not want to do anything that might be seen as going behind his back. This might be better understood if one considers that the safari operator had handed over Z$168,000 to the district council for 1989 hunting revenues. Under the CAMPFIRE arrangement, a big chunk of this money should have been distributed at the ward level. Decisions concerning its distribution should also have been in the hands of the ward.

hunting. Many people in the community had been harassed or arrested by the game scouts patrolling the area or by the local safari operators' assistants who policed the hunting concession area, part of which is Chapoto ward. In addition, the only white men that the local people regularly saw in Chapoto were the safari operators and their clients. As a result, I was immediately cast in the role of safari operators' spy, wildlife department's spy, expressed in the term *Magemu*.[3] In this situation it was very hazardous sometimes to ask even the most innocuous of questions and it certainly was not a good idea to plunge into questions about wildlife. My wife tried this on three occasions with women, after I had been there for some time, enquiring what women thought about the safari operator. The women ignored the question or just walked away.

Previous researchers from CASS (Nhira 1989; Cutshall 1990) had carried out surveys in the area. These surveys were immensely helpful to me and provided very useful and, largely, accurate information. I later received quite a lot of feedback on them from local people. People wanted to know what was behind our questions and what motivated these researchers. They were not satisfied with the account given to them. They felt powerless and worried that the information might be used to arrest them. As a result, I was told that some of this information was not accurate. Some people would make themselves scarce when they knew that the researchers were approaching. Information given, for instance, on the enumeration of livestock holdings would not always reflect the truth as some people feared that the veterinary services were going to confiscate their livestock for being diseased, for not being inoculated, or for other problems posed by officialdom. Others feared that if they were truthful about the number of children they had they might be arrested for not sending these children to school. In general, inhabitants were not sure whether their life-style was lawful, as the state prohibited stream bank cultivation, hunting, fishing with nets and other activities. In the face of officialdom and the apparently whimsical nature of powers up on the escarpment, an important strategy used by many inhabitants is to give inaccurate information wherever possible, until such time as one is sure about the agenda of the person concerned. Once this is established, then local responses become colored with what they perceive as the agenda of the official or visitor. Thus, though VaChiKunda would normally

---

3. My research assistants were also once accused by a drunk man of being involved with the CIO (Central Intelligence Organization).

protest that they are not Mvura, when evangelists from America arrived (briefly by plane) with food and clothing for the impoverished Mvura, this ceased to be an issue. A congregation of about 70 or more VaChiKunda were addressed in English as 'you the Doma people'. Only a handful was actually Mvura (also known as Doma or Vadema, see below).

First impressions are powerful, and a series of items that I had led people to believe that I was associated with a safari operation. I was told that the khaki hat that I wore was the same kind of hat that safari operators used. Secondly, for those who could read English, unfortunately, the model of my vehicle was a Datsun 'Safari'. Worst of all, in my opinion, was that in the first week, ironically in order to 'fit in', I wore two overalls, one was colored blue, which did not cause a problem, but the other was khaki. This suit and color was similar to the one worn by skinners and trackers from Zambezi Hunters, the local safari operators. Given the sensitive nature of this enquiry, and the set-backs associated with these first impression, my personal style in dealing with the situation was multi-stranded. In general, I played down my interest in wildlife and seldom asked direct questions concerning it. On the other hand, I emphasized my interest in agriculture, the collecting of fruits and tubers, religion, marriage, brideservice, local politics, ancestral spirits, kinship, household decision-making, history and 'way of life'. As these domains are all permeated with wildlife issues, I was able to achieve many valuable insights about wildlife issues in this manner.

To avoid the hazards involved in asking direct questions concerning sensitive issues, such as illegal hunting, entry into protected areas, collecting, etc., another method used was walking, listening and watching with people. Walking with people I found was very useful in that it provided a relatively neutral activity. A series of other activities would often spontaneously co-occur; a conversation would start on the nature of brideservice, animals might be seen, a snare might be passed, or a cigarette lit with a traditional lighter. Walking allows people to see you and for you to see them. People walking together share thoughts, and may discuss or experience meanings, codes, symbols, events or objects in the environment. This learning process is the raw material of this study. Thus, the observation of a wild fruit may lead one to discuss the difficulties of collecting in protected areas, where anti-poaching units may threaten one's life. This may lead on to a discussion on someone who has been arrested for illegal entry into the Chewore safari area. At some stage a direct question might be hazarded but one would have to be extremely sensitive in order not to damage the rapport. Thus, an object in the environment leads one to a reflective political discussion, increasing awareness of those involved in the conversation. Methods like this have been explained more rigorously by Freire (1978), but I am not suggesting that this should be the only approach used.

An important issue for discussion in the methodology is the nature of the interactions which I had. The bulk of people in the ward are ChiKunda speakers and ChiShona is usually, but not always, a second language (especially amongst men). Though I had studied ChiShona before entering the field, and had a grasp of it, I found that I could discuss basics but could not converse in the depth that I would have liked. Therefore, I often used the interpretative skills of my ChiKunda research assistants. However, sometimes people would insist on conversing with me in the largely despised ChiLapalapa (a colonial language used for the master-servant relationship, in the kitchen, the mine, etc., but also reportedly used between co-workers who might not share a common language). Initially, when someone switched from ChiShona to this language, I was faced with the dilemma of whether to continue in ChiShona or to follow the initiative. When alone with an informant, I found that this was easier to do than in the presence of others. It was difficult because by using the language both of us could be opening ourselves up to perceived ridicule. Again my approach to these dilemmas was multi-stranded, and I would use English, a poor version of ChiShona, and when the context required it, ChiLapalapa. One important Mvura informant approached me after seven months of fieldwork and asked me if I could speak ChiLapalapa. He felt that we would be able to communicate better with the use of this tool.

Though I have mentioned that extended periods of field research have been carried out, I did not mention that three quite different areas in the ward were used as sites for my research camp, where I lived in a tent and wrote up my notes under a canvas awning (see Map 3). The first site was near the chief's place and I purposely lived next to his messenger so that a watchful eye could be kept on me. The second place was the new school site where the 'democratic' forces embodied in the VIDCOs and WADCOs usually assemble and where the ward meetings are usually held. This site is symbolic of a small, but significant victory over the chief's influence, since he had opposed the building of this school

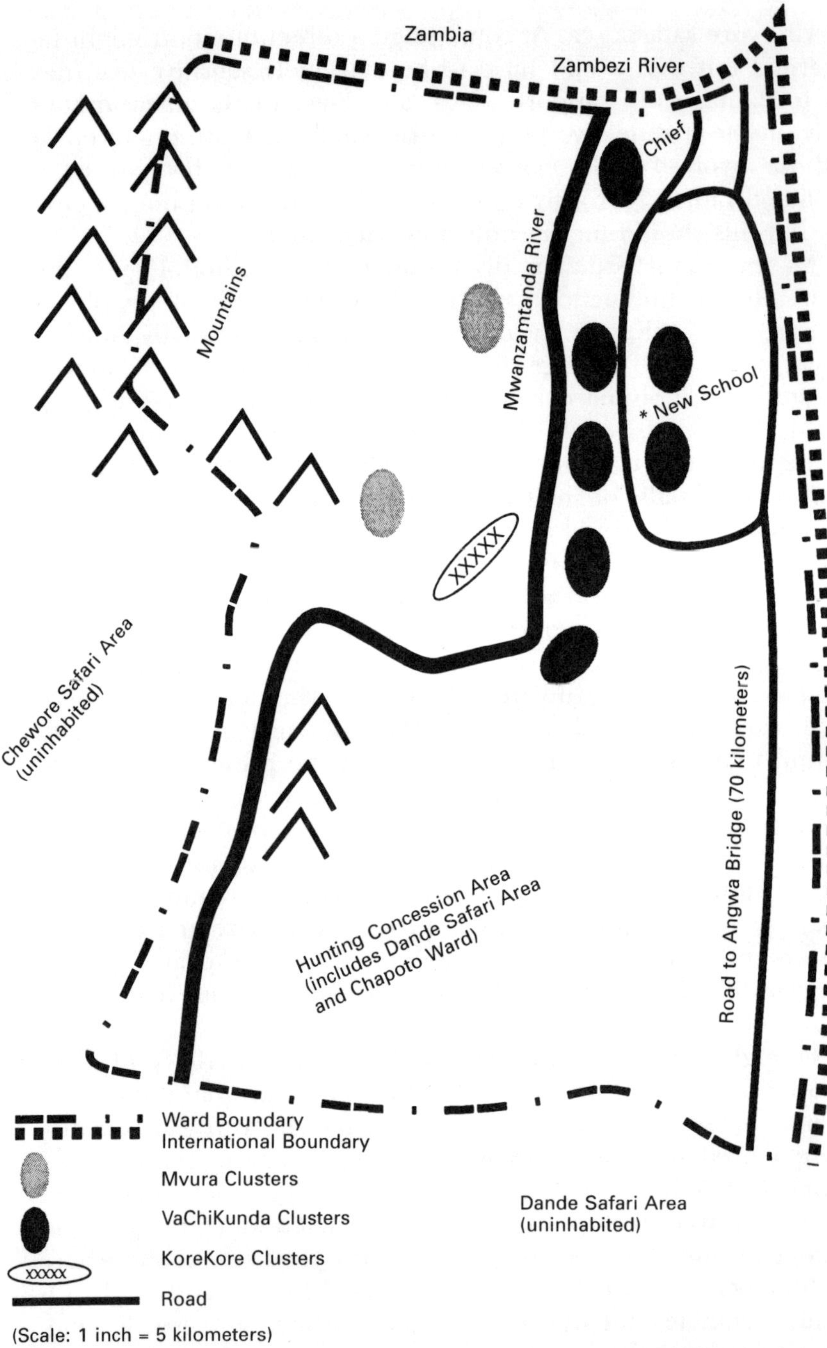

AGRICULTURE, FORAGING AND WILDLIFE RESOURCE USE IN AFRICA

Map 3   Local scenes in Chapoto ward

in the geographical center of the ward. The chief wanted the school to be built near the old school, which was near his homestead, but far away from the bulk of habitation. The last camp that I established was near the southernmost edge of habitation. It afforded easier access to a few remote VaChiKunda and Mvura families living away from the bulk of habitation and it provided very useful insights into how people live and think when, for the most part, quite hidden away from the state. Contrasting uses of different resources were observed including cotton growing in the riverine belt, stream bank cultivation, foraging and hunting. In this situation I lived under the protection and guidance of a headman, with whose family I developed a good rapport.

My policy to safeguard informants and residents was not to include their names when discussing sensitive issues. However, in cases where I do not think that the informant needs to be protected, I have provided full details. In general, both my research assistants and myself were as candid as possible about the research. We explained, in as much detail as necessary, what the purpose and use of the research might be and what its possible effects might be. As far as the ward as a whole is concerned, I do not believe that there was organized illegal activity on anything but a small subsistence hunting scale. As will become clear from a reading of the book, the authorities in charge of enforcing game laws were aware of this long before I entered the field. If anything, I hope this book serves to show how counter-productive some of the enforcement strategies were whilst negotiations about the CAMPFIRE program were taking place.

Geographic Situation and Communication Problems

Chapoto ward (Kanyemba) is a 300 sq. km. area situated along the northern border of Zimbabwe, where the Zambezi river exits Zimbabwe and enters Mozambique to form Cabora Bassa Dam (see Maps 1–3). The ward is bounded on two sides by the international borders of Zambia and Mozambique. Vehicle access to Chapoto ward is via the gravel road down the Zambezi escarpment. The trip is six to seven hours by four-wheel drive vehicle from Harare to Kanyemba, four of which are on the dirt road. When descending from Guruve, the tar ends shortly before making the descent into the valley and the gravel road that traverses the valley floor is very badly corrugated in the dry season and can be impassable in the wet season. When the road is not impassable, the area is serviced by one or two buses a week, which together with the police and District Development Fund (DDF) vehicles are some of the few vehicles that use this road. The Zambezi river is not used by Zimbabweans as a means of transport except by canoe safaris that end in Kanyemba and by the police patrol speed boat. There is no telephone service in the area; at the time of the research the only means of direct communication was by radio. The nearest Zimbabwean center is at Angwa Bridge, which is situated approximately 70 kilometers away.

The area between Kanyemba and Angwa Bridge is the unpopulated Dande safari area. The Dande safari area is unusual in that it is one of three safari areas in Zimbabwe which were formerly designated as Native Reserves. The Dande safari area was formerly part of what is now referred to as the Dande Communal Area which includes Chapoto ward. The area on the western side of the ward is the Chewore safari area. Safari areas are protected areas for controlled consumptive use of wildlife resources, mainly in the form of safari operations. Historically, they have been administered by the DNPWLM, and constitute part of its estate. Areas that were formerly part of the communal areas, such as the Dande safari area, were designed (amongst other things) to bring revenues back to the surrounding areas. Prior to the attainment of 'appropriate authority' status by the district council, funds from these areas would end up in the central government treasury, where the council could submit proposals for local development. After attaining notice of 'appropriate authority' status, these funds accrue directly to council for disbursement to the wards. The council, however, has to pay a nominal lease to the DNPWLM and wards have no legal proprietorship of these areas. Therefore, ultimate control of these areas remains at the center.

On the northern Zambian side of the river is the town of Luangwa Boma. On the Mozambican side is the former provincial capital of Zumbo, which is now in ruins. There are two air-strips in the area, one of which was used to land larger military aircraft during the liberation war (1972–80); both are presently used for canoe safari planes. The nearest petrol station is at Guruve, approximately five hours away by vehicle. The area is spatially extremely remote from the economic and political powers that exist on the escarpment.

One of the more significant extensions of the political and economic power of the state is the Mid-Zambezi Rural Development Project (MZP). The entire valley is being cleared of tsetse fly, and the area between the Manyame and Muzengezi Rivers has been pegged out for resettlement under the MZP. Nothing on this scale is being attempted in Chapoto ward as it is well outside the MZP area. However, as will be shown in the body of the study, this project has influenced ward-level discussions about what should happen in Chapoto ward.

There are a number of issues that are perceived by outsiders as possible dangers in visiting Kanyemba. Local people do not share these fears to the same degree. The first perceived danger is the possibility of contracting a chloroquine resistant strain of malaria said to be rife in the area and to which visitors from the escarpment and elsewhere are particularly prone. The second perceived danger was the possibility of an attack by the Mozambique National Resistance (MNR) who attacked the nearby Mozambican center of Zumbo in July 1989. The third perceived danger is the threat of attack by wild animals.

In the event of an emergency or vehicle breakdown, the remoteness of the area and the poor condition of the road could mean extended delays. In the rainy season there is the possibility that one could be rained in for a month or more at a time. These concerns have a direct bearing on the neglect of the area in terms of development.

Local people, however, have an additional set of fears. The most prevalent are drought and malnutrition, and the crop-raiding activities of wild animals. Generally, local people feel that their area is neglected in terms of development, which they feel emanates from above, that is, the escarpment. They feel that the road is bad, the health services insufficient, and the bus service erratic and expensive. Local people's perceptions of the area will be elaborated on in the text.

Ecological Profile

In terms of the ecological argument why wildlife utilization is appropriate in this area of the valley, four factors are the most important. These are: climate, soils, the presence of tsetse fly, and the presence of wildlife.

Climate

According to the Department of Meteorological Services, Kanyemba falls into the temperature region 'excessively hot' (Buchan 1989: 3). According to Buchan, the mean maximum daily temperatures remain above 30° centigrade throughout the latter part of the growing season, inhibiting effective pollination of Zea Mays (ibid.).

The mean annual rainfall figure for Kanyemba is 691 mm. However, as Buchan points out, rainfall is variable, 'one in four years being below 510 mm. and one in four above 833 mm.' (ibid. 1). Most of the rain falls in the months of December, January and February, though the main rainy season starts in November and ends in March. Mean annual evaporation in this area of the valley (Chirundu) is approximately 2004 mm.

Soils and land use

Chapoto ward is classified in Agritex land use classification as class IV, where rainfall is considered too low for cash-cropping except in very favorable areas. The best agricultural land in the ward is along the alluvium terraces of the lower sections of the Mwanzamtanda river (see Map 2). The remainder of the ward has very low potential for agriculture, owing to steeply dissected land with skeletal soils, rolling to hilly terrain with stony soils, undulated and dissected land with shallow soils and level to undulating terrain with fine grain sandy soils (Anderson 1987). In summary, the agricultural potential of the ward, except for the alluvium terraces, is extremely low because of poor soils, low rainfall and high evaporation.

Tsetse fly and sleeping sickness (Trypanosomiasis)

The presence of large numbers of tsetse fly had meant that there are veterinary restrictions on movement of cattle into the area. Trypanosomiasis and the presence of large predators, such as lion and leopard, restrict the viability of keeping cattle in the ward.[4] This has had an important effect on the cultural ecology, influencing marriage and settlement arrangements, in that brideservice has in the past been an alternative to bridewealth transactions involving cattle. The lack of draught power has influenced the

---

4. According to elders, cattle were kept in Kanyemba in the early part of this century, but as game and tsetse fly populations increased in the protected safari areas, it became more and more difficult to keep them alive.

nature and form of agricultural production especially amongst the Mvura who, to my knowledge, have never owned cattle. For example, Mvura fields are seldom stumped to enable tractor ploughing. In recent years, tractors have been funded by the World Vision organization. Yet, these service a minority of the total households (Cutshall 1990: 26).

A veterinary fence exists approximately 30 kilometers from the southern boundary of the ward. This is to prevent additional wildlife moving into areas which have been or are being cleared of tsetse fly and which are currently inhabited by cattle. According to Buchan, the planned eradication of tsetse fly in the ward, which is part of a larger tsetse eradication campaign throughout the Zambezi Valley, is not likely to occur before 1993 (1989: 19). Given the large populations of wildlife in the ward and its neighboring safari areas and national parks, this may be an optimistic assessment. If this occurs, it would enable people in the ward to have cattle. As Chief Chapoto said to me when I first entered the field and asked him about possibilities for future development: 'We want a fence around the whole ward. We want to kill all the wild animals, wipe out tsetse fly, so that we can keep cattle. Our fields will be safe and we will have cattle to plough.'

Tsetse flies have, in one sense, protected game in the competition with cattle production. Historically, the presence of tsetse fly has often led to the loss of game in large quantities, since game are the host animals for the tsetse fly. Culling host animals was used as a strategy for controlling tsetse fly in those areas where the early white settler ranches were established (Masona 1987: 53). Chief Chapoto's aspirations do not differ substantially from the early white settlers. They started ranches in tsetse infested areas, decimating the wildlife which it is now argued can have higher yields and is more ecologically suited to ecological regions with low rainfall and poor soils, such as much of the Zambezi valley.

The wildlife resource
It is reported that towards the latter part of the nineteenth century, large numbers of elephant in the area facilitated the Portuguese ivory trade (Buchan 1989: 17). Local accounts verify this. However, the resource was reportedly over-exploited and prior to the 1920s there were few elephants in the area (ibid. 17).

Considerable seasonal variation currently exists in both the numbers and diversity of animals in the ward. Mobility of animals may be affected by a number of factors, but the most significant ones for Chapoto ward appear to be movement in search of water and food and movement away from poaching activities in neighboring war-torn Mozambique.

Two aerial surveys undertaken in 1988 and 1989 indicated estimated numbers and densities of large herbivores in Chapoto ward. In 1988 it was estimated that there were 198 elephant, 1,250 buffalo, 13 rhino and 123 sable. In 1989 it was estimated that there were 85 elephant, 225 buffalo, 64 impala and 21 greysbok. No detailed assessments of the smaller game were made in the area.

Annual quotas of animals are set by DNPWLM for the hunting concession area and Chapoto ward forms 19 per cent of the total concession area. In 1989 28 animals were shot in the ward which included: 2 elephant, 1 lion, 5 buffalo, 1 kudu, 4 bush buck, 1 klipspringer, 6 impala, 1 duiker, 4 hippo and 3 crocodiles. Local people could name at least 30 different species of large wild animal regularly present and this should give the reader an idea of both the diversity and number of animals whose presence fluctuates within the ward. The most significant animals, in terms of safari hunting, during my presence in the ward, were buffalo, elephant and hippo.

Chapoto ward appears to be ideally situated for an alternative land-use strategy based on wildlife use. This is supported by the presence of relatively large numbers of wildlife, and its unique, remote situation wedged between two safari areas and a large tract of wilderness area in Mozambique, cut off from the rest of the country by Cabora Bassa Dam. This study argues that this potential is dependent on cultural and political dynamics. Therefore, we now turn to the people who could use this potential.

Ethnicity and Origins

In Chapoto ward there are currently at least three broad constellations of ethnic identity: VaChiKunda, Mvura and KoreKore (see Map 3). People also have combined identities which they use situationally. Thus, ethnic affiliation is made more complex by the instance of some people simultaneously claiming to be VaChiKunda/KoreKore or Mvura/KoreKore. During the bulk of the research period, there were two main constellations of identity centering on the Mvura and VaChiKunda. Towards the end of the research period a new group of KoreKore migrated into the ward. Each of the three groups mentioned can be identified in terms of

AN INTRODUCTION TO CHAPOTO WARD (KANYEMBA)

a set of significant ancestors, the royal ancestral spirits (*mhondoro* – see below), but there is considerable ambiguity and overlap in these constellations.

The majority of people in the ward are VaChiKunda, which means conquerors. They are descendants of a slave army loyal to Kanyemba, an indigenous war lord under the tutelage of the Portuguese towards the end of the last century. Kanyemba was a *prazo* (plantation or farm) holder and his Portuguese name was Jose do Rosario Andrade. According to Beach, by 1884 his family took all the territory from the Musengezi river to the present position of Chapoto ward, west of Zumbo (1980: 153). VaChiKunda regard themselves as owners of the land through their founding ancestor's military exploits. According to oral and written records, VaChiKunda displaced both the raiding Ndebele, who came as far as Zumbo, and the former inhabitants (KoreKore and Vasoli) from the vicinity of the Zambezi river (ibid.: Isaacman 1976). Kanyemba's sphere of influence along the Zambezi stretched as far as the Sanyati river (near Lake Kariba).

The Vasoli and KoreKore were affected by a series of upheavals towards the end of the last century, including raids by the Ndebele from the South, the VaChiKunda/Portuguese from the east and local wars. The Mutapa State, which had resisted the Portuguese and their VaChiKunda armies before, finally relented with the ascendency of Portuguese power in the late nineteenth century. These upheavals affected movements of the older autochthonous groups (Lan 1985). According to oral tradition, they fled across the Zambezi into what is now Zambia in the course of the upheavals (e.g. Chief Mburume). The VaChiKunda, who speak ChiKunda, are a linguistic and cultural assemblage of many river basin groups with origins in Mozambique, Zambia and Zimbabwe (Ntsenga, Tanda, Tserere, KoreKore amongst others), brought together as slaves and warriors to defend the Portuguese *prazos*.

A second major grouping in the ward is the ChiShona-speaking Mvura, also variously referred to as the Doma, VaDema and Deme (Mozambican usage), and more correctly referred to by their *mutupo* or totem *Mvura-tembo*.[5] This group now regard themselves

---

5. Among ChiShona speakers, totems or clan names are inherited from the father and are usually names of animals or parts of the body. Normatively, people are forbidden from eating their totem animal and it is also regarded as incest to have sexual relations or marry someone with the same totem. In the case of the Mvura, in the past, it was usual to marry within the totem. In the text I sometimes refer to the Mvura as VaDema in order to be consistent with other scholars (Nhira 1989; Cutshall 1990).

as basically an offshoot from the main KoreKore grouping under the ancestor Nyamapfeka,[6] although informants say they originally came from Songo near Cabora Bassa. Many of them do not like to be referred to as VaDema or Doma, but prefer to identify themselves with the KoreKore. Their origin may be *Vanyai* (low status dependent men/messengers – see Lancaster 1974: 77) brought into the area by Nyamapfeka, the KoreKore chief, or his descendants in the later part of the Mutapa state. At the time of the fall of the Mutapa state (1868–84), it was defended by dependent young men from minor lineages who, because the Zambezi valley was inhospitable in terms of making a livelihood, were forced to become dependents, bondsmen or even slaves of the wealthier (Beach 1980: 150, 151). These *Vanyai* 'drew their status from their mothers rather than their relatively lowly fathers', because through marriage women could be absorbed into the economy, but not men (ibid. 151). Such men would only serve as *Vanyai* until they were able to marry, after which time they were also absorbed as low-status dependent families. Beach claims it is difficult to understand why these Vanyai did not break away from the state like the VaChiKunda or why they did not become independent cohesive communities. He claims that this may be because the valley lowlands were so poor that the Vanyai were not able to subsist on what they hunted or raided and, therefore, remained dependent on their parent communities. During this period of upheaval, it is likely that the hilly remote areas, with their gullies full of luxuriant growth, in and around the western part of Dande (including Chapoto ward and the Chewore safari area), afforded dependent men of the Nyamapfeka lineage an opportunity to conduct a relatively isolated, protected and independent existence based on foraging. This mode of existence, amongst other strategies, persisted throughout the colonial period and the ensuing war for liberation, until the independence of Zimbabwe in 1980.

These Mvura have historically and mythically been set apart from other ChiShona-speaking people by adopting a nomadic and reclusive existence, which allowed them to resist the influence of

---

6. The Nyamapfeka dynasty has a tradition of descent from the mainstream Mwenemutapa dynasty under Mutota, its founder. This ChiShona-speaking state existed from the fifteenth century to the early twentieth century. Nyamapfeka was of the *Nzou-Samanyanga* (elephant-keepers of the tusk) totem, the ultimate rulers of the state. According to Beach, Nyamapfeka is seen as a descendant of Mutoto's daughter who stole magical powers from his mother's brother in order to conquer the Angwa river area (1980: 67). That is, there were associated lineages such as Nyamapfeka's which became incorporated in the Mutapa state.

the Mutapa state, the VaChiKunda/Portuguese invasion and the colonial state. Today they are geographically and culturally in closer proximity, but marked differences in life-style between them and other Zambezi valley dwellers exist. The option for them to continue living in the post-colonial state, as they did in the past, clashes powerfully with the increased vigilance of the protected wildlife areas (their former home) by militarized custodians of wildlife (who themselves are under threat from organized international poaching operations). Ironically, in my view, Mvura hunters and foragers could play an important role in providing information about poachers, if they were given access to the protected areas for limited use themselves.

The Mvura trace their descent from Nyamapfeka's daughter, Chiguhwa (i.e. they are an appendage to a significant and powerful patrilineage rather than being a significant powerful patrilineage themselves). Chiguhwa, also known as Semwa, and her second husband Chimhako (her first husband was Chimombe) are regarded as their royal ancestral spirits (*mhondoro*). They possess spirit mediums (*svikiro*) who reside outside the ward among the other grouping of Mvura under Chief Chisunga (KoreKore). Chimhako is reputed to have been the Mvura chief, but informants claimed that this institution no longer existed when colonial authorities were conferring chiefdomships on local people.

Chiguhwa is said to have been a very beautiful daughter of Nyamapfeka who won the heart of Chimombe (Chief of the VaSoli, renowned magician and rainmaker), also known to this day as the iron god and sender of the rain. She beguiled him into marrying her, and killed him for the sake of her father, who was his rival. Torrents of blood ensued from the murder and drained into and formed the Musikoti river (a tributary of the Chewore). Chimombe's body floated down the Chewore river and up another tributary, where he disappeared. In his place was found the iron god, a figure of iron (mounted on ivory) which, according to informants, is reputed to have one eye, one leg and one arm. Chimombe, also known as the iron god, is the most important rain-making ancestor in the area.

Chiguhwa was banished for this crime and went to live in the east (i.e. in the direction from which the Mvura are reported to come) and it was said that she and her descendants would not be allowed to marry. Mvura report that they regard Chimombe as an extremely important *mhondoro* and currently still prepare ceremonial salt destined for him via the less exalted spirits as a plea for rain. Lan provides a thorough analysis of this myth in the context of the KoreKore migration into the valley in search of salt and their symbolic negotiations with the autochthonous inhabitants (such as Chimombe) for control of rain through spirit mediums (Lan 1985). Depending on the political currents of the day (i.e. the degree of authority of local spirit mediums), the KoreKore will either claim rain-making powers for themselves, or will defer to the mediums of the original inhabitants. In a similar way, the VaChiKunda, who arrived in the area long after the KoreKore, currently appeal for rain by making offerings of salt and beads via the spirit mediums of the KoreKore (Nyamapfeka, Chikwamba) and the Mvura (Chiguhwa, Chimhako), who in turn appeal to Chimombe, autochthon and rain-maker.

If we are to believe Lan's analysis that conquerors defer to the rain-making powers of the original inhabitants, this in itself is good evidence that the Mvura preceded the VaChiKunda into this area. Versions of oral history that imply they were brought here from Chicoa (Mozambique) by Kanyemba as slaves (see Mombeshore 1987; Nhira 1989; Cutshall 1990) may not be the whole truth. However, some of the independent families, descendents of those who were with Nyamapfeka, may at one time have been attached to the VaChiKunda conquerors and in the course of the upheavals returned to their nomadic way of life. The headman of the Mvura, for instance, talks about a time when Chief Mburume made war on Chief Mpuka (both currently in Zambia). Kanyemba was drawn into the war and the Mvura fled into the hills to avoid the upheaval. As Nhira (1989) and Cutshall (1990) have pointed out, there is an ambiguity about the exact origins of the Mvura, but my research supports the version that they are descendants of a low-status lineage, connected to the many lineages associated with the latter days of the Mutapas, and the ensuing and subsequent upheavals prompted them to adopt a nomadic way of life.

Little has been written about the Mvura people. Their lives and life-styles have been shrouded in mystery, racist mythology and other misconceptions. Falsely described as the two-toed tribe of Africa, they have also frequently been referred to as pursuing a hunter-gathering existence. This is an inaccurate assessment of their life-styles, both now and in the past. According to local informants, shifting cultivation has always been an important mode of production. However, as Nhira (1989) points out, the term VaDema designates a way of life more than just an ethnic differentiation. Perhaps we should say it designates a former way of life marked by nomadism, foraging, storing of cultivated grains to see them through the planting season, reliance on the forest for the rest of the year, and lack of modern technological input. Lan implies that they adopted this life-style in response or resistance to both the Mutapa and the Rhodesian state. Local informants mention the upheavals discussed earlier as a reason, but it is also, in my view, a response to environmental conditions (availability of fruits, tubers and small game in remote hilly terrain) in this remote part of the valley.

Many Mvura informants were unwilling or unable to specify how their ancestral spirits were related to each other,[7] and many informants claimed that their most significant royal ancestral spirits were now those of the VaChiKunda (i.e. Kanyemba and his brothers). They claimed this was so because they were presently living in Kanyemba's area and therefore dependent on him for bountiful resources. There is, however, no ambiguity about Mvura claiming descent from Chiguhwa, identifying themselves more closely with the KoreKore than the VaChiKunda.

The little that has been written about Mvura describes them accurately as shy and retiring (Mtamayi 1959; Bullock 1950). In these earlier accounts, frequently, the difficulty of making contact with people from these groups is described and their lives are shrouded in considerable mystery. This seems to be a result of their reputed uncanny bush-craft abilities, their semi-foraging way of life, and their knowledge of plants and herbs for medicinal, food and supernatural purposes. The myth of two-toedness adds to this otherness. Hughes claimed, in his notes on Chewore history (undated report for DNPWLM), that the Mvura were by far the most mysterious group living in the area.

According to Cutshall, who enumerated household ethnic affiliations in the ward, 70.9 per cent of households claimed to be VaChiKunda, only 14.1 per cent claimed to be VaDema (Mvura), 10.3 claimed to be KoreKore and 4.7 claimed to be other (1990: 11). At the time of Cutshall and Nhira's study, and for the first 11 months of my research period, I think one could argue that there were two main constellations of ethnic identity gravitating towards the VaChiKunda and VaDema/Mvura poles. However, in August 1990, a new segment (about 15 households) of the KoreKore population moved away from Chief Chisunga (Angwa Bridge area).

---

7. This tendency of not being able to elaborate on one's ancestry is, according to Lan (1985), not uncommon amongst low status lineages in the Zambezi Valley.

They claim to have formerly come from within the Chewore safari area and wanted to be closer to their former home. They followed the lead of their spirit medium, Chikwamba, and have settled next to the Mvura. However, though they recognize the Mvura as relatives, they state that they are different from them, both in life-style and in background. Indeed they seem to have more in common with VaChiKunda, in the sense that they are more involved in the cash economy and the broader political and economic dispensation. This reinforces the Mvura ethnic identity as arising from their former semi-foraging way of life, which is perceived as having a low status. It is only since the end of the liberation war in 1980 that many Mvura have partially settled down within the ward. Before this time they were living isolated and non-sedentary lives in the hills of the Chewore Safari area. Both the Mvura and the VaChiKunda constitute small minorities in the broader political economy of Zimbabwe.

Political History Profile

The political past in the spiritual present: Kanyemba the war lord
Since the majority of people in the ward are VaChiKunda (at least two-thirds), and the chief, councillor and senior local officials are all VaChiKunda, they are likely to lead the CAMPFIRE program, if it should develop in this ward. It is, therefore, appropriate that I should spend some time in emphasizing and outlining their history and spirit world in describing Chapoto Ward. The installation of the spirit medium of Kanyemba took place shortly before I entered the field and this is an important political and religious (and potentially ecologically significant) event which will be returned to in later chapters. The installation of Kanyemba was preceded by the death of the spirit medium of Chihumbe (his brother), after being gored by a buffalo. This incident will also be returned to.

In analyzing the ancestral and territorial cults which are found in Southern Africa, we look at the past in order to understand the present. The present can perhaps only be understood by contextualizing and recreating the discourse concerning the past. Likewise, the past is understood or embellished by looking at the present. There is a politically and ecologically important dialogue going on between the past and the present. This dialogue is centered in the belief in ancestral spirits. Schoffeleers (1979) refers to the ancestors as the guardians of the land. Through death good people become spirits (*mudzimu*) who know the future and can cure bad things that happen. Bad people cannot become *mudzimu* (ancestral spirits), either because they are witches or because they have no descendants who can act as their mediums. Conventionally, chiefs in this world are the designated controllers of the land and its people through their ancestors, and when they die they in turn become royal ancestors (*mhondoro* – ChiShona), sometimes referred to as *phondoro* (ChiKunda). These ancestors are the owners of the land and the ecology in a specific spirit province (Garbett 1963) whose boundaries are defined by the *mhondoro*. In conjunction with the spirits of their neighbors, they can control rain, fertility of the soil, pests, crop-raiding animals and the abundance of fruit and other resources in the forest (e.g. honey). They speak of their descendants through the offices of a spirit medium, who himself or herself is usually not related in any way to the lineage of the chief or to the spirit in possession. Furthermore, the spirit medium is often a stranger geographically. In order to understand the dialogue between the past and the present in Chapoto ward, we need to begin with the influential historical figure of Kanyemba who now exerts influence through the spirit world. This dialogue is important in understanding the relations between people and their natural resources and it is therefore also central to CAMPFIRE.

Isaacman (1976) explains that during the scramble for Africa, when Europeans were drawing up boundaries and cutting up territories, it was pointed out to the Portuguese that in order to claim Mozambique as their territory they needed to demonstrate that they were in control of it. Though they had had a presence there since the fifteenth century, the prazo system[8] had taken on a momentum of its own and was no longer accountable to Lisbon, except in name. This was partly because in some areas the VaChi-Kunda war lords with their slave armies who originally were formed to protect the prazos from outside aggression were basically in control.[9] They themselves had often taken over the role of *praezero* (entrepreneur/manager), which had formerly been in the hands of individual Portuguese or their sons, through marriage/cohabitation with the indigenous women. Towards the end of the last century, a number of semi-independent secondary states existed in

---

8. The prazo or farm/plantation was an administrative, political and economic unit.

9. Isaacman argues that this was a form of pre-nationalist liberation movement.

Mozambique, some under the control of VaChiKunda war lords. The most westerly of these states along the Zambesi river was under the leadership of Kanyemba and was named after him. According to Isaacman, the Portuguese conferred the rank of sergeant on Kanyemba in the hope of bringing his activities under their tutelage and thereby extending their influence.

It is said that his badge of office or other medals are kept in the *Dendemaro* (shrine of the royal ancestral spirits (*mhondoro*) in Chapoto ward) and establishing their whereabouts is one of the tests which the incumbent spirit medium had to complete in order to be verified as 'Kanyemba'. Of interest is the fact that the correct way to address Kanyemba in the *Dendemaro* is 'Bon Dias Signore', because, as several informants pointed out, 'Kanyemba and his family are like white men'.

In 1877 Selous, the hunter and explorer, described the VaChiKundas as 'freed slaves or runaway slaves of the Portuguese – most of whom possessed flint muskets and owned allegiance to Kanyemba, a black man who held some official position under the Portuguese' (Hughes n.d.). Selous describes a visit to Senhor Joaquim Mendonca,[10] a Portuguese trader who had a large house, a flagstaff flying the Portuguese flag, many outbuildings and a large village occupied by dependants. During his visit, Kanyemba paid a visit 'in full dress with a large cavalry sword' (ibid.). Selous described him thus:

> a full blooded black man [and] came originally from the Zambezi, somewhere, I believe in the district of Tete (western Mozambique); he has a great deal of power in these parts, having a great number of men all armed with flint lock muskets, over whom he seemed to exercise the most despotic power. From what Mendonca told me, he seems to be constantly making raids upon any people in the neighborhood of the Zambezi who have anything to be taken. Kanyemba, on his island of that name, had a large barrack-looking house and at the back, and enclosed with a high palisade, were residence of the members of his harem, who to judge from the size of the enclosed space must have been pretty numerous. (Ibid.)

10. Of interest to me was the incidence of historical Portuguese names, often distorted through time, which the present VaChiKunda population bear. For instance, the father of the chairman of the wildlife committee was named Mindoka, which I assume to be derived from the name mentioned in Selous' account.

It is usual for the present spirit medium (a woman), when possessed by Kanyemba, to adopt a chastising and domineering manner in line with these historical notes. It is also remarkable that one of my research assistants, whose great grandfather had been a personal slave of Kanyemba and who it is said used to shave his hair, was immediately recognized as such on a first visit to the shrine and ordered to salute.

It would be incorrect to imply that ancestral spirits bear all the same qualities that they had when they were alive. It is true that Kanyemba is remembered as the historical figure of a war lord, but his role as a spirit goes a long way beyond this. Primarily, he looks after his children, his descendants and all those who live within his spirit province or realm. Like a parent, he can withdraw his support if his rules are not obeyed. These rules are not static, they change in response to the changing ecological, political, economic and cultural situations.

The institution of spirit mediums among the Shona is of political significance. The spirit medium speaking with the voice of the royal ancestor may on the death of a chief identify and authorize the 'true' chief from the contesting houses, usually made up from the descendants of brothers. However, among the VaChi-Kunda of Chapoto ward, spirit mediums appear not to have played a significant role in legitimizing chiefs, instead the state has historically adopted this role. See the genealogy (Fig. 2.1) and the account that follows it for evidence of this.

Contesting the chieftainship: the historical construction of chiefly power and authority
The institution of Chief is a central one for understanding why the entity of Chapoto ward exists at all. Early in the twentieth century, through the inception of colonial indirect rule policies, a chieftainship was established in this border area. This is not to say that Kanyemba and his brothers did not come from a chiefly family, but rather that the confirmation and recognition of a chieftainship of a defined area, as part of a broader British colonial dispensation involving district commissioners, was part of the process of subjugation to the colonial state. Likewise, the arbitrary identification of international boundaries bordering the ward was due to political and economic factors emanating largely from Europe, rather than from the local scene. However, the local scene responded to these political and economic forces with an interesting dynamic. Kany-

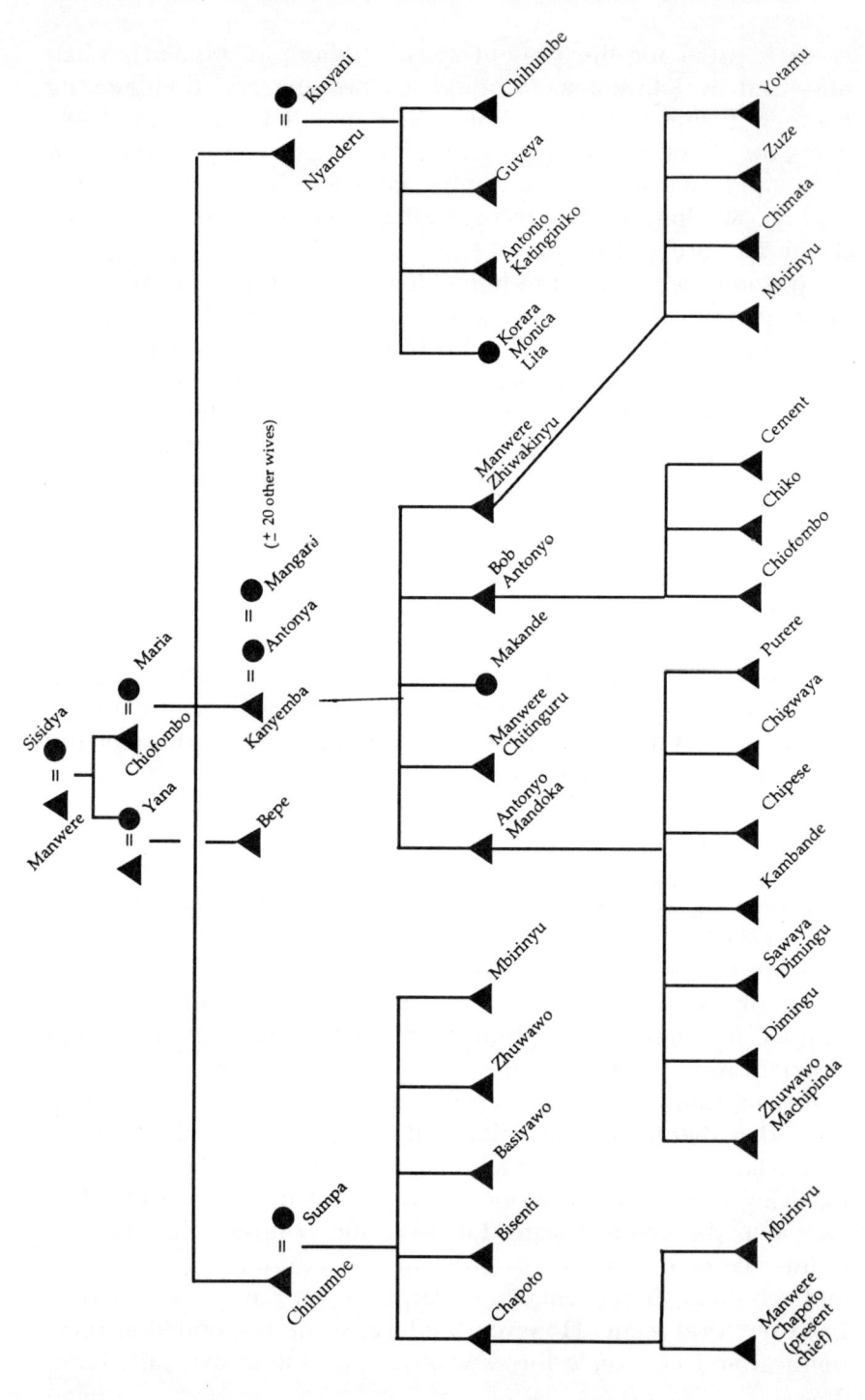

AGRICULTURE, FORAGING AND WILDLIFE RESOURCE USE IN AFRICA

Figure 2.1 Abbreviated genealogy of the spirit world and chieftainship of the VaChiKunda of Chapoto Ward

emba, the war lord who had ben co-opted/used by the Portuguese for purposes of their expansion, was not appointed chief.

A version of oral tradition alleges that the chieftainship had been 'usurped' by the sons of Chihumbe (see Fig. 2.1). At the turn of the century during the demise of the Mutapa influence, the rise of Portuguese expansion and the advent of colonial rule through the British South Africa Company, Kanyemba realized that valuable resources, particularly ivory, were available in the mid-Zambezi area. As he had armed soldiers loyal to him, he decided to co-operate with his father Chaufombo, chief of the VaTanda, in plundering the area. He and his two brothers, Chihumbe and Nyanderu, with the help of his lieutenant Chikohwa, succeeded in expanding their area of influence as far as the Sanyati river. A consequence of driving out the Ndebele, according to oral tradition, was that the local KoreKore would hand over control and ownership of the land to Kanyemba. As a result of these expansions, he set up various forts along the Zambezi and built his base near the junction of the Mwanzamtanda and Luangwa rivers, at the western end of the present Cabora Bassa dam. By the time British colonial rule extended its influence into this part of the world, Kanyemba was quite old. His nephew, Chihumbe's son, had warned him that the white man was after him and would punish him for his military activities in the area. Kanyemba temporarily fled back to Mozambique but promised to return. In his absence, the British colonial authorities implemented indirect rule by appointing Chapoto no. 1, his nephew, as chief. Chapoto claimed right to this position in an alleged ploy to safeguard Kanyemba from their enquiries as to his whereabouts. When Kanyemba returned he was upset by the fact that his brother's (Chihumbe) son had become chief. He protested, but he could not regain the chieftainship, as it had already been conferred, together with pith helmet, walking stick and chain, by the ceremonious and expeditious hand of British colonial power. However, the authorities did allegedly claim that in future generations this could be renegotiated and the chieftainship could move back to the house of Kanyemba if need be.

In contrast to this version of oral history, the district commissioner's delineation report for Chapoto ward (1965) boldly states that at the time that the present chief (Chapoto no. 3) assumed power, there were no other individual contenders for the position. As informants pointed out, it also assumed that the chieftainship should stay within the house of the sons of Chihumbe rather than being circulated to the sons of his brothers (Kanyemba and Nyanderu). As a colonial document, prepared by the district commissioner's offices who were interested in maintaining indirect rule, it conferred authority on the present chief and described him as benevolent dictator, shrewd but guided by the best interests of his people. The chief still has a considerable influence over current events, though these powers have decreased since independence.

The pageant of the past, and the contending houses, play an ongoing role in present local politics over the distribution of scarce resources and the waning of the present chief's power[11] in competition with the more modern VIDCO and WADCO processes. Shortly before I entered the field, two previous ward councillors had come to loggerheads with the chief over development issues. Both of these councillors claimed descent from the house of Kanyemba.

Symbolic of the decline of the chief's power is the siting of the new school. Contrary to his wishes, it was not built at his home situated in the northernmost area of habitation, which would have been an extremely long walk for schoolchildren living in the most southern area of habitation. Instead, it was built half-way between these two extremes, in the most densely populated area, which happened also to be the area where the core descendants of Kanyemba are located. The councillor responsible for arguing for the 'new site', however, decided to move out of the ward soon after this 'progressive' victory over chiefly power.

In general, those who support the chief and/or benefit from his power and authority usually live near him. It is interesting that the present councillor, a relatively young man in his early twenties, lives near to the chief and is related to him. However, like the previous councillor, he has come into conflict with the chief over the siting of the new school and the fate of the old school, which it has been suggested should be torn down and rebuilt at the site of the new school. Also of interest is the conflict over the renaming of the schools. The Ministry of Education recommended that schools should not bear the name of individuals in the community as their descendants would regard them as their property (e.g. Chapoto school is the current name of the school; Kanyemba school is also held to be unacceptable for these reasons). These issues are symptomatic of the conflicting interests between compet-

---

11. The present chief is in his eighties, and has held office for almost 50 years.

ing lines of descent between factions of the so-called 'traditional'[12] authorities. The conflict is further compounded by the newly introduced 'democratic' structures of the VIDCOs. This complex politico-religious relationship between chief, contending houses, spirit medium, WADCO and people is further complicated in Chapoto ward by ethnic and religious differentiation (not everyone publicly honours the ancestors). It is also complicated by competing land-use strategies, which further fragments cohesive tendencies. All these factors will be considered in the chapters that follow, as they have direct bearing on the potential for identifying common property regimes, as envisaged by CAMPFIRE. As argued throughout the book, these cultural, historical and political factors help us to understand the multiple jurisdictions involved in resource use.

---

12. I place both 'traditional' and 'democratic' in inverted commas to indicate that these are hackneyed terms.

CHAPTER 3
Agriculture and Foraging in Competition with Wildlife

Brideservice and Settlement Patterns

Agriculture and foraging practices compete with wildlife in many ways. Vested interests in particular land-use strategies are reflected in the way people organize themselves to use natural resources. Their rights to and jurisdiction over these resources are enveloped in their social organization and culturally defined ways of making their livelihood. In this chapter, brideservice and settlement patterns are shown to reflect the pervasiveness of this competition, in what might appear to be unrelated social factors. Also, population characteristics, and the dynamics and principles of household and cluster organization and distribution, are shown to be important for the analysis of wildlife resource use. These factors influence community projects and the distribution of household dividends earned from wildlife, which are mechanisms proposed by CAMPFIRE for the sustainable use of wildlife.

The population of the ward was enumerated at 1290 residents in 213 ward households (Cutshall 1990: 3). Since then, approximately 150 new residents, or 15 new households (KoreKore), have moved into the ward from Chief Chisunga's ward. Following the lead of their spirit medium, Chikwamba, and in consultation with the spirit medium of Kanyemba and the local councillor, they have settled as of August 1990 on the western bank of the Mwanzamtanda river (see Maps 2 and 3).

The population in the ward does fluctuate as people move to and from the ward. There is also considerable movement of households and household clusters within all segments of the community. This has obvious implications in setting up the possible CAMPFIRE 'wildlife resource area'. As will be shown below, the distribution of the population is indirectly an outcome of the presence of wildlife in the ward.

People regularly move place of residence, both seasonally and semi-permanently, to protect existing or new fields from wildlife, to establish new fields (*munda*) or to protect dry season river bank gardens (*dimba*) from wildlife, to pursue hunting and gathering activities and to move away from or closer to the changing river course. Throughout the ward is abundant evidence of abandoned household sites. A look at previous maps of the area underlines the fact that people have moved in the past and continue to do so in the present. Contingency appears to determine frequency and distance of major household moves as opposed to seasonal movement associated with protecting fields and gardens from wildlife. At least three major factors have influenced moves involving large portions of the community in the last 25 years.

A major move of the population occurred because of the guerrilla war (1972–80). People moved away from the Zambezi River, where cross-border incursions were taking place, and settled upstream on the alluvium deposits of the Mwanzamtanda dry river bed. Towards the end of the war, most of the population were relocated in 'protected villages' in Mashumbi Pools. The Mvura were not relocated, instead, they retreated into the hills conducting both foraging and cultivation.

In the course of these upheavals, many VaChiKunda people moved from the western bank to the eastern bank in order to be closer to the school, the clinic, the bus route and to exploit the available cultivable land on that side. Latterly (1988), the Mwanzamtanda river had flooded its banks and this has resulted in people moving to high ground, close to the bus route and the school, which is currently the center of many ward activities.

The bulk of the population currently live on the rich alluvium soils on either bank of the Mwanzamtanda river, where they compete with wildlife to harvest their crops. The majority of the population, an estimated 900 (mainly VaChiKunda), live on the eastern bank, while approximately 400–500 people (mainly Mvura), live on the western bank. Though Nhira (1989) and Cutshall (1990) identified 10 discrete residential clusters, these clusters are not permanent, static or monolithic. Some of the 10 clusters referred to by the above authors, in my opinion, might be better thought of as constellations of clusters.

A cluster may be usefully defined in terms of a smaller grouping, based on stated kin and friendship relationships. For the Mvura, the VaChiKunda and the KoreKore, the cluster usually centers on a group of brothers and/or brothers-in-law, or more important males who together, with selected affinal and consanguineal kin and trusted friends, live loosely in the same area and exploit the resources to make a livelihood. Constellations of clusters may break up and fuse with each other in a relatively short period of time, but clusters themselves tend to move with each other.

The smallest unit in the cluster can probably be referred to as a household (see discussion on problems in defining household in this chapter). Typically, a group of brothers and one or two brothers-in-law may live in the same area exploiting contiguous *dimba* (river-side gardens) and *munda* (fields) plots and/or foraging, but they will each have their own homestead, as will their parents and their married sons and daughters.

Knowledge of marriage arrangements is crucial information in understanding settlement patterns and household/cluster composition dynamics in relation to resource use. Amongst the Mvura, a preferential marriage in the past affecting settlement patterns has been that between mother's brother's daughter and father's sister's son. Another historically preferential marriage, currently frowned on by spirit mediums[1] and the broader society, is the marriage between a man and his biological and classicatory sister's daughters or granddaughters. Informants state that this happens because individuals cannot afford bridewealth to obtain a wife from elsewhere, but it also makes sense in terms of brideservice and the expectation of uxorilocal residence after marriage, since the bridegroom's services will not be lost to his own group.

In the case of marriage between a man and his mother's brother's daughter, his father may still be in the process of performing his brideservice duties, having adopted an uxorilocal residence. In this situation, it may be more convenient for the son to obtain a wife from his mother's kin and to continue the work and the reinforcement of established ties, which his father may have achieved in supporting his affines. Alternatively, the father may have already performed his brideservice duties and given bridewealth to his affines, which would enable him to bring his wife

---

1. Several Mvura informants claimed that these prohibited marriages used to take place more frequently in the past (i.e. when they were living isolated life-styles in the hills), but nowadays many of them frown on these practices and point fingers at one cluster which is particularly renowned for them. In my view, such practices may have developed largely out of necessity, as outlined in the text, in terms of a shortage of marriageable women. Beach also claims that a possible factor influencing the degree in which dependent men, such as the Vanyai, could form communities of their own, was availability of women (1980: 151).

and children home to his patrilineage. If the son, in this situation, were to marry his mother's brother's daughter and were to go to reside with his affines in order to perform brideservice, this would entail the loss of his services to his own patrilineage. However, if a man were to marry his sister's daughter or granddaughter, this would resolve the problem of having to go elsewhere to perform brideservice and possibly abandoning his own family to starvation.

Simultaneously, this type of marriage would consolidate the cluster, which in this case is centered on a brother-in-law doing brideservice for his affines. This would give incentive either to stay with the cluster, or a part of it, in the affines area, or to move the entire cluster, or a part of it, back to his own patrilineal group.

Both of these forms of marriage can reinforce or split the ties within the cluster. What adds further complexity to the situation is that, though common, these are not the only marriage relationships that exist among the Mvura.

I recorded instances of marriage to sister's daughter, mother's brother's daughter, levirate (as well as the expectation to marry the mother's brother's wife), father's sister's granddaughter and others. Instances of levirate may make sense in terms of brideservice and bridewealth. If a man has performed extensive brideservice duties his wife and children 'belong' to his own patrilineage and they have a concomitant responsibility to look after them. The expectation to marry mother's deceased brother's wife, may be an extension of the idea that men who have successfully completed bridewealth and/or brideservice are to gain the credit of having descendants living after them who are associated with their own lineage, thereby reinforcing them as a *mudzimu* (spirit). If no brothers are available to do this, then the father's sister's (*Vatete*) son is the next best person.

In general, I would describe the Mvura as a relatively, though not strictly, endogamous group in the sense that they prefer to marry within the clan totem (*mvura*) (also see Nhira 1989). This may relate back to Chiguhwa's murder of Chimombe and her banishment from the area, and the allegation that there was a prohibition on marriage with her or her descendants. This prohibition would effectively mean that her descendants would have to marry each other.

Despite the usual practice of endogamy, there are instances of marriage between VaChiKunda and Mvura, but the bulk of marriages take place between the two groups of Mvura, one living near the Mwanzamtanda river under Chief Chapoto and the other living near the Angwa river under Chief Chisunga (KoreKore).

The VaChiKunda, also a patrilineal grouping, appear to have more social mobility in their marriage arrangements. This may simply be because they are economically better off and come into contact with more of the outside world. One of my VaChiKunda research assistants, for instance, had married a woman from Masvingo (700–800 kilometers away). In general, I believe Nhira is correct in pointing out that a son-in-law can choose whether to stay with his in-laws, his own lineage group, or to establish a new home of his own (Nhira 1989: 4). These options may be negotiated with the affines, but each will have its own obligation. If the son-in-law takes the wife back to his own home, or starts a new home of his own, he will usually be expected to pay bridewealth in full, but if he resides with his in-laws and does brideservice he can put off payment of bridewealth to a future date. Informants claimed that brideservice and uxorilocal residence and the bond that develops between brothers-in-law, was more pronounced in the older generation than in the present one. However, many of the existing clusters were centered around a significant set of elders, brothers-in-law or brothers, whose children and grandchildren may have set up households nearby.

Constellations of clusters fall into three VIDCOs (see Map 3). Nyaruparu VIDCO is made up of Chapoto, Pondo and Chimata/Chipese/Black constellations, while Chiramba VIDCO is made up of Kasinjere/Chagaruka, Chiramba and Erad Eria Mtamawo (Manbure, Mugarirahonye) constellations. Chansato VIDCO is made up of Arizhibowa/Zhuwao, Mubinzi/Stone, Chiyambo/Mugonapanje/Bandera and Koranzi/Chaukura constellations. There was talk that the new constellations of Chikwamba will have to form its own VIDCO, but though geographically it is presently part of Chiramba (mainly Mvura VIDCO), they have been incorporated into Chansato VIDCO (mainly VaChiKunda). The residential cluster of Kuhwe, identified as such by both Nhira and Cutshall, should be renamed ('Dumba' is the influential male in this cluster) since Mr. Khuwe and his family have moved his house and fields across the river to join Koranzi and Chaukura. This is a minor point, but it serves to illustrate the changeable nature of settlement patterns in the ward.

Kasinjere/Chaguruka is mentioned as part of Chiramba cluster by Nhira and Cutshall but local people do make the differentiation between Chiramba and Kasinjere/Chagaruka. Similarly, what these authors have referred to as Chimata cluster can be broken down into a number of smaller clusters.

Property Relations and Land Tenure

At the center of the competition between wildlife, foraging and agriculture are the competing claims to land. These are exerted by the state, the erstwhile protector of wildlife, but claims are also exerted by the ancestral spirits, who are the historical and cultural owners of the land and also the proprietors of the ecological health of the area.

All fields and riverside gardens are clearly and unambiguously demarcated. Outsiders might not be aware of the line of demarcation but neighbors will know the exact markers. A resident's field may end at the *masawo* tree in the west, the path in the east or there may be a stone between neighbours in the north. In the case of ward residents, contiguous uncultivated land is claimed by clearing and once a piece of land has been used it remains the property of the user until such time as someone else negotiates for its use and obtains permission from the original user. These general rules apply to ward residents who are cultivating plots near their established place of residence. If someone were not a long-term ward resident, or if someone in the extreme south of the ward decided to cultivate a *munda* and a *dimba* in the extreme north of the ward, different arrangements would have to be made.

Outsiders wishing to settle in the ward, and residents wishing to move their place of residence a long distance within the ward, should consult and request permission from the spirit medium on the wisdom of their intention (e.g., the place they intend to move to might be plagued with crop-raiding animals). Simultaneously, they should request permission from the local councillor, who is the representative of local government at ward level. While negotiating with the councillor, they should also confer with the chief or headman in whose area they would like to live. Once all these people have been consulted and the land is cleared, the new resident is regarded as a member of the community with rights to land.

Amongst the VaChiKunda, when a man dies his widow and his sons will inherit all his property together with his rights to his fields. The widow and her sons, living in the ward, will manage the estate until such time as she dies. When this happens, the property will pass on to the sons who remain in the ward. In the case of levirate (especially among the Mvura), a man's brother will inherit both his wife and portions of his property, which may also include rights to field and garden sites. Thus, rights to land are closely linked to patrilineal affiliation, and this in turn is an elaboration of ancestral history. The owners of all land in the ward are the royal ancestral spirits; patrilineages claim affiliation with these ancestors through paying homage to them if they are outsiders or by claiming descent, if they are related. Those who, for religious reasons, do not honor the ancestral spirits may obtain land by requesting permission from the councillor and headmen/chief, but they also inherit through the patrilineal line of descent.

It is through the ancestors, therefore, that rights to the protected areas of the Chewore and Dande safari areas are claimed by many Mvura and VaChiKunda in the ward. Some VaChiKunda families recall how their parents were cultivating river-side gardens inside the Chewore safari area in the 1960s. Mvura recall the places where they and their parents lived in the past and there is a sense that their ancestors are still there. As has been stated, late in the fieldwork a group of KoreKore, who previously lived in the Chewore safari area, moved down into the ward ostensibly to be closer to their ancestors. This emphasizes the fact that ancestral belief systems are territorially based and are used as a powerful lever in terms of establishing land tenure claims. The politics of the present land tenure system, where large portions of the Zambezi Valley are protected for wildlife by the state, may in the future have to come to terms with conflicting and competing claims over land derived from the ancestral past and land scarcity in other areas. Such claims may become more apparent, if the proprietorship of wildlife in buffer areas next to the wildlife estate succeeds and if income is generated from such proprietorship. Such an eventuality may encourage many people with former ties to the protected areas to appeal to live next to these areas.

Population Distribution and its Relationship to Hunting, Collecting and Protecting Agricultural Practice from Crop-Raiding Animals

As has been mentioned, both the VaChiKunda and Mvura homesteads can be described as a series of clusters. These clusters are usually centered around:

(a) a headmen/*sabhuku*;
(b) economically rich or resourceful male heads of homestead who have attracted other families (frequently affinal or consanguineal kin); and
(c) individuals, particularly brothers in-law doing brideservice, who can be described as 'sharing' in the exploitation of resources of a particular area.

It is worth emphasizing the relationship between brideservice and hunting. The practice of brideservice,[2] I argue, has important significance in terms of wildlife resource use in the ward. In the past, amongst both the VaChiKunda and the Mvura, a marriageable daughter would attract a husband who would settle near to his in-laws and who would provide services to them in the form of agricultural labor, crop protection, building of huts and granaries, and hunting. Through hunting the son-in-law would be able to fulfil his obligations to his wife's family and would also be able to attain much prestige. However, hunting was and still is considered a secret. Reliable informants have pointed out that, despite and perhaps because of the generalized expectation to share resources, individual clusters of relatives (especially brothers-in-law) and close friends (e.g. people who one trusts to hunt with, people who are loyal) keep hunting resources to themselves, as others will be a drain on scarce resources and will obtain power over them through their knowledge that they are engaging in illegal activities.

This is a partial explanation for the many discrete clusters that exist in the ward. Other more obvious explanations for the geographical distribution of the population refer to the system of agricultural production and the measures taken to protect agriculture from crop-raiding animals.

Overview of agriculture
There are two main methods of crop production conducted in Chapoto ward: *munda* or field, wet season cultivation and *dimba* or *dowe*, dry season cultivation. Both VaChiKunda and Mvura currently practice *munda* and *dimba* cultivation, as well as foraging.

---

2. The absence of cattle because of trypanosomiasis meant people did not readily have appropriate 'bridewealth'. Brideservice can, therefore, be seen as a cultural mechanism in coping with the presence of tsetse fly.

Munda *cultivation*

Munda or field cultivation refers to the wet season crop. Both cotton and maize production carried out by the VaChiKunda, and shifting cultivation carried out by the Mvura fit into this category. *Munda* cultivation entails the clearing and sometimes stumping of fields. In general, VaChiKunda tend to cultivate their fields for longer than the Mvura; many of whom prepare new fields or add on to existing fields every year.

A large proportion of Mvura practice shifting cultivation of mixed grains during the wet season (maize, sorghum, *mhunga*) on an annual basis, unlike VaChiKunda farmers who use fields for much longer periods and some of whom grow cotton as a cash crop, and/or maize, sorghum, groundnuts, rapoko (cash crop) and rice. *World Resources 1990–1991*, a report on the state of the world's natural resources, claims that shifting cultivation 'can sustain agriculture indefinitely, even in harsh conditions if fallow periods are long enough' (World Resources Institute 1991: 70). Though Mvura have very poor yields from their fields in general, their agricultural practices have elements in common with some of the most progressive ideas emerging on intercropping.

Since many Mvura do not stump their fields, fields are allowed to recover more quickly from cultivation. Ironically, this is condemned as being a backward agricultural practice by extension agents and by the VaChiKunda, since stumping is required if tractors are to be used. Many VaChiKunda stump their fields to enable ploughing with a tractor for monocropping to pay for use of the tractor.

Another feature of Mvura practice is that they do not plant in straight lines, but in patches or clumps. Each clump of seeds might include a variety of grain (maize, *mungha*, sorghum, *rapocco*) and not just one type. This mixed grain strategy involves less labor than ploughing up an entire field, and the diversity is said to be good for pest and crop-raiding animal control, and provides for a degree of drought resistance. According to Cutshall, Mvura households were far more inclined to grow a 'rational' mixture of grains than their VaChiKunda counterparts (1990: 32). However, Cutshall also identifies the anomaly that Mvura households are amongst 'the smallest agricultural producers in the community, are especially vulnerable to crop failure and in the event of drought, are quite likely to be hardest hit by subsistence deficits' (ibid. 30). While I was in the ward some Mvura households obtained no harvest from their wet season crop.

Dimba *cultivation*

Dimba or *Dowe*, dry season cultivation, refers to garden cultivation that takes place at the river's edge, if not in the river itself (see Plates 1 and 2). This is possible because the dry river bed deceptively holds significant quantities of water which permeate the sand. It is also possible, because the alluvium deposits brought down by the river are frequently found at the river's edge where they are covered with a shallow layer of sand. Crops such as maize, beans, groundnuts, vegetables, bananas, sugar cane, tobacco, cassava, rice, pawpaw, mangoes, sweet-potatoes, groundnuts, beans, sunflower and others are planted in shallow pits.

Amongst the Mvura, *dimba* sites are generally much smaller and less developed than VaChiKunda sites. There is a marked seasonal migration between *dimba* and *munda* sites, which may be as far as one and a half kilometres or more apart. In the *dimba*, temporary grass enclosures are built near to the river bank. Below the bank, mainly maize and other grains are grown in small pot-shaped holes. The well-established banana groves and vegetable gardens of the VaChiKunda are a stark contrast to the more meager cultivation that goes on in the Mvura gardens.

Lush *dimba* sites are particularly attractive to crop-raiding animals. Animals and people compete directly for the sustenance which the dry river bed can provide. Near to the confluence of the Mwanzamtanda and the Zambezi, there is a problem of crop-raiding hippo, while further south down the Mwanzamtanda buffalo cause a lot of damage. Both of these species are highly valuable in terms of safari hunting.

The *dimba* or dry season stream bank cultivation is extremely important as a strategy to survive the extraordinarily harsh weather conditions where the evaporation rate far exceeds the average annual precipitation. In the *dimba*, it is possible to cultivate crops during the long dry season, which otherwise would be impossible. Thus *dimba* sites are relatively scarce and in former times the population appears to have spread out along the course of the river and set up habitation near the *dimba* sites. The reason people want to live near their *dimba* is to be able to protect them from the various wild animals attracted to the crops. Cutshall reports that of the 213 ward households, 185 households reported 678 individual crop-damage incidents for the 1987–8 agricultural year (1990: 56). Notable amongst these animals are buffalo, elephant, hippo, wild pig, bushbuck and baboon which are always looking for new pastures and good supplies of water during the dry season.

As has been pointed out, people (mainly VaChiKunda) also grow cash crops and food crops in *minda* (fields) on the slightly higher alluvium terraces. These are planted at the beginning of the rainy season (November/December) and are harvested in April. These crops also need to be protected from wild animals including wild pig and kudu, as well as those already mentioned. Thus farmers ideally want to have residential sites that are near to both the *munda* and the *dimba*, as it is impossible to be in two places at the same time to protect one's produce. Small livestock such as chickens, rabbits and goats are usually kept at the main residential site and these also need to be protected from predators. In this regard, Cutshall reported that 136 households reported 206 separate incidents involving domestic animal loss for 1987 (ibid. 58).

In practice, the *munda* is frequently a fair distance away from the *dimba*, and at the present time it is not unusual for people to live part of the year near the *dimba* and part of the year near the *munda*. The tension created over protecting one's *dimba* and *munda* sometimes results in a division of labor within the family. For instance, the husband protects the *munda*, while women and/or children protect the other fields and/or livestock at the main homestead. As will be elaborated on, agricultural practice and population distribution can be seen as a form of wildlife management. Social organization is a response to the competition between agriculture and wildlife. The building of a *ntsaka* (hut/shelter) and *dara* (shelter on stilts to facilitate identification and protection from crop-raiding animals) in fields is symptomatic of this competition between wildlife and agriculture. The point is emphasized that residents are actively managing wildlife through protection of their agricultural practice.

Not everyone has access to a *dimba*. Ironically, the reason some Mvura claimed they did not have a *dimba* to grow conventional crops was because they had been told by a safari operator's assistant[3] that the potentially available areas were to be kept for animals. Amongst the Mvura those who do not have access to a *dimba* during the dry season channel their productive activity into exploiting the available fruits, berries, roots and tubers, as well as clandestinely obtaining protein from hunting. A commitment to foraging therefore reduces the potential labor to work in the *dimba*. There is

---

3. The man had argued that Zambian poachers were better than local poachers because they at least killed animals for money whilst the locals merely killed animals for meat.

considerable variation in the degree to which people exploit these resources. Those who are highly dependent on illegal hunting and illegal collecting[4] activities, have good reason not to live in close proximity with many other people. First, the resources in the immediate area would have to be shared amongst all the inhabitants of the residential area and secondly, people should only allow those whom they trust to know that they have access to resources which are obtained illegally. Rivals and enemies can use this information against each other by reporting these activities to authorities or by threatening to do so.

This set of pragmatic arrangements, which has influenced residential pattern, contrasts markedly with ideas about consolidation of homesteads into a single consolidated village. These ideas have been put forward by government as a panacea for many ills, including the lack of 'development' in the area and the assumption that the illegal river bank cultivation is detrimental ecologically in the case of the Mwanzamtanda.

One or two members of the community (e.g. an ex-councillor and a teacher) regularly advocate at meetings the idea implicit in the MZP that progress will only take place if people consolidate their land holdings, consolidate their dwelling areas, and move away from the life-giving river. This entails them moving up on to the higher less-fertile land above the river. In one section of Chapoto ward (Nyaruparu VIDCO) people have done this for two main reasons: to be closer to the new school site and bus route, and to avoid the flooding river. However, it is well known in Chapoto that the land away from the river is not fertile.

People live on the western side of the Mwanzamtanda river (mainly Mvura), I argue, because they have historically had access to resources and a way of life (a combination of gathering, shifting cultivation, hunting, *dimba* cultivation, exchange and employment) that would be denied them on the eastern bank. If the Mvura are resettled on the eastern bank, as has been suggested by government officials, this would make them more dependent upon food for work in the VaChiKunda fields, as most of the arable land is already being used on this side. The ward councillor at one time had in mind that they should be moved up on to the infertile land, away from the river. The idea of moving them has, amongst certain influential people at the ward and district levels, become associated

---

4. People have been arrested for collecting (e.g. *mpama* and honey) in the Chewore safari area, besides the many arrests for illegal hunting, mainly in the form of snaring.

with both progress and CAMPFIRE. It is associated with progress, because supposedly the Mvura will settle down to a 'civilized' agricultural practice, with all its dubious benefits in this impoverished ward (see the case-study of the 'successful cotton grower' below). Moving the population has been associated with CAMPFIRE, because the creation of a wildlife resource area on the western bank is seen as a rational response to maximize revenues from wildlife, since the western bank is rich in these resources and it is argued that a minority of people should not interfere with aspirations of the majority.

If the Mvura were resettled on the eastern bank, it would make hunting and gathering activities more inaccessible for them and it would also create competition over land between Mvura and VaChiKunda households. The few VaChiKunda households who have stayed on the western bank (Mambure, Mugarirahonye and Dumba) argue that the land is much more fertile and readily available on this side. Living on this side also offers hunting and gathering opportunities and two of these households own guns. These VaChiKunda balance these advantages against the dubious advantages of living on the eastern bank. These include being closer to the school, the road (bus access), the clinic and the extension of the power and authority structures of the state (the chief, the police, the VaChiKunda VIDCO, the agricultural extension officers, etc.).

In the case of the Mvura, if one does not have the means to obtain clothes for a child (often exchanged for honey or labor with the VaChiKunda), or if one cannot adequately feed her/him, sending that child to school is hardly a priority. Besides, even amongst the generally more affluent VaChiKunda, children provide an important source of cheap labor. Living on the western bank, away from authorities, provides a degree of autonomy which appears to be valued highly.

Reliable sources from Chiramba[5] (the Mvura VIDCO on the western bank of the Mwanzamtanda river) told me that if the government, in the name of development or as part of an alternative land-use strategy (e.g. wildlife utilization), forces people to be

---

5. The argument against moving to the eastern bank is couched in the agriculturally biased value system of the broader society. The argument is stated in terms of there being a lack of fertile land on the eastern bank. On probing, it was discovered that the real reason why people wanted to stay was because they would have access to the resources within the forest. In the past these have sustained them through the drought years, before the advent of drought relief distribution or other aspects of 'development'.

resettled on the eastern bank, they will not succeed. All those Mvura living on the western bank will flee into the hills to pursue foraging activities, as they did when the Rhodesians attempted to force people into 'protected villages' in order to reduce contact between guerrillas and locals during the guerrilla war. I have visited the site where Chiyambu, the headman of the Mvura, lived during this time. It is in a thickly wooded stream valley, not far from present sites of habitation. There is a water source there and flood plain, besides the stream that was used for cultivation. Honey collection, *mpama* (a tuber) and other tubers, fruits and berries, as well as hunting, are all accessible. Chiyambu was only discovered living there at the end of the war. I believe there are many such sites in the area and since the Mvura have few fixed assets and receive few benefits from the present situation, it is easy to see how they could move on at a moment's notice.[6] At present, they move seasonally within their present location. Historically, as will be explained in more detail later, Mvura often practised shifting cultivation during good rainy seasons. They stored their grain harvest in bark containers and hid them, while they foraged during the dry season. The grain would then be used up during the next planting season.

Foraging and the Mvura (*VaDema*) Dilemma

In the past, the Mvura had a number of different strategies which they used to survive in their mountain fortress home, known as Chiramba kaDoma.[7] These can be described as collecting, hunting (usually small game), shifting agriculture and other employment and exchange. Today, the range within which they can pursue their hunting, collecting and subsistence activities has been greatly reduced. This is because of the implemented controls on illegal entry, hunting, and collecting in the protected areas (in this case the Chewore safari area, and the hunting concession area, which includes Chapoto ward), which used to provide them with their

---

6. After the onset of the widespread drought in Southern Africa, with the failure of the 1991/2 rains, it was reported in the local newspaper that many Mvura had returned to their former way of life.

7. The eastern part of these mountains form the boundary of Chapoto ward, and most of the Mvura in the ward now live at the foot of these mountains.

range.[8] Their way-of-life is a casualty, clashing, as it does, with the powerful vested interests in wildlife. Particularly, they are caught in the cross-fire in the war over the protection of the rhino and the African elephant. Anti-poaching units, with legal indemnity to shoot and to ask questions later, have instilled in the Mvura a fear of pursuing activities that are vital for their sustenance.

A letter written from the provincial headquarters of the DNPWLM to the district administrator's office, underlines the way the problem has been perceived in the past by this authority. The letter explains that yet another family of Mvura had been apprehended by the national parks scouts and points out that the individuals involved were engaging in subsistence activities (i.e. foraging). It requests the administrator to provide more drought relief to the Mvura, in order to prevent them from engaging in such activities. The assumption is that provision of drought relief would prevent people from engaging in cultural activities, such as hunting and collecting. This serves to illustrate that while DNPWLM is, on the one hand, looking for progressive and innovative ways of using resources sustainably for the benefit of local people (e.g. CAMPFIRE), there are quite different perspectives and interests exhibited both within and between different government departments. This is a key stumbling block in the CAMPFIRE program and it is well illustrated by the relations between the Ministry of Local Government (district administration) and the DNPWLM, whose agendas do not always cohere.

Honey-collecting and the collection of a wide range of fruits, berries, tubers, worms and other items has been a very important feature of the Mvura way of life in the past and it continues to be

---

8. The Harare newspaper, *The Herald*, had a spate of articles on the plight of the VaDema people in mid-1990. One editorial stated that, 'drought, in the majority of cases has a devastating effect on the lives of people, especially those with no history of agricultural practice and the impact is disastrous. This is how the famine is likely to effect the Dema people who last received what they say is insufficient drought relief more than two months ago. These people have no idea of how to cope with a drought situation' (*The Herald*, 14 September 1990). The irony in the last statement is that the knowledge of coping with a drought situation is patently very strong amongst the VaDema. The reason they are presently suffering is not because of lack of knowledge, but because there is a paramilitary operation (anti-poaching activities) preventing them from implementing their knowledge on how to cope successfully with the harsh valley environment, through hunting and collecting strategies. So often whilst in the field I heard VaChiKunda cotton growers or agricultural and other extension officers say of the Mvura, 'they do not know how to practice agriculture'. I then thought of a conference I had attended in the US on sustainable agriculture. I realized that many ideas in the Mvura practice would be endorsed by progressive agricultural thinkers. As outlined in the text, some of these might be: mixed grain strategies, not using hybrid seeds, not ploughing with a tractor but using a hoe and thus causing less oxidization of the soil, and not stumping trees.

an important mainstay of life in the present. However, in Chapoto ward there is considerable variation in the degree to which individuals rely on collecting (and hunting and fishing for that matter). In general, both hunting and collecting are limited within the ward itself and the richer resources of the Chewore are beyond the reach of many who would like to have access to them. This is not because they are incapable of getting access to these resources, but because they fear being arrested by game scouts and anti-poaching units active in this area.

In general, there are two categories of collecting. First, there is the collection of the most accessible resources within the ward itself. Secondly, there are those who take the risk of arrest and enter the Chewore safari area or venture further into the hunting concession area, protected by law and by the game-scouts and anti-poaching units. Local informants reported that game scouts had warned them about entering the hills that border the Chewore (i.e. the massif – a portion of these are well within the ward). Rumor has it that there is the possibility of, at worst, being shot on sight and, at best, being arrested. Mvura are apprehended or arrested for illegal entry into the Chewore safari area, as well as collection, fishing, hunting and snaring within the ward itself. Considerable fear therefore exists among the Mvura population about being apprehended whilst moving around, even within the boundaries of the ward. Few people in the ward know where the boundaries of the ward are and these boundaries are artificial, as they can be arrested for snaring and hunting within the ward (often by the safari operator's personnel who are protecting his concession).

Within the last 15 years, Mvura had been living inside the Chewore or near to its boundary, and, according to local informants, had been issued with snares by the Rhodesian government. After 1980, when it became possible to implement stricter controls on the management of protected areas, the Mvura were wooed by politicians and government officials down from the hills with promises that there was a new and better way of life for them in the new Zimbabwe. The assumptions behind this included the notion that this would entail their embracing a settled more civilized way of life. The corner-stone of this, of course, would be an increased reliance on settled agriculture, a potent bias in the broader Zimbabwean value-system. Implicitly, foraging, the life-style which had enabled them to resist the influence of the state, would be forfeited and 'development' would replace it. This might include health care, education, participating in the democratic processes at village and ward levels, and benefiting from the various extension and other services available from government. These would include: drought relief and proposed programs concerning water and sanitation, or incorporating them in such programs as CAMPFIRE.

Unfortunately, Chapoto ward is one of the badly neglected parts of Zimbabwe, and the quality and quantity of what might be referred to as development are sadly lacking. The promises and hopes of 'development' may prove to be false hopes. In general, the Mvura have attempted to benefit from the little that is available in both the foraging and development worlds. However, from their point of view, it is not yet clear what the benefits of 'development' are. The World Vision program in the ward, for instance, has built a number of boreholes. All these boreholes exist on the eastern bank of the Mwanzamtanda river and are much too far away from Mvura households to be of any use. Almost all of them are too saline to be used for drinking or even cooking. Besides, Mvura have adequate supplies of water from the natural springs at the foot of the massif and from shallow wells in the dry Mwanzamtanda river bed itself. The latter is also the source of the drinking water for the VaChiKunda population on the eastern bank of the river.

A small portion of Mvura children attend school.[9] This means that they are not involved in other activities that might be more necessary for short-term survival, such as working in the fields of the VaChiKunda for as little as a bowl of maize meal a day, collecting available fruits and berries and small game, or guarding their own fields from crop-raiding animals.

Another prominent symbol of development, or rather the lack of development, in the ward is the clinic, situated between 15 and 18 kilometers away from the furthest Mvura households and relatively far away from the other residents in the ward. It is hoped that this clinic will be moved to a more central location where people will be able to make use of it with more ease. However, when one considers that there are a number of well-known herbal specialists among the Mvura and that they do not place much faith in western medicine, we might well ask what is the perceived benefit of a new clinic for them. In contrast to development, foraging, if allowed, offers the tangible necessities of survival.

---

9. CAMPFIRE community projects funded from wildlife revenue often focus on schools and clinics.

Collecting fruits, tubers, and berries
The forest is not what it seems, neither is the apparent vacuity of Mvura life. By this I mean that outsiders have judged the Mvura to be poor, lacking in knowledge about how to farm, and to be somewhat inferior and uncivilized. Many VaChiKunda have said to me, of the Mvura, 'they are too shy to stay with people like myself' or 'we have tried to tell them the importance of the clinic and school, but they don't understand. Their children run away from school because they have no clothing.' A visit to one of the Mvura makeshift shelters, a look at the limited material resources they have, and their meager untidy fields (see Overview of Agriculture, pp. 73–80 above), might reinforce the bias that they need to be told how to live. However, the ink in which their knowledge is written is for the most part invisible to us and it is only when we try to see through their eyes that we realize the richness and potential of that knowledge. Walking with Mvura was like taking a pair of glasses which allowed one to see things for the first time which one had passed by daily. For example, within a radius of 500 meters from his abode, a Mvura informant could identify most of the following edible plants and describe how to prepare them. I present them here because this indigenous knowledge is as important as, if not more important than, the more recent agricultural practices of maize and sweet potatoes cultivation introduced to the area as late as the sixteenth and seventeenth centuries. The following account is not comprehensive, but it gives the reader a sense of the importance of indigenous knowledge in regard to the most important edible tubers, fruits and berries, and gives ecological flesh to the essentially political nature of the presentation so far.

1. The *Mandapanda* (pods) of the Mpakasa plant (Lonchocarpus capassa) are ready in October. Pods are emptied and boiled in water. They are prepared in the same way as beans.
2. *Bonongwe* (Aerva leucura) leaves are boiled as relish with tomatoes. These are not available in the dry season but are ready in December/January. These plants are not weeded in the fields of the Mvura because they are known to be relish.
3. *Ngayi* (Vangueria infausta) is a tree which provides fruit. It is sometimes used as a porridge sweetener.
4. *Mutukuta* (Piliostigma thonningii) is used to cure influenza. The leaves are boiled with water and it is drunk as a tea. The ancestors knew that it could cure.

5. The *Muteme* (Strychnos madagascariensis) plant has a fruit like a hard shell which one has to break open to eat. It is ripe during January and February. One usually takes the inner kernel and roasts it on the fire.
6. The fruit of the *Mutondo* plant (Cordyla africana) is known as *matondo*. It is yellow and sweet like a mango. One waits until the fruit drops from the trees before picking. These are not cooked but are eaten 'on the way'. They are ready in December and January.
7. *Bepe* and *Guruvi* (Taka leontopetaloides) are poisonous but edible tubers. The toxic substances in these tubers may be leached up to four times in boiling water. An agent for aiding this process is the Kapikira plant (Amplocissus africana).
8. *Masawo* (Ziziphus mauritiana) is widely collected as a staple by both the VaChiKunda and Mvura population. It is a small but very tasty fruit. These fruits are both eaten 'on the way' and collected and dried for later use during the hot dry months before the rains come. People will usually not cut down a *Masawo* tree if one happens to be in their *munda*. The fruit is also used to make an alcoholic drink. My 14-month-old daughter developed a healthy appetite for these (see Plate 3).
9. *Matohwe* (Azanza garceana) is also a fruit which exudes a sweet brown mucus. Some years the tree does not bear fruit, as occurred in the 1988/9 season when heavy rains fell.
10. The *Mnonde* tree (Xeroderis stulmannii) bears pods which contain edible beans. These are ripe in August. They are boiled and cooked in the same way as beans. They are only eaten in dire famine.
11. The *Ntacha* (also *Matatya*, Berchenia discolor) bears a fruit that ripens in February, which is often eaten by monkeys. It is used as a porridge sweetener. One boils it and then takes out the pips. The residue is used as a sweetener or relish.
12. *Nzviru/Horongwa* (Cleistochlamys kirkii) is a black fruit, which ripens in February and can be used in the same way as *Ntacha*.
13. *Nchinga* (Friesodielsia obovata) provides a sweet fruit which ripens in February. The fruit should be peeled, the juice can be squeezed out and it can be used as a porridge sweetener.
14. *Nsomo* (Sclerocarya birrea) provides a fruit that is ready in October. One cuts out the inner parts that are hard, and grinds them to make a peanut butter-like substance. I have seen the plant unweeded in the fields of the Mvura.

AGRICULTURE AND FORAGING IN COMPETITION WITH WILDLIFE

15. *Tobva* (Cerototheca triloha) provides a relish, similar to okra. It can be used throughout the year. Tastes best when boiled with tomatoes and salt.
16. *Nynkatewe* (Achyranthes aspera) is used during the summer season. The leaves are boiled to make relish.
17. *Chifoyo* (Coccinia aodensis) provides a tuber similar to sweet potatoes but not as sweet. It is not poisonous and people can eat it raw. It can be obtained anytime, but in October it shrinks.
18. *Chigaratongwe* (Dioscorea asteriescus) provides a white bulb. This is troublesome to prepare as the juice within is poisonous/toxic. It should be left overnight to soak in water, and the juice should be squeezed out in the morning. If in a hurry it can be squeezed out in water twice. The residue is left in the sun to dry, it is then pounded. The meal is white and is cooked in the same way as sadza (maize meal).
19. *Nchenje* (Diospyros kirkii) provides a fruit ready in September/October which, like most of the fruits mentioned, is collected by both men and women, and taken home raw, where it is stored in gourds for the next day's use. It is sweet. The ancestors used to eat both the buds and the outer shells of this fruit.
20. *Nsvanzva* (Ximenia americana) provides a relatively large fruit which is ready in December. It is sweet 'like Coca Cola', and eaten raw 'on the way' or is taken home for the children.

The following fruits, tubers and leaves (amongst others) can be found within a day's walk of my camp at Mr. Mugonapanje's. Some of them can only be found on the higher massif (e.g. *mpama*), but many can also be found in the lowlands.

21. *Mpama* (Dioscorrea odoratissima) has long been known as one of the staple foods of the Mvura. It is a tuber which grows, amongst other places, in the gullies and stream banks, on the western sides of the Massif that forms a border with the Chewore safari area. It is of great interest because those who exploit these resources replant a section of the lower stem to be used in future years. The tubers are large and have to be boiled four times to extract the toxic juices. The outer skins have to be peeled and the substance is then ground, dried and cooked in a similar way to maize meal. Small groups of three or four men and/or women will usually

collect a sack-full each. If they do not have food they will prepare *mpama* before returning home, but if available they will have made *mukati* (cakes of green mealies/groundnuts and maize) to sustain them on the journey. The preparations can then be done at home.

22. *Muchabobo* (Commiphora mossambicensis) is a root used as a fertility drug/aphrodisiac but can also be used as a means of obtaining water, or to obtain its 'sweetness' while out walking in the forest. Generally, one uses one's ubiquitous small axe to unearth and peel the tuber, one then chews a portion of it and spits out the residue. A common ailment among many Mvura is extremely enlarged testicles (the size of cricket balls). It was claimed that this ailment was a result of taking too many fertility/aphrodisiac drugs.
23. *Madzungwe* (Emminia antennulifera) is a tuber/root used for obtaining sweetwater. According to a scientific paper (Skelton and Matanganyidza 1978), it also has amylolytic qualities and can be used to stop fermentation in beer.
24. *Chikuri* (Ipomoea Shupangensis) provides a very sweet non-poisonous bulb. After the skin is peeled it can be eaten raw. It does not lose water during the dry season and can be eaten at any season.
25. *Dzungu* (Cissus trophae) provides a fruit which can be eaten raw and which is usually ready in April.
26. *Ntengeni* (Ximenia caffra) provides a red fruit which is used as porridge sweetener.
27. *Cafafeya* (Cucumus hirsutus) provides a cucumber which is ready in February or March. It is found in both the high gullies and the lower lying territory.
28. *Muchecheni* (Ziziphus abyssinica) is similar to *masawo*. It provides a fruit that ripens between August and September.
29. *Nsombori* (Eriosema shirensi) provides a small bulb which can be eaten any time, one usually peels the outer skin with one's teeth.
30. *Mtudza* (Flacourtia indica) provides a fruit that is red when ripe in October and November. It is bigger than *masawo*.
31. *Mungoye* (Vitex payos). In VaChiKunda it is known as *Chubhu*. This provides a black fruit when ripe and it is frequently eaten by school children, who may have no other form of sustenance with them on the 15 kilometer walk to school. It ripens in March, April or May.

The forest is not a homogeneous barrier to successful agriculture as it is to many of us. It is full of known and named resources that have practical uses. It is the Mvura supermarket. In order to be operational and effective, individual foragers require access to a wide range of goods. It is not sufficient to be confined to the one shelf, as we all know. According to a key informant, this generation of Mvura eat mainly *matondo, horongwa, ntacha, usika, mpama, manyanya, nyuchi* (honey) and *masawo*.

Informants claimed that people were not collecting as many fruits as they used to in the old days. Some claimed there was no need to, since 'long back there was not enough maize, nowadays there is no reason to collect fruits because maize is available'. Patently, however, maize was not available in the quantities required to maintain relative health and, of course, maize by itself is not sufficient to do this. It was pointed out that people are getting more sick these days than in the past. But the informant concerned did not know why. In his mind, it was not related to diet. It was recognized that it was best to have maize and the other cultivated grains, as well as fruits of the forest, as it was pointed out that these fruits were drought-resistant. However, lurking in the minds of many is the idea that foraging is dangerous, that it is unsafe for women to go by themselves to collect *mpama* because they might be apprehended by the national parks game scouts and they would not know what to say to them. A further irony is that, in the eyes of the state, foraging in protected areas is illegal, hunting is illegal, fishing is illegal, stream bank cultivation is illegal or the areas are allegedly restricted for wildlife. Mvura do not produce enough food from their wet-season crop to see them through the year, hence their earlier dependence on foraging. Systematically, though perhaps not with intent, the state apparatus is reducing people's survival options, and instead of foraging many Mvura now work in the monocropped fields of the VaChiKunda. In my opinion, this is a far less sustainable practice than their own limited exploitation of resources.

In the past, the Mvura accrued surpluses from their foraging and hunting activities. It is claimed that exchange of meat, *hari* (clay pots) and other items for maize and clothes took place between Mvura and VaChiKunda. According to VaChiKunda informants, it was very easy to obtain a bargain from Mvura who did not realize the value of the resources they were exchanging. Exchange still continues but, needless to say, the exchange of meat for other items is not spoken about. Instead, everyone talks about exchanging maize for a *hari*. Usually a pot is exchanged for the amount of grain which it holds. As it becomes more difficult to conduct foraging activities, Mvura have become a source of cheap labor in the fields of the VaChiKunda. Thus foraging has been replaced by providing labor to the VaChiKunda maize and cotton fields.

There is an opposite side of this picture of exploited, intimidated, starving people at the whim of minor officials and people with guns. The picture has been documented to a certain extent (Bullock 1950: 35; Mtamayi 1959) and it is reinforced by myth and limited empirical evidence. It is the picture of the Mvura tracker who cannot be tracked. 'He who cannot be tracked' does, I believe, exist. Some VaChiKunda say that the Mvura can disappear in the forest if there is danger by holding up their forefinger. A VaChiKunda research assistant and I both marvelled at the manner in which we were guided through remote parts of the forest with buffalo lurking under thickets and amidst other dangers. We noted how little noise is made when the individuals involved walk through the forest. Walking is culturally defined and walking silently and sure-footedly and slowly, and knowing what noises are possible threats and which are not, is a skill developed from youth. Remarkable, also, is the sense of being 'at home'. Here is a hidden spring (*ntsantsa*), source of sweet and drinkable water. Here is a tree which holds the treasure of three fat worms (*macenta*) to be taken home as a treat for the children. Here is a root which bears water, a life-saver in the dry heat of October and November. But best of all, here is plump young bush buck or a kudu calf that has lost its way. When you have not eaten meat or other sources of protein for a few weeks, when your children are starving and have distended *kwashiorkor* stomachs, who would not cast a spear, carried of course in self-defence, at such treasures provided by the forest and the caring hand of one's own ancestors in their land?

If one knows that one cannot be tracked, the decision is easier to make. In the remote parts of the Zambezi Valley there are no scribes as such and few if any people have access to the daily newspaper. News, evidence and events are frequently transmitted in quite a different way. The sand, the soil, and the dust bear the marks of almost all activities of interest. Where did one's neighbor go this morning? His tracks lead in the direction of his *dimba*. Has Chidota gone to the meeting? Yes, there are his tracks, but they are walking with someone else . . . Ah! those are the shoes of Mary Charuma . . . A buffalo was here this morning, but it is safe now as it went in that direction. The record of events on remote paths or passes may stay for a month of more (in the case of a kill they may stay for years), and thus documentation is provided for all those interested to know what animals or humans have done. The tracks mean nothing to the uninitiated, they may mean the difference between life and death for those who depend on them. The difference between the two views is essentially a cultural difference.

Some Mvura bragged that they follow the game scouts' tracks and know when they enter the area. They can pursue them and embark on their own activities when the scouts have finished their patrol. Others explained how they would wear a common brand of shoe (police issue) and then remove them before entering a path which bore many other footprints on the way home. Others boulder hopped down river beds or stood only where there was grass so as to leave no record of their presence. It is interesting that one does not merely have to be concerned about the present, that is, whether a game scout catches one in the act, but also about the future, in the sense that those tracks will be a vivid visual picture of what has happened in the past and may lead the cunning scout on to further information which may convict the unsuspecting illegal hunter and collector. There are core bases or *misasa* (grass and thorn scrub scherms) which are used by Mvura entering the Chewore, as well as hidden base camps. Fires may be lit at night to roast meat, etc. so that the smoke cannot be seen. Fires may be made in pits so that no light escapes from them. It was rumored that the DNPWLM had a machine which could detect fire from a long way away. Young men, under the tutelage of a widely experienced hunter, may go into these areas for a month or more at a time.

Fencing the Mvura

Given this situation, it is not surprising that many Mvura are not convinced about the benefits of a possible CAMPFIRE fence to keep wildlife out of their productive areas. The first fear is that the fence would be to keep them out of the areas where they go to collect and hunt. The second fear is that they would be fenced in, that is, imprisoned, as was attempted by the Rhodesians. If a fence is to be of benefit to them, they claim it should go along the boundary of the ward and cross the Mwanzamtanda just before it enters the hills in the south west. It should have many gates to provide them with access to their collecting and hunting activities. In a sense, this is largely defeating the object of the fence which is to protect agricultural practice, in order to have a community resource area for the management of wildlife. The question is, will they effectively be deprived of their land, in the name of wildlife resource management, as has happened to them in the past when they were living in the Chewore safari area? A possible alternative to fencing is that they play a role as custodians of the Chewore, in exchange for access and limited hunting in that area. This might be a strategy to overcome the many biases toward the Mvura. A precedent has been set for this in the relatively culturally homogenous Mahenye ward, Gazaland district, where negotiations have started between DNPWLM personnel and local people who want to form a hunting club or guild (Child personal communication). This raises the question of how one could control and implement such an idea in the culturally heterogenous Chapoto ward. In the present climate of antagonism and distrust that has emerged between these people and the official militarized custodians (the anti-poaching units, safari operators, wildlife scouts), the prospect seems unlikely. Furthermore, as Nhira (1989) points out, any specialized treatment of the population based on ethnicity is likely to create ill feeling.

Household Identification and Composition

Up to this point the competition between the various land-use strategies in Chapoto ward has been described in general terms. Since the CAMPFIRE program attempts to involve the smallest accountable units in the proprietorship of wildlife resources, we now turn to the specific questions associated with agriculture, foraging and wildlife in specific households.

Households are often taken as the basic units in rural Zimbabwe. This term has acted as a key concept in survey research conducted in the ward (see Cutshall 1990). However, it is sometimes difficult to identify what a household constitutes. If the household is to be a basic unit of analysis, we need to have some idea of what it refers to. An example of a working definition of what constitutes a household might be the group of people who regularly eat together at the same hearth, engage co-operatively in food production or other forms of economic activity, and share enduring commitments to mutual social welfare. Household often implies a reference to physical features such as buildings, structures, or enclosures, and these may explicitly or implicitly be equated with the 'household'. The physical and relatively permanent feature of 'the house' is an important connotation of 'households', and we would not be wildly wrong if we made the assumption that households live in houses or huts or even shanties with some degree of permanence. However, would we accept that a household constitutes a structure used for crop protection in one's field or garden? Similarly, in what sense do the grass scherms in which some Mvura live during the dry season constitute households? Definitions of 'the household', in the case of Chapoto ward, have to be sufficiently broad to encompass the marked degree of movement of households or parts of households that occur within the ward. Assumptions about the relative permanence of physical dwelling structures, as indicators of households, has to be carefully reviewed (see Plates 4 and 5). As Cutshall points out in his baseline survey of community households,

> though a concerted effort was made to contact and interview every existing household within the community, it must, however, be admitted that a few households were omitted from the present survey either because the households were 'abandoned' during the survey periods or because the households had no fixed residential locus where they could be contacted by members of the survey team (ibid. 2)

Of the 213 households in the community identified by Cutshall, 72.8 per cent of them comprised a single family unit (i.e. parent[s], their progeny, or married/unmarried adults without children). The remaining 27.2 per cent, according to Cutshall, were 'composite' households containing from two to six discrete family units. A relatively small proportion of these households were polygynous, the remainder consisted of married or divorced household progeny, who were considered by the household head to be regular residents of his or her household. There is room for ambiguity here, as married or divorced household progeny could claim that they form separate households within the proximity of their kin and are likely to do so when presenting themselves for drought relief distribution or other benefits (wildlife revenues?) designed for households. Furthermore, the fairly common observance of the institution of brideservice means that sons-in-law initially go to live with their wife's patrilineal kin and may remain living in the proximity of such kin after brideservice has been honored (uxorilocal residence). In this manner, clusters of affinal and consanguineal kin emerge. In this sense then, household is a loose segmentary identification depending on whether people choose to identify themselves as constituting a discrete household or as being part of a larger cluster constituting a larger grouping which can break down depending on circumstance. The mean household size according to Cutshall was 6.06.

Cutshall correctly points out that although composite households are widely distributed (existing in all the major constellations of clusters except for one), Mvura households are more likely to be composite households than VaChiKunda households.

A relatively large percentage (24.4) of the total number of households were identified by Cutshall as female headed. 'These were usually older widowed or divorced females who had established an independent household in the proximity of a male kinsman or females whose husbands were regularly resident in areas outside of the community' (ibid. 5).

In regard to migrants, Cutshall enumerated 93.8 per cent of the individual household members as regular full-time members of the community. The bulk of the remaining group were males engaged in seasonal or wage labor activities outside the community.

Household/cluster agricultural activities
Cutshall identified 97.2 per cent of the population as having reported some kind of agricultural activity for the 1988 season. He observed that size of plot varied in accordance to size of households (larger/composite households have larger fields), available labor resources, household ethnicity (Mvura have smaller agricultural operations), season (*munda* cultivation is larger than *dimba* cultivation), and method of cultivation (fields which are cultivated with the aid of mechanical inputs are generally larger than those fields cultivated by hand) (ibid. 25). The average size of fields is relatively small (five to eight acres) (ibid.).

Differential access and use of tractors was marked. As Cutshall has pointed out, only one Mvura household used tractors in the ward. This is explained by Cutshall both in terms of geography and in terms of ethnicity. Geographically, since Mvura live on the western bank of the Mwanzamtanda, it would not be wise to attempt to take a tractor across the river when it floods. However, if the river floods, it is likely to flood only during the peak of the rainy season and there are many bone-dry months prior to the onset of rains when it would be very easy to cross the river. During the two rainy seasons when I was in the field, it was possible to cross the river except at the height of the rainy season. This would indicate that the geographical explanation is not an adequate one and I was led to believe that the reason was essentially a political and economic one. The higher-status families, on the eastern bank, largely monopolized the use of the tractor. These could afford to pay the costs set down by the World Vision committee for use of the tractor, and were more involved in decision-making regarding the tractor. Cutshall also observed that female-headed households were less likely than their male-headed counterparts to use mechanical inputs.

Cutshall reported that during the 1988 season 91.3 per cent of the population reported they cultivated both *dimba* and *munda* in the dry and wet seasons respectively (ibid. 28). Those households who did not conduct both types of agriculture included Mvura clusters, who were used to relying on foraging and/or providing labor during this period, and new migrants, who may not have had access to riverside plots because the available land had been used by the households that were already there.

The following crops were identified as having been grown by households during the 1988 season (in rank order of the frequency distribution in terms of households): maize, vegetables, mhuunga, bananas, groundnuts, cotton, sorghum, beans, sugar cane, rapocco, tobacco, cassava, rice and sunflower. The actual proportions grown for each crop and the average yield per household was not collected by either Cutshall or myself. Cutshall points out that such information requires an accurate assessment of acreage under each crop, which would be an extremely time-consuming exercise unless one had access to an aerial survey. Informants were not able to make accurate assessments on acreage. Furthermore, harvests were not bagged, so no quantitative data were available on this. Perhaps the most important reason why one would hesitate to collect this information is because annual yields are extraordinarily varied, depending on the extremely erratic annual rainfall, and data for a single year would not give the reader an accurate idea of agriculture in the ward. 95.8 per cent of households grew maize and Cutshall points out that only 7.4 per cent of the households which planted maize reported that they sold any of their maize crop. Thus maize is the most important crop for cultivation purposes, in that most households plant maize. My observations support the notion that maize is the most important part of the household diet, except in those households which harvest little or no maize. Not surprisingly, Cutshall found that maize is also the food crop that has the most reported crop-damage incidents from wildlife. Out of a total of 678 crop-damage incidents reported for the 1987/8 year, 558 incidents were to maize. Interestingly, Cutshall identifies vegetables as the next most common crop grown by households and indicates that 67.5 per cent of households plant vegetables. This of course does not tell us anything about the quantity of vegetables planted, merely that many households do plant vegetables. Many of the vegetables are grown during the winter season in the *dimba*. Thus, for most people in the ward, the summer wet season provides them with their staple maizemeal from which *sadza* (maize porridge) is made. The river-side garden or *dimba* cultivation, amongst other things, provides them with vegetables to make relish for the *sadza*. In many of the more wealthy households, *sadza* and relish is eaten twice a day, while other households may substitute sweet potatoes or beans as a meal in themselves. Those more impoverished households, which did not have enough maize or beans to see them through the season, may have to resort to foraging/drought relief and/or food for work to supplement their food supply. Cotton-growing households frequently purchase maize with the cash they receive from their crop to supplement their own maize crop.

Cutshall also, interestingly, points out that cotton was only grown by 15.5 per cent of the ward's households (ibid. 33). Cotton production appears to be on the increase, both in terms of the sizes of plots under cotton and in terms of households entering cotton production. The donation of the World Vision tractor may be one incentive to plant more cotton. As I have pointed out earlier, shortage of labor is a more serious limitation to crop production than shortage of land. However, shortage of capital outlay to pay for ploughing is a crucial restraint amongst the less-wealthy families. This may be a relevant factor in assessing the possible impacts of household distribution of dividends from wildlife in the community. Some of these revenues may be used in paying for increased agricultural production (ploughing, clearing, etc.). One of the results of increased participation in wildlife resource utilization by the local community may, ironically, be to increase agricultural production (especially cotton) in areas of the ward.

Cutshall makes some important points about household variation in using mixed grain strategies as a means to combat the risks of drought (ibid. 29). He argues that grains such as sorghum and *mhunga* (unlike maize) are drought resistant and that it would appear to be rational to plant a mixture of grains rather than relying solely on maize as a staple. As has been pointed out, maize, unlike millet and sorghum, is not indigenous to Africa. However, during the period (1988 season) for which he asked the question, 52.5 per cent of the total number of households in the ward at the time planted only maize (ibid. 213). 22.7 per cent planted maize, sorghum and mhunga, while 72.7 per cent planted maize and mhunga and 5.2 per cent planted maize and sorghum. As has been pointed out, Cutshall underlines the fact that Mvura are more likely to have a mixed grain strategy than their VaChiKunda counterparts, but also points out the anomaly that Mvura are more likely to need drought relief assistance.

A number of factors may be involved in explaining why so many people rely exclusively on maize. Cutshall mentions the ethnic differentiation, the emphasis of the agricultural extension officer, and dietary preference as possible explanations. I emphasize that the variety of foods grown in the *dimba* may offset the risks of solely growing maize as a wet-season crop, and this may be an important factor in explaining why more people do not diversify their grain production.

Though maize is sold locally, there are very few households who produce surpluses of maize. As has been pointed out, those wealthier VaChiKunda households who do have surpluses can exchange them for Mvura labor. Most crop production is for domestic consumption, not for cash cropping. The main exception to this is, of course, the cotton crop which is grown exclusively for cash. Bananas and tobacco are also sold for cash and I came across instances of the sale of *masawo*. However, the main source of cash income from agriculture is cotton production. This is an important source of cash used for paying school fees and buying necessities. The following account of the most successful cotton-grower in the ward in 1990 illustrates many of the dilemmas associated with competing land-use strategies involving the balancing of cash crops and food crops.

Cotton-Growing

Mr. Samson Dumba – successful cotton grower

Mr. Dumba (see Plate 6) was the most successful cotton-grower in Chapoto ward in 1990. In total, he produced 10 bales of cotton and received a cheque for just over Z$1,700 (approximately US$400 at that time), for his family's pains, from the cotton-marketing board. This figure was unusually high, since many farmers I knew produced two or less bales. Out of 14 cotton-producers in the southern portion of the ward, the average was 3.1 bales. Cotton is evaluated according to grade and paid by the kilogram. Some bales, therefore, weigh more than others. Mr. Dumba's cotton was graded as: one bale of grade B, five bales of grade C and four bales of grade D. The highest price he received per kilogram was Z$1.18 for the grade B bale.

Cotton was first introduced into the ward in 1985 and some farmers are tending to mono-crop cotton in their *minda* (the *dimba* still provides a diversified source of food) in the hope of obtaining larger cash takings. Basically, this is a switch from maize-production to cotton-production. Maize meal can, if necessary, be bought at the subsidized rates, thus achieving the food supply forfeited from the losses in the often unreliable maize crop. However, many farmers do plant both cotton and maize.

In working out his profits, Mr. Dumba withdrew the amount charged for transport (Z$30 per bale before the gulf crisis), plus the amount paid out for pesticides and the hire of the pesticide sprayer from his neighbor, the cost of hessian bales and string, but did not include any payment for his own labor or that of his wife and her children. Family labor was not considered a cost, though the enlisting of Mvura to work in the field is, I believe, more likely to be considered a cost. Neither did Mr. Dumba factor in the inflation rate in Zimbabwe. According to some sources, this is said to be an alarming 30–40 per cent per annum and is exacerbated by the drastic rises in fuel cost. Even prior to these drastic rises, which have increased the price of production of all commodities in Zimbabwe, if we use the minimum wage for labor as an indicator of the value of labor, it was clear that Mr. Dumba's family was making no profit on his 1990 cotton crop. The implication is that the majority of less successful cotton-growers were making an outright loss, in terms of the value of their labor.

Mr. Dumba, his wife and two children prepared for, protected, harvested, and attended to the cotton crop over a period of nine months (November–July). Though he also had successful harvests from his maize crop, it is true to say that the bulk of the labor and time spent on crop-protection went into the production of cotton. This included preparation of the fields, planting, weeding, protecting from crop-raiding animals, spraying and pest control, harvesting, grading and baling. The minimum wage in Zimbabwe at the time was Z$155.90 per month (US$32) for an agricultural or yard worker who does not live on the premises. This is taken to be the cost of paying and supporting an individual's total requirement and in the current inflationary situation the figure is low. Admittedly, it is a figure which takes into account the urban situation where rents and transport to and from work have to be paid. However, other costs are accrued in remote areas, particularly the cost of transport. My observation was that many commodities were often more expensive in the ward than in the towns. If we use this figure as a relative indicator of general financial well-being in comparing successful cotton-growing with agricultural or yard labor, it may be useful.

Mr. Dumba, his wife, and two children under fourteen years of age attended to the cotton crop as a team. Certain periods of the year were not as arduous as others, but I estimate that the amount of labor including crop-protection was at least equivalent to one full-time adult worker for nine months. If we apply the agricultural worker monthly figure, this labor is worth Z$1,403. We must add on to this the cost of transport, which was Z$300, and the cost of hiring the spray equipment and purchasing chemicals (estimated to be at least a further Z$70). In addition, we must include the cost of purchasing the hessian bales, string and tags. A very conservative estimate of costs incurred by such a successful cotton grower for his 1990 crop was about Z$1,773.

The cheque Mr. Dumba was so pleased to receive was almost equivalent to his costs. The only way in which profit can be rationalized in this case is by underestimating the value of family labor. This particularly refers to female and child labor, since men often are the ones who control and spend the income derived from the crop. There is variation in this, in the sense that some male householders would consult all members who had contributed to the cotton crop as to how the money should be spent. A wife might request plates or cooking oil or school fees, while a child might request clothing or bus fares, etc.

Mr. Dumba's agricultural production differs from other VaChi-Kunda cotton-growers in that other cotton-growers tend to use more Mvura labor at times of the year when intensive labor is required. As has been mentioned, this is basically a transaction of food for work (see below).

The significance of Mr. Dumba's decision to grow cotton is that cotton-growing may become a substantial threat to the existing natural resources in the valley. Other areas, particularly those closer to the escarpment, such as the MZP, show that escarpment dwellers and existing stream bank cultivators are expanding their agricultural practice into wooded areas that potentially are the habitats of a wide range of fauna and flora. Clearing woodland to grow cotton may not be wise for many reasons. The high costs of transport and other inputs such as pesticides, may become prohibitive. But more importantly, can we be assured that there will always be a good price for cotton on the local and world markets? Once the trees are cut down and the land is cleared, successive years of cotton-growing will degrade the soil and may lead to poor yields. If there should be a slump in the price of cotton, because, for instance, synthetic fibers encroach into the market, cotton-growing may be discontinued, but the resources of the valley will have been depleted and it may take a long time to build them back up.

Kanyurira ward recently decided to give Z$200 dividend to households from wildlife revenues. Many cotton-growers in Chapoto ward did not receive as much from their cotton-growing. Though it may also be true that the market for wildlife resources is a foreign one and is also a fickle market, wildlife has proved to be a resource that can do well in valley conditions, if properly managed.

Family members are not the only people whose labor is undervalued in cotton-production. In many cotton-growing households, Mvura assist in stumping fields, weeding and harvesting in exchange for a daily ration of maize meal. This means that they do not have the time to work sufficiently in their own fields or forage. Though female and child labor is undervalued in the case of Mr. Dumba's cotton, in many VaChiKunda fields Mvura labor also is undervalued. One possible reason is because Mvura no longer have access to their former means of livelihood in the Chewore safari area.

Despite the fact that I argue that Mr. Dumba is making a loss from the point of view of rational economics, from his perspective he has done exceptionally well. Other farmers obviously also think cotton-growing is a good option, as it appears to be spreading. I believe this is so for reasons that have been outlined above, namely that the price of maize meal is subsidized therefore making it more attractive to grow cotton than maize or other food crops, which otherwise it might be necessary to grow in larger quantities.[10] The second reason is that male, female and child labor is not included as a cost of production. This is not to imply that cotton-growers do not also plant maize, but there is evidence that cotton-growers do buy maize at the subsidized rates. If such subsidies did not exist and the cost of maize was higher than the returns on cotton, I believe this would mean that fewer people would plant cotton.

The next illustration is that of a household cluster, which more closely resembles the life-style of the majority of people in the ward who do not plant cotton. It illustrates a more conservative and historical strategy based on diverse exploitation of available natural resources. As has been mentioned, state regulations prohibiting or restricting hunting, fishing, foraging, stream bank cultivation, etc. tend to threaten this type of diverse exploitation, while encouraging monocropping. This is not to say that cotton-growers do not also take advantage of multiple resource opportunities. Almost all cotton-growers, for instance, have both *munda* and *dimba* cultivation.

A Diversified VaChiKunda Household Economy: A Strategy For Survival

Both VaChiKunda and Mvura households have historically had diversified economies. Crops are grown in both the *munda* and the *dimba*, and foraging, fishing and limited hunting continues to be an important source of food. In addition to state regulations, to some extent cotton-growing for cash poses a threat to this diversity, since it requires a lot of labor. However, there are many households that have not started growing cotton. The following illustration gives the reader a picture of decision-making and household economics in a non-cotton-growing household cluster.

Household cluster, *nimbi* – as we shall call it, constitutes a core

---

10. One could also argue that people grow cotton to be able to afford maize, since maize is unreliable. If maize yields are good then cotton profits can be used for alternative purposes; if they are poor then food can be purchased (Derman: personal communications). However, the degree of yields from diversified *dimba* cultivation, during both the wet and the dry seasons, also affects the decision to grow cotton (a non-food crop). *Dimba* cultivation provides an important source of food, and cotton is not grown in the *dimba*. The long-term implication of this is that *dimba* cultivation supports the growing of cotton by hedging the bets against household food deficit.

male head of household, his three sons, his divorced daughters, his married daughters and sons-in-law. His neighbors are all *sahwiras* (bond friends) or in-laws. The residents of the cluster either work in the fields of the household head or else they have their own fields near to his. The household head claims ownership of the *dimba* and of the *munda*. In general, he supervises the work of the women and children and other labor going on in these fields. However, if he is away, his wife makes decisions and reports back to her husband. If they divorce, the wife has no rights over the *dimba* or the *munda*. The men of the household clear and stump the fields, but they may enlist Mvura to help do this heavy work. Women generally do the planting, while men are cutting poles and collecting thatching grass. If weeding or other tasks are excessive, the wife may prepare beer to recruit labor through a beer party. Men usually protect the fields at night from crop-raiding animals, whilst women and children stay at the main homestead. If crops are growing both in the *dimba* and in the *munda*, this may pose a logistical problem since, in the case of this household, the homestead is not situated near either the *dimba* or the *munda*.

Harvesting is done by both men and women, but men may also have to build storage sites (*chigota*). The maize that is harvested is eaten or sold or used to prepare beer. Corn and sorghum are also used to make *sadza* (grain meal). Vegetables, groundnuts, beans, watermelons, paw-paws, bananas are all important sources of food. Sweet potatoes are often eaten at breakfast when they are available. The household head does not grow cotton because he claims that he cannot afford to buy chemicals to spray the cotton. He was also, correctly, concerned that these chemicals might poison his family.

The money earned from the sale of any surplus food is usually used for buying other necessities such as soap, salt and cooking oil. Money earned from the sale of beer is also used to purchase necessities, such as blankets and clothes. While, in general, the man in consultation with his wife ultimately makes decisions concerning money, it is recognized that women put a lot of work into specific extra tasks, such as brewing beer, and any cash obtained from such sources is considered to be theirs to decide upon. In cotton-growing households, there was variation in the degree to which women were included in decision-making on money. Some households had a liberal policy of dividing up the cash revenues to all members involved in the cotton crop, while others left control in the hands of the male household head.

The head of this household also earns some money as 'the messenger of the spirit' (*Kambande*). His duties include cleaning the clothes of the spirit medium, collecting herbs on instruction from her, cleaning the area around the *Dendemaro* (shrine), calling the spirit by blowing the trumpet (*unda*) and taking messages. This is an inherited position, because he is descended from one of Kanyemba's slave attendants. He also supplements his income by building storage bins for others, fishing and, in the past, making log boats.

His family also gather *masawo* and make liquor or porridge from it. Other items gathered include *masenda* (worms) and *ntowe* (worms). Hunting is usually done by men using snares while women use mosquito nets to catch fish. Herbs are used to treat hunting dogs; they are obtainable from the spirit medium.

In contrast to this VaChiKunda household cluster, the next two case-studies illustrate the relationship between a Mvura household and the available natural resources, both in terms of their present life-style, emphasizing labor in exchange for food, and their past life-style, which emphasized foraging. It also underlines how the broader issues related to the control of poaching (national policy and the role of the safari operator and DNPWLM game scouts) impinge directly on their productive activities.

Home Economics and Decision-making in a Mvura Household – Past and Present[11]

This household consists of eight people, that is six children and two parents. The man is the head of the household and makes all the important decisions in consultation with his family. He is still working out his brideservice for his in-laws with whom he stays. He helps his in-laws in a number of ways and is not allowed to move away from them until brideservice is complete. If he finds 'food for work' opportunities in the fields of the VaChiKunda, he is expected to share this food with his in-laws. If he goes into the forest and finds honey, when he returns he will share this honey with his mother-in-law. He and his wife should always be thinking about what strategies they can use to obtain food for their family. Every member of the family should decide what to do in order for them all to survive the season; they should all go in different

---

11. Mvura text as narrated by Chidota Kaputi (research assistant) and adapted by the author.

directions in order to find something to give the children. This might include going into the mountains, as well as working for food (i.e. foraging and provision of labor).

They faced fewer problems before settling in the ward (within the last 12 years), because they had a different life pattern. Maize and grain from shifting cultivation was stored in portable granaries (bark bins) (see Plate 7) until the next growing season. In the intervening period they would move through the forest, collecting and hunting, while their granaries remained inside a web of thorns hidden and secured from baboons and other crop-raiding animals. The stored grain would support them while they were working on preparing the next season's harvest. While wandering through the forest, they would live from tubers and edible fruits. *Bepe* was favored because one can make *sadza* from it after withdrawing the poisons. If the wandering family came across a good area for *bepe, guruvi* or *mpama*, they would settle there for a week or more while elderly women prepared meals from the tubers. While they did this, the men would try to kill small game and birds or fish in nearby pools. Women also hunted and fished.

While in the forest they did not have spirit mediums who were with them, but they honored these spirits by visiting the spirit mediums of those people who were sedentary. These spirits knew that they had children in the mountains and whenever they had problems with their way of life, they would ask for assistance from spirit mediums.

They had no headmen. The first headman was appointed by the first Chief Chapoto, who was designated chief by the colonial authorities. Under the colonial dispensation they were considered to be under Chief Chapoto, even though they were regularly moving through the forests. In these early days there was plenty of food and exchange took place between the VaChiKunda and the Mvura (e.g. Mvura gave food and meat for VaChiKunda clothes and maize).

These days there are major problems of hunger and disease. They can hardly go for a single day into the forest to collect honey. This is because the game scouts will arrest them there, but it may also be because the spirits have been neglected as there is a shortage of food in the forest. Herbs that can cure the various illnesses are plentiful in the forest, but access is prohibited.

If they work in the fields of the VaChiKunda, they will only receive enough food for a single day and the next day they will be hungry again. If they have no food before they start their employment (they may not have eaten for three days or more), they may have to borrow a day's food from the owner of the field, in order to give them strength to work in that same field. If they owe the owner of the field a day's work, it will be very difficult to go for a day without eating while they pay this debt off. If they are working in the owner's field, it will mean that they will not have time or strength to work in their own field or to go into the forest to look for food.

The state apparatus, through the creation of protected areas for wildlife and through the enforcement of prohibitive regulations concerning hunting, fishing, foraging and stream bank cultivation, has contributed to the effective reduction of the diversity of survival options used in the past. The following narrative again illustrates that foraging was previously an important component of brideservice, that the spirit is seen to control resource opportunities, in terms of foraging and hunting, but game scouts make it necessary to curtail or forgo these options.

Brideservice, Endogamy, Rain, Foraging and Prison: A Mvura Case History[12]

Mr. K is married to a woman from Angwa (70 kilometers away by road) and lives next to his brother-in-law. As he did not pay all the *lobola* (bridewealth) required by his in-laws, he is expected to work for his in-laws. Mr. K remembers that in the old days men used to marry their sister's daughter or even the daughter of their mother's brother. Although these practices still continue among some people in the ward, Mr. K was very opposed to such practices and believed that the reason people married so closely within the family was because they had no money to pay bridewealth. The children of parents who marry within the family, also marry within the family. Genealogies, which I traced, generally supported this notion. According to other informants, the spirit mediums have forbidden such practices, but they were common in the past.

Mr. K had not fulfilled his obligations to his in-laws. If he were to die, his children would belong to his wife's family and not to his, because *lobola* (bridewealth) had not been paid and neither had an adequate amount of brideservice been offered. In the old days, the young man would perform tasks for his in-laws, such as

12. Text adapted by the author and research assistant from narration by K.

hunting and foraging. These days one is arrested by game scouts or safari operators for hunting or foraging.

In the old days, crops such as maize, cucumbers, pumpkins, sorghum and millet were grown. During times of drought, they could rely on wild food which was near to their homes, such as *mpama, manyanya,* and honey. When the first honey of the year was collected, they were expected to make a new *hari*, fill it with honey, and present it to the spirit medium as a way of respecting the spirit, who is the owner of things in the forest. Honey was very important because it helped them to survive when the tubers (e.g. *mpama* and *manyanya*) were shrinking, owing to lack of water. They believe current shortages of honey and other forest products occurred because people were ignoring the spirits. Chinyensva, Chimhako and Kanyemba were all important spirits in people's daily lives. Chimombe is considered to be like God, he is the most important spirit because he brings rains. Without rain there is no harvest, neither in the forest nor in the field and there is no life. Appeals for rain are made by sending gifts of salt, clothes and other items to Kangora (Nyamapfeka). Kangora will give these to Chinyenzva and Chinyenzva will give it to Chimombe.

Before, when they were living in the mountains, there was plenty of food. All the problems of hunger started when Chief Chapoto (i.e. the authorities) called everyone to come and settle near the Mwanzamtanda river. Even during the liberation war they had no problems as they never came into contact with the freedom fighters. This year the rains are bad and the crops did not grow, but they cannot go and fall back on *mpama* and *manyanya* because they are so far away and the game scouts are so strict.

He was once arrested for poaching by a game scout who found the skull of an animal he had killed many years previously. He was beaten and had to serve two months in prison. He said it was better to die of hunger than to trap an animal for food and be caught by the authorities again. This was an experience that should not be faced twice in a person's lifetime. He will never tell anyone that someone else is hunting, because that is a sign that he himself is also hunting.

Accounts like this one underline the manner in which state regulations have curtailed traditional forms of resource exploitation. There is a genuine fear about being apprehended for subsistance activities, especially hunting. Such informants are faced with a losing proposition. Their current agricultural practice and labor for food exchanges do not adequately meet their needs. Simultaneously, the time-tested supplementary activity of foraging and hunting is becoming more and more difficult.

Household/Cluster Animal Holdings

As mentioned earlier, there are no cattle in the ward. However, Cutshall established that there are five households in the community which own a total of 44 goats. My first camp was next to one of these households, that of the chief's messenger, and I vividly recall how frequently leopard would visit at night to see if they could procure some of his stock.

The most significant animal holding in the ward is poultry, and Cutshall enumerated 72.3 per cent of the households as owning chickens or ducks. Mvura households, according to Cutshall, were less likely than other households to have poultry and when they did have poultry, they tended to have less stock (1990: 38). The mean number of poultry owned per household was approximately 14, and when we consider that, at any given time, at least half of these would be too young to harvest, having chicken for dinner was a rare and wonderful occasion. Despite this, my neighbors regularly cooked chicken for me in return for some small favor I had done.

When Cutshall enumerated domestic animal loss from predators, 95.5 per cent of households reported animal loss in the preceding season (1988). 77.9 per cent of the poultry-owning households reported at least one incident of poultry loss.

Pigeons and rabbits are also kept in the community, but the number of households which have these is very small. Many households have tried to keep dogs in order to give warning when wild animals are near and for use in hunting, but these dogs appear to be a treasured delicacy for leopard and while I was in the field several dogs were lost in this manner.

Household/Cluster Foraging, Hunting and Fishing.

Subsistence hunting, in any form, is illegal. Foraging in the hunting concession area (i.e. the ward) is frowned upon by the safari operator, foraging in the protected areas (Chewore and Dande safari area) is illegal, and fishing with nets is prohibited. It is, therefore, difficult to obtain accurate information on these activities. However, having lived through two dry seasons in the ward, I was able to observe that many ward households rely on one or more of these activities to supplement their food supply. I have already outlined in detail the type of indigenous knowledge that exists amongst the Mvura in regard to fruits, tubers and berries. In this section, I simply would like to highlight some of the activities which are relied on by a broader section of the population.

Of considerable importance to many ward residents, regardless of ethnic affiliation, is the fruit of the *masawo*, which is widely collected as a staple by both the VaChiKunda and Mvura. It is a small, but very tasty fruit. Each tree yields a large harvest of fruit, and towards the end of the dry season I have observed families who have been eating little else. The fruit is also used to make an alcoholic drink. Unlike many of the tubers eaten by the Mvura, no elaborate preparation is required for the *masawo*, in terms of extracting toxins. An added benefit is that *masawo* grow in the riverain belt where the line of habitation is and people do not have to go far into the forest to face the double danger of wild animals and armed safari operators or anti-poaching units to obtain it. During the research period, I isolated this tree as being the single most important fruit supplement to household food supply for a wide cross-section of the population. It was not at all uncommon to see elevated racks of *masawo* drying in the sun at most households towards the end of the dry season.

In an attempt to find out how regularly the *masawo* and other food items appeared in the diet of selected households, I asked members of households to note down how many times a week they would eat the fruit when it was in season. Of course, there was a great deal of variation depending on the economic status of the households, their size, ethnic affiliation, annual rainfall and other variables, but my overall finding was that many people regularly (three times a week) ate main meals which included *masawo*, for at least six weeks in the year. The reason I emphasize this is because so often foraging is not considered to be a part of the household economy. In endeavoring to find out what natural resources mean to local people, it seems to be vital to include their foraging activities. The devastating 1992 drought has made many agriculturalists, throughout Southern Africa, supplement their agricultural practices with foraging.[13]

Likewise, hunting and fishing activities are important in terms of added protein in the diet. Recently, many of the VaChiKunda of Chapoto ward, who are currently settled next to the Mwanzamtanda river, were living on the banks of the Zambezi river. The Mwanzamtanda river for much of the year is a dry river bed, with a few isolated pools in which small quantities of fish live. The Zambezi river, on the other hand, flows strongly throughout the year and harbors a range of edible fish, the most common of which is the Tiger fish (*Hydrocynus vittatus*). Fish in the diet has played a bigger role in the past than it does in the present. There are two main reasons for this. The first is that people have moved away from the Zambezi river because of the Rhodesian war, and secondly because of DNPWLM regulations concerning the prohibition of fishing with nets, except by a local defunct fishing co-operative, means that individuals cannot fish for their families, except with lines. The defunct co-operative was allegedly not successful because of 'corruption'. Some people who live in the most northern portion of the ward, do spend a large portion of their time fishing with lines in the Zambezi and selling the fish to other residents. However, the largest quantities of fish that I saw for sale had been caught in Cabora Bassa Dam (Mozambique), where no implemented controls on fishing exist.

Mvura clusters, in the southern portion of the ward, do fish in the isolated pools in the Mwanzamtanda river bed, but have frequently been arrested for this. In the past, VaChiKunda women used to use mosquito nets to fish in these pools, but these days they fear that they will be arrested for fish poaching by the DNPWLM. Consequently, DNPWLM regulations affect diet, and this in turn makes people search for methods to obtain the abundant protein that surrounds them.

Subsistence Hunting for the Household Pot

As many people in the ward have been arrested for hunting, it is very difficult to obtain accurate information on the quantity of hunting that goes on in the ward and the role that game meat

---

13. According to a BBC news item, 39 million people in Southern Africa were in need of drought relief food distribution; 18 million of these faced the threat of starvation.

plays in the diet of households. There is also diversity in the degree of hunting carried out by different households. I emphasize that this is extremely sensitive information and refer the reader to the methodology for more on this subject. Though selected households were asked by research assistants what role game meat played in their diets, some people were co-operative whilst others were not. Research assistants were instructed not to pursue this question if the informants were not willing to discuss it, as it could possibly jeopardize my entire research project. After a legal safari operator kill in the ward, where the carcass was donated to the people, it was noticed that game meat was eaten more freely or openly. But otherwise, when asked how much meat was secured for the pot, or for other purposes, most households were unco-operative. Others claimed that, at times, they ate two or three meals a week which had a portion of game meat. Circumstantial evidence gave me an overall picture of how much game meat was eaten by households, such as the arrest of local people for poaching, the discovery of snares by the safari operators' anti-poaching unit, or the isolated incidents when I myself came across people attempting to hide meat, or the rare occasion when I was offered meat. Even the simple evidence of cooking smells in the evening gave me an idea of how regularly people ate meat in the vicinity. My considered opinion is that all residents do eat game meat on occasions and this is broadly verified by informants, but these occasions are, for the majority of households, rare.

Simultaneously, however, there are certain households in the ward which are renowned for hunting and which, I do believe, rely quite heavily on game meat for their maintenance. However, these households constitute a small minority. In general, people's fear of being caught snaring prevents game meat from being a regular feature of their diet. One only needs to be caught once in order to find oneself in gaol and therefore much precaution is necessary. Though instances of trading or exchange of meat do occur, these too are rare.

Household/Cluster Decision-making

As has been pointed out earlier, a household or a cluster of households, usually center on significant affinally or consanguineously related males. Women (usually widows, divorcees or 'abandoned') may also head households, but frequently they situate themselves next to male kin.

Decision-making concerning agricultural production, foraging, hunting and the distribution of income, usually occurs along a continuum between two extremes. The one extreme is that the significant male, within the household, makes all decisions concerning both production and distribution of food or income and does not broadly consult those who participate in production. At the other extreme, decision-making concerning these matters is a negotiated group decision with inputs from all those participating including children. The most common form of decision-making is negotiation between senior members of the family. A variation of the first extreme is that if a man has to go away, for any purpose, his wife or wives may be delegated authority to manage production in his absence.

In the case of *dimba* cultivation, women tended to exhibit more control over production than *munda* cultivation. *Munda* cultivation, especially when cotton was planted, often tended to be supervised by the man of the household. Again, there was much diversity in this and I came across instances of authoritarian male management as well as participatory decision-making on behalf of the group. This was most marked when it came to the distribution of cash income from the cotton crop. In some families, all members who contributed to the crop were consulted on how the money should be spent and were asked what they most needed. Young boys might say they needed clothes, the woman of the house might suggest pots or cooking oil or school fees, and a man might suggest bus fares or hoes or blankets. In other households, the man would not even tell his wife and children how much money had been accrued from the cotton crop and would attempt to monopolize control of the money and minimalize the amount given to his family. Frequently, such practices would end up in dispute and possibly divorce.

In contrast to cash cropping, decisions about foraging appear to be far less centralized and more situational. The head male of families that engage in foraging might make general plans about where they should live and which areas they should go to in search of food (or food for work), especially if these areas included prohibited areas where one could be arrested for illegal entry. Yet, such a head would not be able to monopolize foraging take-off for himself as some cotton growers do.

Women who brewed beer, as an alternative source of income,

were usually regarded as being in control of that money. With this money she might buy[14] items for the household, contribute to the school fees of her children or buy items for herself.

This chapter has outlined some of the local level, cultural and political dynamics, and vested interests associated with agriculture and foraging as it is related to wildlife issues. So far, the focus has been on local units of analysis such as the household, the VIDCO and the ward. The next chapter attempts to place these dynamics into the broader cultural and political field.

---

14. 'Buying' is not as easy as it sounds. There are two room-sized stores in the ward. Both are understocked and charge exorbitant prices. The best option is to ask a relative to buy something for you when they go up the escarpment.

CHAPTER 4

The Cultural and Political Dynamics of Wildlife Resource Use in Chapoto Ward

> The DNPWM Respects Animals More Than Human Survival.
> (Mvura Elder and Herbal Specialist)

Chapter 1 makes it clear that wildlife resource use cannot be understood in isolation from the multiple jurisdictions under which it is controlled and used. Political, economic and social factors interact with the ecological conditions supporting the productive systems discussed in the last chapter (such as agriculture, foraging, wildlife utilization). The broader concerns of political economy are, therefore, an important focus of this study which must not restrict itself to micro-social organizational issues at the ward level. Diffuse relations between human beings and resources within the wider political and economic dispensation can directly affect outcomes at ward level.

In this chapter, the multiple jurisdictions concerning wildlife are shown to coincide with the differentiations within a series of social organizational levels. A discussion of these factors is followed by descriptive material which depicts how some of the more marginalized and impoverished Mvura fit into this broader picture. In order to make analytical intentions clear, a diagrammatic representation is given of the interaction of levels of social organization, productive systems, competing demands, and vested interests in the ecological resource base (Fig. 4.1). These are the factors that buttress the various competing or ambiguous rights to wildlife in the ward.

An important feature of Fig. 4.1 is the various productive activities, such as cotton-growing, stream bank cultivation, shifting cultivation, hunting, foraging, exchange and employment, engaged in by ward residents. These are shown to be in a direct relationship with the changing ecological resource base. However, this resource base is influenced, directly or indirectly, by a number of other factors, some of which emanate from situations and forces largely removed from this remote ward. The complex relationship between ivory trade, poaching, the presence of anti-poaching units,

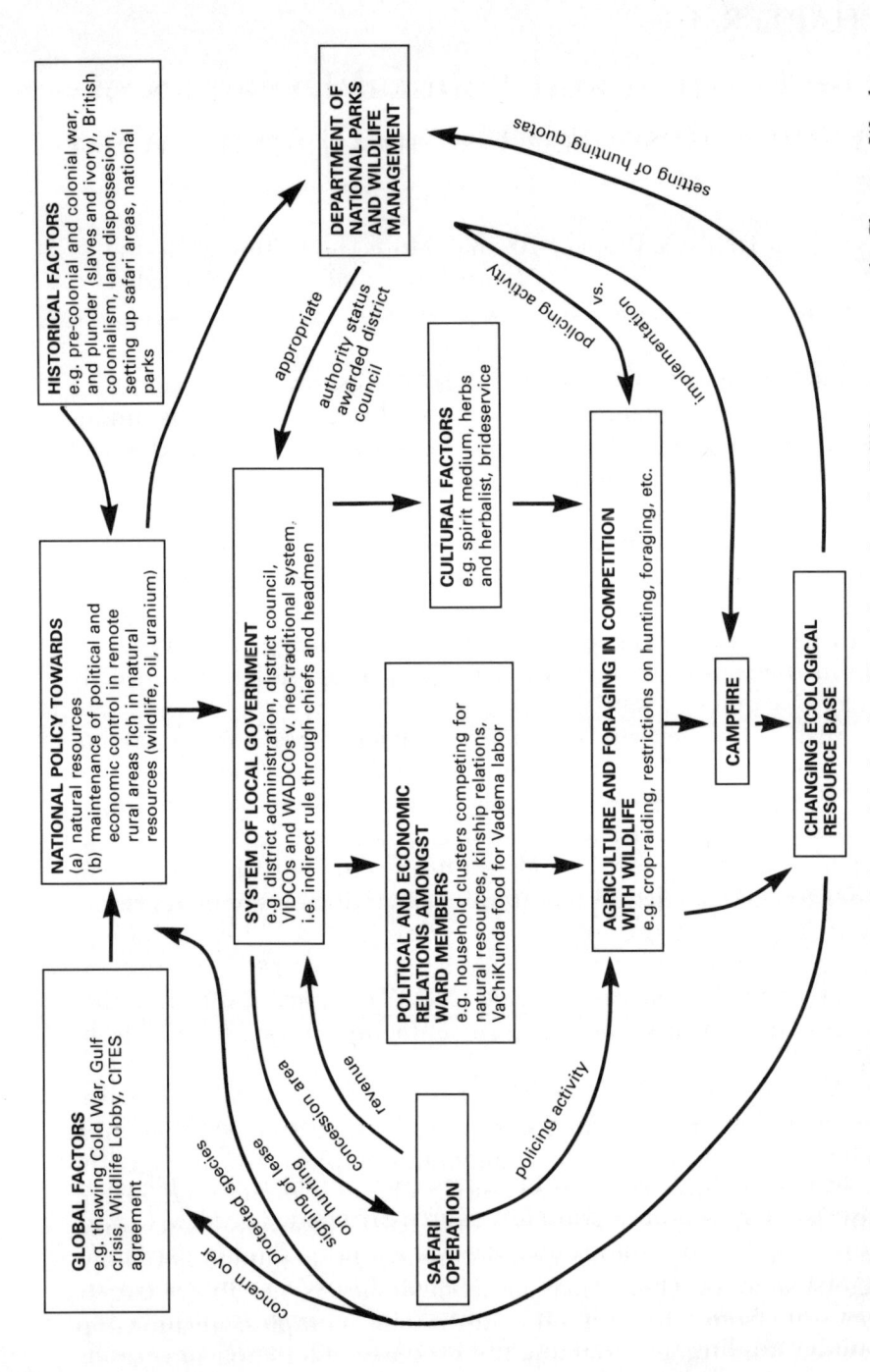

AGRICULTURE, FORAGING AND WILDLIFE RESOURCE USE IN AFRICA

Figure 4.1 Diagrammatic summary of the political and cultural dynamics of wildlife resource use in Chapoto Ward

and the influence of the CITES ban on ivory trade in making Zimbabwe and other Southern African countries seek alternative marketing mechanisms for their ivory resources, are good examples of how the local resource base might be influenced by global factors. Global factors, such as the thawing cold war, have also had a direct bearing on Zimbabwe's decision to undertake an economic structural adjustment program in an attempt to liberalize the economy. Therefore, national policy is closely linked to global politics.

Likewise, historical factors, another feature of Fig. 4.1, sometimes have a direct and immediate bearing on how the resource base is used. The ward itself is largely a creation of colonialism, as are the safari areas which surround it. The notion of 'the king's game', that is, that wildlife belongs to the state and that the state protects the wildlife from the people in the common interest and that of posterity, is a very powerful legacy. It appears to be an important factor in the largely alienated and negative attitudes which people presently have towards wildlife in the ward.

Current national policy towards a professed decentralization of wildlife resources (excluding, however, interdependent resources like uranium and oil), is also influencing the use of resources at the local level, and since local government authorities and the system of local government (district council, VIDCOs, WADCOs, councillor and committees) are the vehicles through which this decentralization is to take place, they have an obvious significance in terms of resource use. But equally important is the neo-traditional system of government used prior to independence, which relied on the chief and headmen for many administrative and judicial functions. The conflicting or overlapping interests between these two systems may in themselves be crucial factors in the success or failure of such programs as CAMPFIRE. Conflicts between the two systems may have important impacts on the local resource base, especially if some people feel excluded and alienated from a resource management regime. Such conflict may lead to such a regime being undermined.

Political and economic relations at the local level within the clusters (e.g. the institution of brideservice, child labor), between clusters (e.g. competition for scarce riverside gardens) and between vested interest groups (e.g. VaChiKunda food in exchange for Mvura labor, Faith Apostolic Mission Church members versus those who honor the ancestral spirits) are all important in terms of understanding the changing resource base. Of particular importance is how the wider global, historical, local government and national policy issues impinge on these local dynamics.

For instance, the royal ancestral spirits are (for most residents) the owners of the land and largely are seen to control the ecological resource base. They are not, however, involved in the official custodianship or proprietorship of specific resources, except unofficially as religious functionaries. Though ancestral spirits are renounced by a section of the community, such as members of the Faith Apostolic Mission Church, they have considerable cultural influence on the way people think and behave, even on those who renounce them, in regard to the resource base. The safari operator and client, by virtue of his concession lease signed with the district council, also claims ownership of wildlife resources in the ward and such conflicting claims are central to an understanding of the sustainable use of resources in the ward. Chapter 6 is devoted to the question of competing claims to the wildlife resource and Fig 4.1 is relevant in elucidating these competing claims.

Global Factors

Global interests in the environmental crisis and the competing stances taken on conservation through utilization, as opposed to conservation through protectionism, as exhibited at the CITES debates, have a direct bearing on how wildlife resources are managed in Chapoto ward. One could argue that the increased global awareness and appreciation of wildlife and the environment has led to increased anti-poaching units in the Chewore safari area. That is, the attempts to combat increased poaching of rhino horn and ivory has directly affected or curtailed foraging activities in protected areas.[1]

Zimbabwe has opted to support the trend for conservation through sustainable use and is trying to redress the policy of protectionism. This is not solely a response to parochial Zimbabwean concerns about the future of its own resources, it is part of a global concern about the future of environmental resources. Such international concern is made politically evident through the lan-

---

1. Another obvious example might be the influence of the Gulf war. This was a catalyst for the increase in fuel prices in Zimbabwe, which directly affected cotton growers whose transport costs per bale were dramatically increased, thereby reducing profit margins until commodity prices rise, and possibly making it less attractive to grow cotton as a cash crop in the long term.

guage used in project funding and aid and trade agreements at international level. The global concern with bio-diversity, the concern for conservation and sustainable use of environmental resources, therefore, influences national policy as well as projects like CAMPFIRE. Global concern is often supported by large amounts of financial incentives and other opportunities. Lobbying and fund-raising in America, for instance, can directly affect regional and national policies, which in turn affect outcomes at the local level in remote wards. To ignore the impact of money, technology and idea flows from global through regional to the local level is to ignore a major vested interest in local wildlife. The CITES debates on banning the ivory trade vividly symbolized this political and economic reality. It emphasized that local, district and national controls have to accommodate regional and global vested interests. Likewise, global interests in local outcomes cannot overlook the important role of political and administrative structures at national, provincial, district, ward, village and household levels.

Though some global trends or factors like the CITES agreements may have a direct and immediate effect on how resources are used locally, others are played out on a much longer time-scale and are intricately intertwined with the historical factors which have shaped the present. This is a major challenge for analysts of the global goal of sustainability of natural resources.

Historical Factors

The advent of colonialism had a very strong impact on the diversity of land-use strategies available in this part of the Zambezi Valley. Over time, wildlife became the property of the state which led to dispossession of land and resettlement, while protected areas and national parks were set up. Populations at the turn of the century were a mere fraction of what they are today (the 1901 national census estimated the African population to be 500,000) and in many communal areas in Zimbabwe there is now considerable land shortage.

Land was a key motivational factor in the civil war which ended in 1980. Though there is not a problem of land shortage in Chapoto ward, in the sense that the ward is only habitated in one area, there is effectively a land-shortage problem, because residents are denied access to natural resources, which the land supports within the ward. Historically, despite protective policies, people have survived in the valley by cultivating in both the dry (stream bank cultivation) and wet seasons, by foraging natural resources and by subsistence hunting. Yet government policy has attempted to reduce land-use strategies by stating that stream bank cultivation, subsistence hunting, fishing with nets, foraging in protected areas and shifting cultivation are all illegal or frowned upon. Cotton-growing, on the other hand, is actively encouraged by agricultural extension agents, despite the fact that drought relief maize is irregularly delivered (i.e. there is a deficit of food).

The state and the historical factors which have shaped it, are subtly exerting pressure on farmers to increase cash cropping as a viable way of life. Yet, even in the case of 'successful cotton-growers', cash cropping tends to underestimate the value of labor (see case-study in Chapter 3), and it is not clear that cash cropping of non-food crops such as cotton is a long-term option in valley conditions. In these conditions a diversity of survival strategies would be a better option. While condemning *dimba* cultivation, the state has to date turned a blind eye to it in the ward, but the MZP 'resettlement program' is essentially moving people away from the rivers because stream bank cultivation is not considered a sound policy.

In the past, the state leased out Chapoto ward as part of a hunting concession area, which is policed by the safari operator and his assistants. Under the CAMPFIRE program, this arrangement continues, but revenues accrue to district council. From the average person in the ward's perspective, the safari operator is still policing the wildlife resources in the ward and though the revenues from the concession lease are intended to benefit locals, this really has not yet impinged on the average person's life-style.

Generally, the state apparatus has impoverished people by reducing their land-use strategies. It is in this context that the CAMPFIRE program needs to be located, and it needs to show that it can reverse this trend.

System of Local Government and National Policy Towards Natural Resources

During colonialism, the mechanisms through which the state maintained political control in remote areas was through the offices of chiefs and headmen (indirect rule). At the present time, the system of local government is based on VIDCOs, WADCOs, and councillors who are represented in a district council (see fuller description in Chapter 1). The district council is run by a chief executive officer who, in the case of Guruve district, is also the district administrator (previously known as the district commissioner), a senior executive officer and a council chairman. Councillors from each ward are represented, but the structure is essentially a top-down hierarchical structure. Thomas (1991) argues that decision-making at district level is didactic because the District Development Committee has no democratic representation (see Chapter 1 for a description of local government structures). This committee is chaired by the district administrator and is responsible for district development plans which are presented for approval to district council. Thomas indicates that the potential for district councils to be coerced by their executive is therefore high.

The decentralization of the proprietorship of wildlife from the central government to the selected district councils is the start of what is officially hoped to be a grass roots proprietorship of natural resources. However, there are a number of problems associated with such changes. First, the state differentiates between different resources, there being different state mechanisms, institutions and laws involved in controlling water, forests (Forestry Commission), soil, minerals, wildlife (DNPWLM), etc. Ecologically and socially, these resources are holistically intertwined. Secondly, in the case of wildlife, the Wildlife Act (1975) provides provision for the district councils to be designated appropriate authorities for wildlife, but no legal proprietorship exists in current legislation for wards to take this responsibility. Realistically, ultimate control does not lie in their hands. In this sense, CAMPFIRE may not constitute decent-ralization, but a form of 'indirect rule'. A third major problem is that vested interests in these resources developing at higher levels such as the global, central or local government levels may militate against such vested interests developing at local levels. Further-more, the development of vested interests at the local level does not mean that the smallest accountable units (the households?) will develop such interests, it may be more likely that rural élites will emerge who capitalize on the resource opportunities.

Political and Economic Relations at the Local Level

As in the foregoing sections, the following exposition is written with Fig. 4.1 in mind and is a summary of relations that have already been mentioned. In Chapoto ward, the local élite is a fragmented grouping of VaChiKunda household clusters, competing and co-operating with each other for a range of opportunities, including *dimba* sites, *munda* sites, meat from legal and illegal kills, labor, church benefits and other resources emanating from both within and without the ward. An important division is that between the house of Kanyemba and the house of Chihumbe (see Chapter 2). Another important division is that between the followers of the spirit mediums and the followers of the Faith Apostolic Mission Church.

A common problem, for all in the ward, is that of crop-raiding animals, but the most impoverished people (mainly Mvura) in the ward are the ones who suffer the most because their foraging activities have been curtailed by game protectors. One attempt at coping with this imposition is to work in the more wealthy people's fields in exchange for food, which means that they cannot spend as much time working on their own fields. The Mvura people are currently caught in a circle of poverty, which marginalizes them from the dominant political and economic processes.

For all groups in the ward, kinship, marriage and brideservice play an important role in the micro-economy. In many areas of the ward labor shortage is more crucial than land shortage as a limitation to production, since there are still unoccupied areas of fertile land that could be used. Women, children and sons-in-law (through brideservice) are vitally important in providing this labor.

In terms of the wider economy, as early as 1908, Kanyemba was an area for recruiting labor from Zambia and Mozambique for the colonial expansion, but today surprisingly little migrant labor occurs.[2] People who have left the ward to go and work elsewhere tend to stay in those areas for long periods of time and generally do not plough back much income into the ward. A number of people from the ward have been relatively successful with their careers and some hold top positions in government. However, there is no visible evidence of development in the ward itself that has been generated by these sons (not daughters) who have out migrated and are upwardly socially mobile. This, I believe, is because the ward is not considered to be an economically viable concern, despite its rich potentials.

---

2. Cutshall (1990, 3) emphasized that 93.8 percent of household members were regular, full time residents, the remaining 6.4 percent included both secondary school students and migrants. I encountered instances of both VaChiKunda and Mvura labor migration. Older VaChiKunda men often mentioned that they had spent a period in their lives working on commercial farms. There were instances of Mvura finding employment on now inactive mines in the Chewore safari area. In general, VaChiKunda were more likely to have spent time in wage labor outside Kanyemba.

The descriptive material below elucidates the themes identified in Fig. 4.1 and the ensuing analysis. They are presented to complement and balance the political economy approach, favored in the diagram, by illustrating the importance of individual decision-making, interaction, and choice-making. The descriptions illustrate components of the diagram and the broader points which they make are related to the diagram, whilst at the same time giving flesh to these abstractions. In order to give the reader a picture of the manner in which valuable wildlife resources are controlled or policed within the ward, I have included an account of my own research experience of these activities. The safari operators' anti-poaching activities are the result of a number of factors identified in Fig. 4.1. The policing activities reflect the concerns of the wildlife lobby and the global concerns over the threat of loss of species such as rhino and elephant (global factors). Historically, they are an outcome of the colonial and Rhodesian establishment of protected areas. Furthermore, these activities reflect national policy towards such resources, which is influenced by the aforementioned factors and which enables the safari operator to lease the concession from the district council, which in turn is ostensibly there to manage wildlife resources in the best interests of local people. The following account indicates that there is considerable disjunction of goals and objectives in relation to the decentralization of the wildlife resource between the district and the ward levels.

Mr. A of the Animal Police

Mr. A is a hunter who works for the safari operators. His anti-poaching activities are infamous in the ward. Once I heard him telling a group of local people that the 'Zambian' poachers who kill rhino for the horn are superior to local poachers who kill for meat only. They at least have realized that wildlife is a resource worth a lot of money, whereas local people only think of its value in terms of meat. Mr. A pointed to his forehead and said that the next poacher he caught would get one there. I later heard that a Zambian had been killed by the safari operators' outfit.

Sadly, Mr. A and his colleagues, on several occasions,[3] searched people's houses for snares and smelt their pots to see if they had

3. Usually at the end of the hunting season.

been eating meat. The assumption being that if their pots smelt of meat, then they must be poachers because they were too poor to buy meat. The bulk of these anti-poaching activities were targeted against the Mvura. At the end of 1989, the safari operators policed the concession area with an anti-poaching unit led by Mr. A. The first victim was Mr. Chiyambo; they checked the pot on his fire and harassed him. Next they went to Mr. Kindon's residence, and told him to show them what he was cooking. He at first refused, but after being threatened he opened his pot. Inside the pot were some fish. The men wanted to know where the fish were caught and what method was used to catch them. Mr. Kindon replied that he had caught them in the Mwanzamtanda using fishing lines. Fishing lines were acceptable, but using fishing nets of any description (e.g. mosquito nets) was illegal. They did the same at Mr. Eria's home, before continuing to go through the bush searching for snares. After this incident, people believed that Mr. A was using spies in the community to monitor illegal hunting activities. During the research period, there were cases of people being arrested for poaching both within the ward and outside it. However, to my knowledge, no local person was convicted of the crime.

Though the state apparatus tends to withdraw survival options through facilitating such protective practices, it also irregularly provides an external and frequently unreliable source of food through drought relief distribution. The infrastructural set-up of local government is used to disburse these necessary hand-outs, which are targeted for drought years. The following statements, made by a Mvura informant, contextualize the role of drought relief amongst the other sources of making a livelihood (working for food, foraging, etc.).

Drought Relief Dependency: The State Taketh Away and the State Giveth[4]

Mr. S told us in November 1990, that for the Mvura, food shortage was a big problem. Drought and lack of time to prepare their fields had resulted in poor or no yields. Food was obtained by

---

4. The text is a paraphrase of the informant's statements.

working in VaChiKunda fields,[5] by making *hari* and from state drought relief, which was late. If one member of the group happens to obtain some bananas in exchange for labor, he/she will have to share these equally with the rest of the group because you cannot eat while watched by others who are starving. State drought relief, at that time, was distributed on the basis of 'food for work', and though Mr. S claimed that he had already worked for his drought relief to date, he had not received the maize. Consequently, he has no other choice but to work in other people's fields. As a result, he will not have time to grow his own crops. In essence, he will be growing his own crops in someone else's field,[6] but will not reap the benefits for his labor. The amount of food given him for a day's work is eaten the same day, so there is no way he can afford to stop working. If drought relief arrives, he may be given a small respite, which will allow him to plant some crops of his own. He will also use some of the drought relief maize as his seeds. (Many Mvura had, in desperation, eaten the maize seeds which should have been planted for the next season.) However, drought relief is never enough. If they decide to go into the forest to look for honey (i.e. if they embark upon alternative drought relief foraging activities) they may follow a honey guide bird, but when they arrive at the hive there will be no honey and the time spent on following the bird will have been wasted. This year's drought was the worst in a long time because the life-giving forest, which usually saves them in times of drought, now provides no food. If they go into areas of the forest where food is available they will be arrested by DNPWLM game scouts. Last year they had gone into the forest and came across scouts, but they were lucky because the scouts did not see them.

Sometimes they spend two to three days without eating anything and usually they will only eat *sadza* once or twice a week. The safari operators are also a problem. People are dying (according to Mr. S) and have no relish, yet the animals are ironically waiting around their homes to eat any crops they may plant.

As has been mentioned, protecting fields from crop-raiding animals is one of the most fundamental issues affecting social

---

5. VaChiKunda cotton fields and vegetable gardens situated on rich riverain soils were better situated and tended than the Mvura fields.

6. This is not to be taken literally. Mvura provide labor alone. No other inputs, such as seeds, are provided to the VaChiKunda. Mvura usually work alongside VaChiKunda families in such fields. Some of the more arduous tasks, such as clearing and stumping fields, may be contracted out to Mvura, in which case this may be their responsibility alone.

organization in the ward (this issue is dealt with extensively in Chapter 5). It is argued that settlement patterns, building of huts, look-out platforms and granaries are part of wildlife management.

The description which follows, is a pastiche of my own experiences, and it illustrates many of the themes identified above. Global, historical, national and district vested interests in wildlife, need to be contrasted with the manner in which local resources are perceived by those who are themselves perceived to be the 'poachers'. The following account illustrates the notion that local people do not legally have access to many local resources, that such resources (e.g. rhino) are deemed to be highly valuable, yet living side by side with these valued resources are people who often do not obtain enough food to eat. It also conveys a picture of the dangers and potentials which the forest offers and shows how removed the micro-world of the Mvura appears to be from the broader political and economic issues outlined in the diagram. On separate occasions, I was guided through the forest on foraging trips by Mvura and the findings are documented in Chapter 3. The purpose of documenting the following walks is to convey an ambience of the people and the place. Though the professed purpose of the second walk was to visit the place where Ntsinguni emerged, I was more interested in how Mr. Eria and Mr. Mtamawo related to the natural resources within the constraints outlined in Fig. 4.1.

Walking with Mr. Eria: A Case-study of Self-reliance and Poverty in the Midst of Plenty

Mr. Eria is the brother of Mr. Chiyambo, who is the headman of the Mvura of Chapoto. Mr. Eria lives on the western side of the Mwanzamtanda, in an extremely remote area of the ward, near an abandoned safari camp. The first time I met Mr. Eria was at about seven o'clock on a cloudy rainy morning near his home. He stood with an air of dignity and local knowledge, in the rags that served as clothes. We told him we were going to visit Mr. Mtamawo, a renowned herbal specialist and hunter, who lived away from other households near the border of the Chewore safari area. Without hesitation, he picked up his *dipa* (spear); it was still early in the morning and it was an overcast cool day, so buffalo might still be lurking in the undergrowth. He walked silently and slowly along the path which led through thick jesse (riverain woodland) and he did not appear to be wary of buffaloes and other dangerous animals. We walked through the cleared area used as a common field by a number of families, where individuals share the burden of crop protection imposed by crop-raiding animals.[7] On arriving at Mr. Mtamawo's, we were told that neither he nor his brother-in-law nor his son-in-law was available. They had gone into the hills in search of 'tobacco'; a euphemism for a range of foraging activities including hunting. Everything at Mr. Mtamawo's, besides a few pots and some ragged clothes, was hand crafted from available resources. Clay pots were being made to exchange for maize with VaChiKunda. The intriguing portable granaries, made from the bark of a large tree, could be seen up in the *dara* (small hut on stilts). Grass rattles and traditional guitars were assembled from the immediate resources.

From Mr. Mtamawo's house a grand view of Kamota and Membgwe, two mountains of the massif where the Mwanzamtanda river disappears between them can be seen. On the western face of this massif are a number of landslides. It is said that *Ntsunguni*, the water spirit, emerged at one of these land slides. Water unexpectedly started to pour out of solid rock and ran down into the Mwanzamtanda. We asked Mr. Eria to accompany us to the place where *Ntsunguni* had emerged, but he refused because it was a cool cloudy day. He claimed that wild animals would be actively moving around and it would be very dangerous to attempt such a visit. He told us to return on a sunny day and this we did about three days later.

Though we had set off from my camp early in the morning, by the time we reached Mr. Eria's house, approximately 10 kilometers away, it was extremely hot. Mr. Eria was at work clearing trees from his field, but he agreed to walk with us to the place where *Ntsunguni* had come out of the side of the mountain. On the way we again visited Mr. Mtamawo and this time he was there.

His wild and fiery eyes reminded me of those of an old lion (see Plate 8). He seemed to be defiant of state power and all that it represented. We sat down on a grass mat together, watching the women moulding a *hari*, which would be exchanged for food. I

---

7. This mechanism of coping with wildlife will be discussed in more detail in Chapter 5.

asked Mr. Mtamawo about the old times.[8] I told him that it had been written in books that the Mvura were non-sedentary foragers and were not agriculturalists. He told me that this was an outright lie and that in the old days people used to cultivate fields. Books were full of lies, in his opinion.[9] He also said it was a lie that people used to move about from place to place. They did move their fields on an annual basis, but in general they were sedentary.[10] Other informants point out that shifting cultivation was an important strategy of survival, but they also indicate that after harvesting, seasonal movement through the forest, hunting and foraging was the normal way of life.

After this conversation, we continued on our walk with Mr. Eria. We passed the grass enclosure of Mrs. Mtamawo senior, whose ancient and dilapidated body was crouched over a plate of meal. She is the oldest of the Mvura, but unfortunately from a research point of view quite senile.

Mr. Eria walked sure-footedly along what was clearly an animal path. Mvura do not make conventional paths and seem to avoid straight lines. It is remarkable how circumspect their paths are. It is also remarkable that when walking in the forest they will tend to take one route to reach their destination and a different route to return.

Our present path, judging from the spoors and droppings left, was clearly traversed by many different types of animals. These animals included elephant, buffalo, bush buck and others. This area was more densely forested than others we had passed and Mr.

---

8. Of all the people in the ward I would say that his way of life most closely resembles the Mvura's past way of life. He stubbornly refuses to work for food in the fields of the VaChiKunda, seems to despise western medicine, and is himself renowned as a great herbalist and hunter. Towards the end of my research, Mr. Mtamawo fell ill with a wasting sickness, which seemed to be related to kidney failure (too many toxins in the tubers which he had eaten?). He could not walk and his legs were reduced to bone. People said that when he died, his family would move closer to other people and to the school. They also said that when Mr. Mtamawo died, a great deal of herbal knowledge would die with him. I tried to persuade him to visit a doctor in Mvurwi on the escarpment, but he said he wanted to die at home not far away from his ancestors. Besides, where would his children get the money to bring back his body to this, his land?

9. A shocking lie written about in books is of course the notion that Mvura are two-toed.

10. Mr. Mtamawo's response must be considered in the light of considerable intimidation by the custodians and keepers of the wildlife resource and his reputation as a hunter. It must also be remembered that this discussion took place early on in the research and that Mr. Mtamawo had just returned from 'tobacco' collection, a euphemism for foraging and/or hunting. I know that at this time Mr. Mtamawo suspected that I was working for the safari operator or the DNPWLM. This, I think, explains why he chose not to be accurate about the past.

Eria walked with evident knowledge and confidence. In one instance, before I had heard or seen anything, Mr. Eria gave us a sign to stop. Shortly, I heard the sound of galloping hooves approaching fast and darted for the nearest tree, but my companions stood their ground. The buffaloes had stirred, but not before Mr. Eria was aware of them. Shortly after this, Mr. Eria's attention was drawn to a tree, where many ants were crawling. Using the axe which he had carried on his shoulder, he dexterously chopped open a section of the bark. We were still in earshot of the buffalos, which are renowned for stealthily following and hunting down people who come upon them suddenly. My research assistant pointed out that Mr. Eria chopped the wood without making too much noise and without making a fuss that might antagonize the buffalo. He pulled out two fat worms (*masenda*) from the tree and clasped them in a split stick. He carried these worms for the rest of our journey and when he returned to his house he gave them to his daughter to eat.

We crossed the Mwanzamtanda and the prints in the sand were testimony to the many animals that crossed at that point. We followed the game path diagonal to the river, but later left it in order to set a course for our destination. We avoided the dense bush where animals might be resting from the midday heat and climbed the hill by following the stream bed that had been formed by the water and rock slide. This geological feature had spontaneously occurred when *Ntsunguni*, bringer of floods and wind, had emerged. We stopped in the dry stream bed, hot and exhausted. Kuyeri, my research assistant, dug in the sand below a boulder and to my great surprise the hole filled with murky water. It was November 1989, the hottest period of that dry season.

We waited for the sediment to settle. The taste of that water is especially memorable for its sweetness. Though both Kuyeri and myself were considerably younger than Mr. Eria and a great deal better fed, we were both wilting in the heat. I estimated Mr. Eria to be in his early fifties; he showed no sign of stress and walked slowly and determinedly to the rock face. He showed no trace of sweat, though his cough indicated that he was not in the best of health. A few months later, Mr. Eria developed a persistent swollen foot, which he put down to someone having snared him with herbs on a path (sorcery). A western medical explanation would more likely be 'poor diet'.

On arrival at our destination, we sat and gazed at the view of Lake Cabora Bassa and the meandering Mwanzamtanda river course below us. Mr. Eria searched in his pouch and folded some tobacco into the dried outer leaf of a maize cob. He then produced what looked like the shell of an old size D torch battery. A bottle top served as the lid. Inside the battery was a small quantity of cotton, a small piece of metal like part of a chisel, and a stone. By hitting the chisel against the stone at the right angle a red hot splinter would be directed into the cotton at the bottom of the battery shell. By blowing on the cotton, Mr. Eria lit his cigarette. I was struck by the independence and ingenuity of the device. It symbolized how people like Mr. Eria take whatever comes to hand to meet their needs. How less helpless he seemed in comparison with the many other Zimbabweans who were totally dependent on the production of matches and the efficacy of the transport and marketing networks; at that time there was a chronic shortage of matches in the country.

While smoking his cigarette, Mr. Eria noticed a young bush buck. At home his children were badly malnourished and particularly in need of protein. I could see my companions were sorely tempted to hunt it. They knew that the consequences of doing so might heavily outweigh the benefits, and at this time Mr. Eria was not quite sure what I was doing in the area.

On our way down, we took a different route and Kuyeri said this was a normal procedure since anyone who had been tracking us would have identified the water source we had made and could wait and surprise us there. Mr. Eria pointed out to us the faint spoor of a rhinoceros. I believe only the best trackers, displaying a keen attention to detail, would have detected this faint track. I thought about Mr. Eria's family's poverty and how highly valued a rhinoceros is considered by both wildlife conservationists and international poaching syndicates. Here indeed was dire poverty in the midst of one of the world's most highly prized resources.

We were led to another source of clayey water that emerged on the side of the hill; it also had a sweet and fragrant taste. Spoor indicated that elephants had recently visited this source. There were snares for smaller game and thornbush placed strategically around the waterhole. From there, we meandered down back to the Mwanzamtanda river joining it at the deserted field where Mr. Dumba had found lions eating his maize cobs. From there we passed a dry season pool in the river, near two magnificent trees, where the safari operator's old safari camp had been situated. In camps such as these, international clients pay exorbitant daily camping rates and hunting/trophy fees. At last we were back at

Mr. Eria's home where he gave his daughter the two juicy worms to eat.

The children were playing hunting, with miniature spears and axes, which had been forged in the fire by their father, who made his own spears. I did not notice that any child played the role of game scout or safari operator. They would have been representing the political ecology more closely if they had done so.

I would like to end this chapter by again referring the reader to Fig. 4.1. The material above illustrates the broader point that the productive systems and the changing ecological resource base found within Chapoto ward offer people a life-style which largely competes with a far more lucrative and business-like use of resources conducted by externally based entrepreneurs, such as the safari operators, who are facilitated in this task by virtue of national policy and the system of local government. These in turn are directly buttressed by global and historical factors.

CAMPFIRE currently attempts to convince local people that resources should be protected, because they are valuable to the safari operator and his clients, who in turn pay a concession lease to the district council who in turn, in consultation with ward representatives, may decide on how revenues may be used. At the time of writing, in this ward such revenues have been directed into building a new block for the school, but no ward debate took place on this issue and few people knew that the new school block was partially funded by revenue from wildlife resources. Mr. Eria and Mr. Mtamawo certainly did not participate in such debates, as I have never seen them or their families at ward meetings. Secondly, sending children to school is a low priority for these residents, since clothing and feeding their children must come first. When we talk about wildlife utilization and the benefits of wildlife for these people, the two worms which I saw Mr. Eria giving to his daughter come to mind; this for him is the type of significant, albeit sometimes illegal, contribution wildlife utilization makes to keep him and his family alive.

For those people in Chapoto ward who were historically foragers, and for those who have relied on stream bank cultivation, the state has effectively been working to deprive them of the diversity of land-use strategies necessary for their healthy maintenance. Despite this, by virtue of living with wildlife, they have a limited jurisdiction over the resource. This limited jurisdiction has to be seen in the context of global factors, historical factors, national policy and the system of local government, which have all played an ongoing part in influencing how resources are used and controlled in the ward. Competing rights, jurisdictions and vested interests in the wildlife resource influence how people cope with wildlife. This is the subject-matter of the next chapter.

CHAPTER 5
Coping with Wildlife

Wateya Waya Wachemera Mampepo.

When you set snares, you have asked for trouble, you must be brave and prepared for trouble.

The following conversation was overheard by a reliable informant while he was doing some casual wage labor with other VaChiKunda residents. The dialogue illustrates how tempting it is to kill for the pot, especially crop-raiding animals. It also underlines the social sanctions that come into play when one takes the risk to hunt. Despite these sanctions, there is a mutual understanding about the need to obtain meat and prevent crop damage.

B: If I had a gun I wouldn't leave elephants and animals to go around. I would kill.

P: You would not have a problem of [lack of] relish, people would know [that you have killed an animal] because you will give [relish] to relatives and you would be reported.

Comment: It was common knowledge that Mr. Tauro's wife spread the news about P.'s recent illegal kill. She was given a piece of meat to give to Mr. Tauro in his capacity as spirit medium. As a result, P.'s sister went around grumbling 'why didn't you give to me, and yet you are giving to others.' P. realized that by giving something secret, you make it public. The discussion continued:

M: Even if you get a bush buck, it will be heard by people and the game rangers will go to see what's wrong. Then you will be discovered.

B: I will go at night when people are asleep.

T: My cotton is always being taken by kudu, I'm planning to set snares. If kudu is killed I will eat with my own family, so that others won't report me; not like what happened to V. [V. was arrested for snaring a kudu and attempting to sell the meat].

Z: I heard a bush buck screaming near your [B.'s] field.

B: I did not put snares near my field.
P: Just admit because we are not all sell-outs; we won't report you to the game protectors.
B: (secretly to a friend) I'll be all right this evening.
Z: If everyone was allowed to kill. If everyone had guns, there would be not one single animal left. We would learn how to eat baboons (currently taboo). It is better if we kill illegally because we kill one and then stop, kill one and then stop. It is better if we hand over management to the wildlife committee.

Comment: The others disagreed, they all wanted guns.

It is a mistake to think that wildlife management constitutes only what is done by the formal authorities (i.e. the DNPWLM, the local safari operators, the district council, the wildlife committee). Natural resource management is not simply a matter of committee-ing at the local level. Committees are the current thrust of the CAMPFIRE program, but I would argue that such committee work could be strengthened by more recognition that the household/cluster directly manages wildlife on the ground. As T. says above, ['If kudu is killed I will eat with my own family, so that others won't report me.' In this chapter, both formal and informal wildlife management activities are described. First, the manner in which the family clusters cope with wildlife is described, then other more formal mechanisms are described, including PAC by DNPWLM. Lastly, the local wildlife committee and their relation to the community is explained. These issues are important, because they illustrate the practical ways in which rights of access to wildlife are manifested.

Both Mvura and VaChiKunda manage wildlife in a direct way. Wildlife management at the local level includes the management of both fauna and flora, and primarily this management entails spending an inordinate amount of time attempting to prevent animals from eating people's crops or damaging them. Wildlife management activities can be split up into individualized family/cluster activities and collective activities and beliefs. Wildlife management activities are centered on the family unit, which conducts agricultural production, foraging and other forms of food production. Individualized family management activities mainly occur at night when the animals move away from the heavily forested or remote areas into the cultivated areas on either side of the river. This causes direct competition between humans and animals.

It is useful to describe the behavior of the animals which are thus managed. In Zimbabwe there are distinctions which can be made between animal populations that are hunted and those that are protected in national parks. A further distinction can be made between animal populations which exist contiguous to human settlement engaged in agriculture and other subsistence activities, and those which do not. In Chapoto ward, we are dealing with the management of animal populations that have been and continue to be hunted and which live in close proximity to human populations. We are not dealing with the 'tourist/game viewing animals' one might find at Mana Pools or Kariba. The latter can be seen during the day in close proximity to human activity. In Chapoto ward, animals (baboons are the exception) generally make themselves scarce during the day and only emerge at night. The entire landscape of the area changes when night falls. Few people move around during nightfall and those who do usually carry spears for protection. People will usually not go far into the forest on a cloudy day, as they believe animal activity will be greatly increased.

Measures and mechanisms used to ensure the protection of family and property during the night frequently have to be prepared during daylight hours. Thus when we talk about time spent on wildlife management activities, we are not simply talking about the hours when wild animals are physically present. We must include the time spent constructing or involved with the following protective mechanisms and also the time spent on crop protection. Note that all of the following refer to the household/cluster economics, centered around the immediate family.

Construction and Use of *Dara*

The *dara* is a grass hut on stilts, about one and a half to three meters above the ground (see Plate 9), and *chibarakawo* is a grass enclosure. These structures are built in the field (*munda*) or river bank garden (*dimba*) depending on the time of year. In the case of the VaChiKunda, the male head of the family, with his wife, may sleep in the field in one of these constructions. Other members of the family may stay at the main homestead (*nyumba*) where they protect small livestock, such as chickens, rabbits and goats, as well as food that has been or is being prepared. Such food might include dried or fresh fish and meat, as well as the grain and other crops stored in granaries. Special protective structures are built for all types of small livestock. Some of these are particularly innovative (see pictures of chicken coups, Plates 5 and 10). Therefore, settlement patterns and construction of living space is a response to wildlife. The location of one's fields is also important because neighbors can buffer one from crop-raising animals. In more densely cultivated areas, fields in the center of cultivation are prized because they are surrounded by neighbors who will be protecting their crops and will give the alarm when danger is near. In the case of Mvura shifting cultivation, joint fields have the same advantage. This is especially relevant in the remote riverain woodland field areas where there are many problems with crop-raiding wildlife.

Fencing
In an attempt to prevent or dissuade crop-raising animals from entering fields, and also to prevent animals from entering living areas, fences made out of thin branches of trees tied together with reed or grass, or simply clumps of thorn brush, may be placed strategically especially around the *dimba*. The later method is used by some of the more remote Mvura households, who at times are surrounded by potentially dangerous animals such as buffalo, lion, elephant and leopard.

Fire
Fires are kept alight in both fields and living areas. If elephants are in close proximity, throwing a burning torch in their direction may be risked, but this may provoke a charge. In the dry season, bush beside a dwelling place or field may also be set alight. Forest fires are widespread in September and October, especially on the massif. This may be accidentally caused by honey collectors using fire to smoke bees out of a hive, but there may be other reasons. The fires may be a deliberate attempt to clear the bush or they may be set in an attempt to drive animals towards snares. I was not able to conclude exactly why such fires existed, however, initial evidence from Kanyurira ward indicates that fires are not as accidental as might be thought. In the 1990 dry season, the usual widespread fires did not occur in this ward. A possible reason for this may be the increased awareness of the value of natural resources (Murphree: personal communication).

Beating of drums and tins
This is probably the most common way in which to make animals aware of one's presence and to suggest that they move on else-

where. On countless occasions I was awakened by the beating of tins or drums by my neighbors. I adopted this method myself, and when awoken by buffalo eating grass nearby or by the guttural growl of a leopard, I would hit my tin bucket gently and rhythmically, gradually increasing the volume and speed of the beating, in the same manner as my neighbors did.

Stones and slings
Frequently one finds heaps of medium-sized stones in the fields and river bank gardens. These stone heaps are strategically placed and may be thrown or slung at buffalo, kudu, bush buck and elephant, at one's own risk. As one informant, who threw a stone at a buffalo, only to find that it charged him and that he narrowly escaped with a leg wound, said, 'I know now exactly how very dangerous a buffalo is and I will never throw a stone at a buffalo again.' Another informant, who had witnessed a woman being badly injured by a buffalo, said, 'If I see a buffalo coming into my field, it can take the whole field and I will not do anything to deter it.'

Mutedwe *(Bark String with Tins)* – *Used to startle animals*
A length of bark rope can be an effective startling mechanism. Usually tin cans filled with stones are tied to the rope, which may be as long as 50 metres. Usually the rope emanates from the *dara* or other enclosure and stretches across the field. One informant claimed that he usually slept soundly and that a sixth sense would wake him when animals were raiding his field. If this happened, he would reach out from his sleeping mat to the rope and give it a few hefty pulls. He claimed that this usually worked. This particular informant was blind (see Plate 11).

Scarecrows
This is not a popular method but I have seen them used in Chapoto. I believe they affect both diurnal and nocturnal creatures. Scarecrows often include a white object, which is noticeable both during the day and at night.

Axes, spears and poison
There are three main types of spears. The most commonly seen spear is a fishing spear (*mondo*). *Mondo* is made from a lean sapling and has a narrow metal head, like a spike. The spike is wound on to the wood with metal strips.

A more heavy-duty spear is the *dipa*. It has features on both ends of the wooden handle which is over one meter long. The head of the spear is wide and may have serrated edges, the butt of the spear is formed from a short sharp axe-like wedge of metal, often used for digging. The spear may be used to kill animals caught in snares or as a heavier protective measure for hand-to-hand-hoof-paw combat. Another heavy-duty spear is the throwing spear, *mondo*. This is a long spear with a tapering metal head. Such spears are rare these days.

Informants claimed that both poison and herbs may be applied to spears to make them more effective. The common 'traditional' axe is a ubiquitous weapon.[1] A wedge of sharpened metal, often part of an old leaf spring, is inserted into a knob kerrie shaped handle to form a light and wieldy axe. I awoke one night from an uproar to find one of my research assistants had apprehended a leopard that was trying to get at his chickens. He had used an axe to frighten the leopard away.

Catapult
When I first arrived in the field, young boys would hide their catapults when they saw me. These can be used to kill birds and also as a means to harass animals intent on crop-raiding.

Snares
If one is caught using snares, there are heavy penalties. Arrest and trial before a magistrate in Guruve, Karoi or Chinoyi is the normal procedure. A gaol sentence usually follows and one is incarcerated for six months or more in the company of thieves, muggers and other dangerous characters. Besides the risk of apprehension, the business of checking one's snares can also be very dangerous. I was informed that if a buffalo, elephant, lion or other large animal has been caught, that animal may gain super strength when one approaches it. Extreme caution and good timing are therefore vital. Given the current climate of anti-poaching activities, there are many good reasons why people in the ward are frightened to set snares. On the other hand, if members of one's family are going to die from malnutrition and if animals or drought have

---

1. These days the axe is a more commonly used weapon because anti-poaching patrols who find people with these axes are not as suspicious as they are with an individual carrying a spear.

consistently prevented one from reaping a harvest, the risk/benefit equation changes and snares may be laid with discretion.

The setting of snares requires knowledge of the usual game paths and water holes used. Game paths may be encouraged by removing or placing obstacles (thorn bush) on the route to water. Single snares may be put in place, but it is far more effective to use lines of snares (*chinga*) in strategic places (water holes, game paths). To enhance effectiveness, snares should be treated with herbs. Individuals specialize in particular types of snares. Some favor relatively light-weight snares geared for smaller animals while others are experienced in using cable or heavier snares for larger animals. Very light snares made from grass or bark are used to catch pigeons and smaller fowl; these are usually sprung snares. A supple sapling or branch is used. Conservationists may be glad to know that young boys who are keen to build wire toy vehicles have been known to raid lines of snares set by their fathers.

If one is persistently cursed with crop-raiding animals, the temptation is great to place snares in or near one's fields. The risk of doing this and being reported by an enemy or an official is high. At the end of the hunting season the local safari operator's anti-poaching squad moves through the area looking for snares (especially near fields). For example, at the end of 1990, they found some snares near Mr. Chiyambo's brothers *dimba*. Mr. Chiyambo (the Mvura headman) happened to be collecting tobacco from his brother's *dimba* at the time. Two young, well-nourished, carnivorous men (one black and one white) beat the poorly nourished Mr. Chiyambo until he 'confessed' that he had laid the snares. He was then taken with others, treated in the same manner, to the police camp from where he was sent up to Guruve to be 'tried'. At the Guruve police station he pleaded his innocence (the snares belonged to his brother) and the police dropped the case. He returned to Kanyemba, visibly shaken by the experience.

When I spoke to him, he told me that he thought the safari operator's personnel were permitted to beat and arrest people for laying snares or even for suspecting that snares had been laid. In fact, the safari operator's personnel should have a member of the national parks staff with them when conducting anti-poaching activities. Furthermore, they do not have a right to assault members of the public.

Guns

I know of only five male household heads who have guns. The common gun is the 'gren gun' or single-barrelled shotgun (see Plate 6). If licensed, these guns may be used legally to shoot at certain crop-raiding animals. They are ineffective against buffalo, elephant and larger game. One informant vividly narrated how a buffalo paused briefly, after he had fired a shot near its eye, before destroying his banana trees. Herbs are important for guns and their owners. After two baboons were shot in a granary by a single shot, people accounted for this by explaining that the owner of the gun had used herbs. All of the mechanisms mentioned so far are centered around household economic activity, in contrast to these are the formal mechanisms of wildlife control and management through the wildlife committee, the DNPWLM guns and the safari operators' guns.

DNPWLM guns

More effective guns are carried by the DNPWLM officials at Mashumbi Pools who have a briefing to conduct Problem Animal Control (PAC). The wildlife committee in Chapoto may radio through to Mashumbi Pools that a problem animal has destroyed or damaged crops or threatened people. The officials there may come down themselves to hunt the animals or they may request that the safari operator's personnel conduct the PAC. This may also be done as part of a formal hunt if a client is available. However, these formal mechanisms of PAC have sometimes backfired and personnel sent out to do PAC have caused problem animals. On one occasion, a buffalo allegedly wounded by a DNPWLM personnel later seriously wounded a woman who was collecting grass. Another example of the creation of problem animals, is that of the elephant kill at Mr. Phineas Charuma's cluster. On this occasion children from these homes ran out towards the oncoming elephant with excitement, neighbors later explained how they could hear the bullets ricocheting through the grass. The elephant was literally peppered with shots (many heavy-calibre rounds were used and automatic weapons were used intermittently). It finally thundered to the ground within 20 metres of Mr. Phineas Charuma's home. The rifle fire was aimed in the direction of the homesteads. A wounded elephant bull (6,000–7,000 kilos?), heading in the direction of homesteads, poses a large problem. One of the hunting party armed with an automatic weapon was a cartographer who had never hunted elephant before.

This incident illustrates how the goals and objectives, conceived by CAMPFIRE planners, outside the ward, can be interpreted and perceived in quite a different way at the ward level. The 'rationality' of the program is that the people who live cheek by jowl with animals will have an incentive to develop a sense of propriertorship for animals. This is the normative level (what should happen) which planners often operate at. The normative plans are in this incidence confounded by pragmatic choices at the district and ward levels (what actually happens). First, the district council chooses not to involve the ward broadly in decision-making concerning the 1989 revenues from the safari operation in the ward. This in turn influences the wildlife committee at the ward level to believe that there is no vested interest for them in this operation, as they have seen no benefits from this source. They have, however, had benefits from PAC. By reporting a problem animal they usually bring about a kill. Selling the meat from a buffalo resulted in a credit with the district council of over Z$400. Selling the meat from the elephant resulted in a credit of over Z$1,000. Since the highest return that an individual received from the 1990 cotton crop was just over Z$1,700 and most individuals received less than Z$600, this indicates that such sums are regarded as high and provide a good incentive to report or invent problem animals. In this case, as one of my research assistants pointed out, the elephant was innocent. It had not damaged fields or property; it had not threatened life. It had been visiting the community for a few days prior to its death without causing any harm. This elephant was a trophy bull and therefore, could have brought the community as much as Z$60,000 from a safari hunt. However, in this case the committee wanted to kill the elephant, because they felt they would get a return from it, whereas they felt they could not be sure that they would receive a return from safari operations. Project CAMPFIRE, therefore, becomes project PAC. This was one of the ward's introductions to the concept of 'money in the coffers from animals'.

The officer in charge of PAC was not present at this incident. His subordinates handled the affair. He later explained to the community at a ward meeting that, in fact, they had lost money by killing the elephant and that the incident was a big mistake.

This could have provided an informative learning experience for the community, but one factor militated against it doing so. That factor was that the ward had received no perceived benefits from revenues going to district council from the safari operation and so these statements did not strike any chords in them.

Whilst discussing 'guns' as a mechanism of wildlife management at the local level, it would be very wrong to omit the role played by the safari operator and his clients. However, this topic will be discussed in some detail in Chapter 6 and I therefore restrict my comments to a few observations. The effectiveness of the safari operator in the habitated part of the ward is to some extent dependent on local knowledge. Local people are keen to inform the operator where animals are, as this may provide a brief respite from crop-raiding activity. However, the safari operator is primarily concerned with obtaining the bag for his client and not for PAC.

The Distinction between 'Poaching' and Illegal Hunting by the Local Community

In mid-1989 local informants reported that 19 'poachers' from Zambia were killed in the Chewore safari area, which shares a common boundary with Chapoto ward. One of my research assistants was instrumental in the capture of one of the 'porters' in this group. This porter was paid 4,000 Zambian kwacha to carry food for the two hunters/poachers. The individual, who was apprehended near the research assistant's house, claimed that he came from Kafue (Zambia) and was engaging in this activity as he had no other work or employment.

The attitude of local people to poachers of this kind is generally negative and many say that they support the harsh methods used to apprehend them. This is probably because local people feel that if anyone is going to 'poach' the resources, it should be them since the resources are within their area. However, it is also pointed out that the anti-poaching unit and the *Magemu* (anyone who is concerned with the management or protection of wildlife) will now shoot anyone in the Chewore safari area on sight and ask questions later (a perceived consequence of giving indemnity to anti-poaching units). This is allegedly done because 'poachers' were setting up ambushes for such anti-poaching units, by using ruses of various kinds. The poachers are generally seeking rhino horn and/or elephant tusk.

Cultural Beliefs and Practices Associated With Wildlife Management

Collective beliefs and practices that stretch beyond the interests of individual household clusters and immediate families, are also important coping factors at the local level. There is evidence from elsewhere in southern and central Africa (Marks 1984; Matowanyka forthcoming), that 'traditional' laws (i.e. collective management rather than individualized management) exist or have existed for controlling access to particular species of wildlife. In particular, I am thinking of the notion that people are forbidden to eat the meat of their totem. It is true in Kanyemba that certain species are not killed or eaten, because of prohibitions arising from the belief system and general cultural mores concerning what constitutes acceptable food. Lions are associated with ancestral spirits and some lions are said to be the physical manifestation of ancestral spirits. Pangolins are also regarded as having mythical significance and are, in general, regarded to be the property of the chief. Pythons are not eaten 'because no one eats snakes'. Crocodiles are not eaten, because their bile is full of witchcraft and this poison will bring about certain death. Baboons are not eaten because they are regarded as vermin. In general, predators such as leopard and the smaller cats, and scavengers such as hyenas, are not eaten. Despite these general mores about what is culturally appropriate to eat, there are perhaps surprisingly few other prohibitions which are taken seriously. The prohibition on eating one's totem which other writers have referred to, largely does not exist in Chapoto ward. As it was descriptively explained to me 'everyone enjoys their own totem'.

In regard to fauna, it is true that limited areas of land are regarded as protected or sacred areas. Such areas include graveyards, areas around the shrine for the spirit medium (*Dendemaro*), certain large trees, areas associated with mythological figures such as *Ntsinguni* (the water spirit) and some springs. It is also true that such beliefs could develop if the locus of natural resource management is returned to the local level. However, at the present time such beliefs do not appear to be significant from a conservational or natural resources management perspective. The probable cause of this is a political and economic one, since this population has been dispossessed of much of its rights to use land.[2] Under these circumstances, it is not surprising that elaborate mechanisms for protecting natural resources do not exist. Well-established individualized management strategies exist, but collective management processes are not well developed, although the potential to engage such collectivist mechanism does exist (see next two sections).

Cultural Conceptions of Natural Resources, Herbs and the Spirits of the Forest

Both the Mvura and the VaChiKunda know the importance of herbs (usually roots and tubers) for the physical and psychological welfare of individuals and the collective. A herb can broadly be defined as any substance which has magical qualities. They are usually pieces of root or foliage that have been acquired from the forest, but they can also be animal products (e.g. lion dung) or other odds and ends. Herbs are of crucial importance for many aspects of life. They have an extremely wide range of uses and can be used to ensure fidelity in one's wife, to inflict swollen feet and ankles on one's enemy (frequently also a dietary complaint) and to cure or prevent snake-bite. They are also used to protect one's field from pests and crop-raiding animals and to give one success in hunting. However, herbal knowledge, like hunting, is a jealousy guarded secret. I believe it is no accident that renowned herbalists (mainly men) are often also renowned as successful hunters. This makes sense, since a successful hunter knows the craft of the forest. He knows how to survive from the resources found therein – the roots tubers, berries and fruits, the hidden springs, and the herbs are all an integral part of his hunting life.

Many of the secrets of the forest are told to him by his father, with whom he will have done a kind of apprenticeship. I believe that a crucial element, even a control on hunting and on the

---

2. Both VaChiKunda and Mvura have been dispossessed of their rights to use land and natural resources under colonial rule and the ensuing protectionist policies associated with the establishment of safari areas and national parks along a large stretch of the Zambezi Valley to the west. The Mvura previously lived in the Chewore safari area and the VaChiKunda, under Kanyemba, had forts on islands along the Zambezi, which effectively controlled trade. Kanyemba and his forces were virtually neutralized by agreements between Portugal and Britain on the limitations of each others territory. Both groups became subject to a colonial management regime, administering local land and resources.

exploitation of natural resources, is the combined efficacy of herbs and the spirits. Herbs are psychologically and physically enabling; they give one the right heart to deal with the dangers involved, and they give one the strength to deal with them. If one does not have herbs, one may encounter all kinds of obstacles. Taking herbs accounts for a steady heart, a steady hand and a good aim. They may be eaten or they may be carried on ones' person in a small bundle tied with cloth and string. Incisions may also be made with a razor blade on one's face or other parts of one's body and the herbs may be rubbed into the wound. Herbs are not only employed on the person, they are also used on guns (in the case of the VaChiKunda; Mvura do not have guns), snares and spears. Even dogs may be given herbs and Mtamayi (1959) reports that lion dung was fed to dogs to make them courageous hunters.

Individual hunters usually select their own herbs, each hunter having a particular specialty. Hunters who co-operate and trust each other may also exchange herbs and techniques for apprehending animals. For instance, a hunter may specialize in snaring buffalo and big game using cables, whilst another hunter may specialize in smaller game using thinner wire. *Chinga* (a line of snares) may be used or individual snares may be set. Much of the knowledge about illegal hunting is acquired through observing one's father or grandfather. However, family spirits also appear in dreams and visions. For instance, one might appear to be walking in the forest with the person, while the spirit will be pointing out which herbs one should use, where one should place snares, and where an abundance of animals can be found. This is a secret dream only to be shared with one's sons, who will usually use the same herbs.

There are four main categories of herbs:

(a) those administered for sickness or for medical reasons;
(b) those administered for good luck, success and protection (including protection of fields from pests and crop-raiding animals);
(c) herbs used against one's enemy (particularly worth mentioning are herbs used to insure that one's wife is faithful); and
(d) herbs used for hunting and bush lore (including poisons, protection of paths).

Both herbal specialists and spirit mediums administer herbs. In the case of the Mvura, the spirits of the VaChiKunda are the owners of the land. The Mvura spirits (e.g., Chimhako, Chinyenzva and Chiguhwa) live outside the ward[3] and they obtain many of their herbs (e.g. for serious illness) by consulting these mediums. As has been stated, for the Mvura, the placing of herbs at a crossroad or on a path can snare unwanted intruders or enemies and this tends to make people circumspect about their movements. This may be one reason why Mvura tend not to make single paths from point A to point B, but prefer to be cautious and choose a different way each time they need to travel. Considering their non-sedentary and largely fugitive life-style in the past, and their fear of apprehension by game protectors, it is interesting that such mechanisms controlling the nature of paths have become established as part of the belief system.

During my stay in the area, Mvura claimed there was a shortage of honey in the forest. An explanation offered for this was that no honey had been taken to Kanyemba and kept in the *Dendemaro*. A supply of honey in the *Dendemaro* or given to the spirit medium would ensure that a plentiful supply of honey could be found in the forest. The same applies to other natural resources including, of course, meat from animal kills. After a safari operator's kill, I was told that fewer and fewer animals would be found in the ward because the safari operator had ignored giving the spirit medium a piece of the meat from the kill.

This symbolism is an excellent idiom for expressing the fact that the natural resources of the area are alienated from the people. It is also a powerful expression of a range of political implications. An obvious one is that illegal hunting is the factor which outside observers would claim causes fewer and fewer animals to be found in the ward. However, this local explanation has a deeper explanation than this, it implies that there is a relationship between honoring the owners of the land (the spirits) and the ecological health of the area. The explanation also implies that illegal hunting (an important factor in determining the numbers of species) can be controlled by the spirits of the land. Such factors make me question whether the 'appropriate authoritics' for wildlife should not include spirit mediums and herbal specialists at the local level. Most of these ecological authorities at the local level have nothing to do with the administrative appropriate authority; the district council up in Guruve. They are largely ignored by planners.

3. See section on Mvura in Chapter 2 (pp. 52–8).

We now turn away from the cultural coping mechanisms to the formal mechanisms, proposed by CAMPFIRE for coping with wildlife in Chapoto ward.

The Initial Wildlife Committee

Under the CAMPFIRE program, ward wildlife committees are elected in the various wards. The chairmen and secretaries of these committees, together with the ward councillor, sit on the district wildlife committee which is responsible for most of the decision-making concerning revenues from wildlife in the district. Amongst other things (see chapter 1), disbursement of revenue may include compensation to individuals for particular instances of crop-raiding, if the committee decides to do this.

The first wildlife committee was elected in Chapoto ward (some informants used the term appointed) at the instigation of the chairman of the district wildlife committee (September 1989). The chairman of the district wildlife committee arrived in Chapoto and called a meeting at short notice by informing members of the community whom he met along the roadside. No advance notice was received by the community, who are usually informed of events, meetings, etc. by the school children or by the chief's messenger. As a result, the meeting that was held did not represent the entire community, but only a small portion of it. Likewise, the wildlife committee that was elected did not represent the interests of the entire community but only a small portion of it. Specifically, the committee had no representative from the Mvura segment of the community, though it did have one member from the western side of the Mwanzamtanda river. Ironically, it could be argued that those people who do not live by the roadside are the ones who are most likely to have more contact with wild animals, hunt, and possess skills in tracking, animal behavior, etc. These people, however, did not hear about this meeting when the wildlife committee was formed. As a result, the elected committee reflected both a geographical and a political bias. Of the six-member committee, the three most important members (chairman, secretary and treasurer), all came from the same immediate area. These three were all related through marriage and they were all members of more influential VaChiKunda families. The remaining positions were for committee members without specific charges. Though subsequent committee members have been appointed and members who were not active have been dropped, this initial lack of equitable representation still exists.

Revenue from Wildlife

District council has a right to a percentage (not more than 15 per cent) of net revenue drawn as a district council levy on wildlife revenues. However, in Guruve district in 1989 the council also drew a 10 per cent District Management Fund and put aside 20 per cent of net revenue as a capital reserve (Guruve District Council Financial Report to District Wildlife Committee 9/11/90). The Guruve district council is also accountable for current expenditures drawn against gross revenue. In 1989, this amounted to almost 45 per cent of gross revenue, stated as Z$299,387,00 in the district council's financial report. In 1990, similar percentages were set aside for council. Effectively, this means that the council is placed in control of relatively large sums of money. Besides submitting a copy of the district wildlife committee's annual report to the director of DNPWLM, the main check on how the council conducts its affairs is through the participation of local leadership in the district wildlife committee. Another important check or balance is the participation of the NGOs discussed below.

In the initial stages of CAMPFIRE, NGOs including ZimTrust, WWF and CASS play an important collaborative role in helping to monitor, evaluate and implement the project. ZimTrust has a briefing as the implementing agency, whilst the latter organizations provide necessary research and consultancy services. WWF and ZimTrust have both provided funds for capital items, such as fencing (frequently required in the community's land-use plan), necessary to get projects off the ground. There is no formula as to how the program will be implemented in each communal area that volunteers for it. Since there are varied ecological and socio-economic circumstances, the program has to emerge through a process of negotiation with those involved. This is ideally a type of participatory action research, whereby the research itself brings up possibilities and alternatives, which it is to be hoped have a basis in local thinking and local ecology.

An illustration of revenue distribution from wildlife took place in Kanyurira ward, approximately two and a half hours away by vehicle from Chapoto bordering on the banks of the Angwa river. Local people in Kanyurira, in negotiation with the district council and the NGOs, agreed on a land-use plan to fence their productive lands in order to protect them from crop-raiding animals. The remainder of the ward is used as a communal resource area where a safari operator, employed by the district council (initially aided by ZimTrust), may take clients willing to pay relatively vast amounts of money for hunting. The money accrued from the safari operation is ultimately controlled by the district council, and once they have withdrawn their costs of other allocations and the percentage owed to them, they are briefed to credit the remainder to the local people, who decide at a ward meeting how the funds should be distributed.

It was agreed that a fair way of calculating the amount of revenue due to a ward would be according to the schedule of hunting fees. Thus those wards where animals were shot would accumulate the trophy fees values in Zimbabwean dollars (e.g. a male elephant at the time of the research would earn Z$7,500 in trophy fee). From the 1989 revenues (totalling Z$47,310), Kanyurira ward decided to provide Z$7,000 for furniture for the local school, set aside Z$8,110 for a tractor or other contingency, spent Z$15,000 on clinic reconstruction, and the remainder was divided as a Z$200 award to (approximately 102) predominantly male[4] household heads. This, I believe, was the first time that revenue from wildlife or natural resources had been distributed at the household level, anywhere in Africa. Masoka/Kanyurira ward, therefore, has a very high media profile and attracts much international interest.

Revenues in the same year were also accrued by the district council from Chapoto ward, though unlike Kanyurira, the safari operator in Chapoto ward has signed a concession lease with the council. The hunting concession area includes the ward, the contiguous Dande safari area and a portion of land north of the Angwa river in Chisunga ward. Revenues handed over to the district council amounted to Z$168,600. By January 1991, no one in the ward could adequately account for what had happened to these funds. The district council, in its annual financial report for the district wildlife committee, claimed that the Chapoto school had been built (would be built?) with funds accruing from 1989 wildlife revenues (Z$53,012), but local people were not informed that the funds for the school had accrued from wildlife revenues, neither were they informed that the funds belonged to them and that they

---

4. This dismayed many of the women in the ward.

could decide what to do with them.[5] On the contrary, in one instance, local people had been led to believe that funds or resources emanating from district level were personally given to them by officials, implicitly in exchange for votes. Local people argued that the funds for the school had already been allocated from a separate source, known as the disadvantaged school vote. Thus, in the initial stages of CAMPFIRE, a façade of community participation may be machinated at the district level. This façade is for consumption by the NGOs and other interested parties. In reality, an authoritarian top down approach leaves local people in the dark, in apparent compliance with district and local government objectives, which, from the perspective of the ward, appear to be to maintain control of revenues due to the ward. The lesson to be learnt is that the way the program is introduced at ward level is very important and may influence people's attitudes for a long time thereafter.

According to the CAMPFIRE document, safari revenues for Chapoto ward should accrue from at least two and possibly three sources in the future. The first source is revenue from the trophy fees accumulated from animals shot in the ward, which forms 19 per cent of the concession[6] in terms of hunting quotas. In 1989, a total of 28 animals were killed in the ward: one male and one female elephant, one male lion, five male buffalo, one kudu, four hippo, three crocodile, four bush buck, one klipspringer, six impala and one duiker (Buchan 1989: 18). I estimate that the total revenue accrued from trophy fees for these animals was Z$19,380. In 1990, the total revenues accruing from trophy fees to the ward from the safari operation kills within the ward (ten animals, including two elephant) was Z$24,070.

---

5. By June 1991 senior ward members such as the teachers and the headmaster were satisfied that Z$47,000 (from 1989 revenue) had been spent on materials for an additional school block, and were told that a balance of Z$6,000 existed at the district council. However, individuals had not been broadly consulted on the allocation of these revenues; the ward had not participated in the decision-making process. This is partly because the main communication link between the district council and the ward (the ward councillor) was not an effective means of communication over this issue. There are many possible reasons for this; one of the most important being the build up of vested interests in the resources at the district level.

6. The concession lease is a contractual agreement between the safari operator and the district council. It permits the safari operator to bring clients to hunt within the concession for the duration of the hunting seasons covered in the lease and to set up camps for this purpose. However, the operator has to stay within the quotas laid down by DNPWLM. The duration of the lease, in the case of Chapoto ward, was short term because the council wanted to keep its options open.

PLATES

1. Mvura *dimba* on the banks of Mwanzamtanda River

2. Close-up of *dimba* cultivation showing round holes in which maize is grown

3. Close-up of *masawo*, an important edible fruit from the bush

4. A well-maintained homestead belonging to a VaChiKunda cotton-grower

5. A Mvura dwelling-place, showing pyramid-like chicken coop (right foreground) and thorn-bush fence (behind boy) to keep out animals

6. Mr. Samson Dumba, a VaChiKunda cotton-grower, posing with gun

7. Mvura 'portable granary' (*chibande*) made from woven bark, and a clay pot inside a grass enclosure

8. The late Mr. Mtamawo (Mvura) with part of his family. (He was a renowned herbal specialist, hidden away from the state)

9. A *dara*, a raised sleeping-platform for guarding field at night. (Note bark rope (*mutedwe*) which is tied to tin cans with stones inside them to startle buffalo, kudu, etc.)

10. Ingenious suspended chicken coop, with spiked deterrents for predators and thorns underneath

11. Mr. Bandera with bark rope tied to tins to startle animals. (Mr. Bandera, who is blind and carries a white stick, has a member of his family (left) illustrate how bark rope tied to tins in the field can startle animals. Thorn-bush in foreground keeps animals and children away from *masawo* tree)

12. A buffalo, the safari hunter's dangerous prize

13. Spirit medium (in black hat) with cooking oil outside chief's store during a drought relief distribution of maize

14. A safari operator (left) with two Spanish clients determined to hunt buffalo

However, a second source of revenue, identified by the CAMPFIRE decument, is that 'a community sharing a common boundary with a national park, safari area or state forest would receive a proportion of the income from that area' (Martin 1986; 47). Since Chapoto ward is bordered by the Dande safari area in the south and the Chewore safari area in the west, an amount should be added to the figure accruing from safari operations within the ward. In 1989, the district council reported that it divided up the revenue from the Dande safari area between the wards that are contiguous to it. This increased the Chapoto ward revenue from the estimated Z$19,380 accruing from kills within the ward to Z$53,000. According to the CAMPFIRE document, a percentage of revenue from the Chewore safari area, which borders the ward in the west, should by the same token be distributed to the ward.

In the case of the Dande safari area, control of revenues falls under the appropriate authority status accorded the district council.[7] Starting from 1991, the district council has to lease the area for a nominal fee from the DNPWLM. In the case of the Chewore safari area, which falls into a different province, revenues go directly into the treasury, and according to Martin (personal communication), there is a long way to go before these funds will be distributed to wards.

Local people in official positions are aware of some of these complexities, but they feel that there is nothing they can do about them. A number of people believed that the district council was hoarding their money. Such perceptions are extremely important, even if they may be regarded as totally unfounded by district and local officials. One reason for their importance is that they mark the degree of participation in decision-making by the ordinary people (as opposed to one or two spokesmen for the ward) living in the ward.

There is a danger that what CAMPFIRE may do is replace one centralized bureaucracy (DNPWLM) with another slightly less centralized institution (district council) in the management of wildlife. The hope, expressed by colleagues in the NGO's, is that pressure emanating from the DNPWLM, the Minister for Environment and Tourism, the NGOs and the local people speaking through their councillor and wildlife committee, will influence the district coun-

---

7. These revenues should be shared between the wards which border the Dande safari area, namely Chapoto and Chisunga, but at the end of the research period (mid-1991) no criteria had been established on how to do this.

cil to devolve responsibility and benefits further. The hope is that local capacities for managing and 'utilizing' local resources will emerge as the project proceeds and that appropriate local institutions will become proprietors for the resource. The researchers from the CASS, WWF, ZimTrust and the DNPWLM can and have played an important role in increasing local awareness of possibilities for wildlife utilization and in aiding institutional and economic capacity in those wards where the project has had initial success. However, the fact that wards are dependent on a district level institution as the appropriate authority for wildlife is, from my research point of view, problematic.

The Problem of Empowerment

Local government and the district council is perceived, in Chapoto ward, as not merely an administrative institution, but also and primarily as a political institution. By this I mean that local people are constrained by feelings of political inadequacy and dependency in their dealings with this institution. As has been mentioned, they are at the whim of political forces beyond their control. As one informant pointed out, in talking about the guerilla war, 'We heard rumors but we did not know that there was a war until 1978. That's when things started happening in this area. Shortly after, we were moved to the "Keeps"[8] in Mushumbi Pools.' Another informant asked me almost a month after the 1990 elections what the results were. Few newspapers reach the ward to update the government workers (teachers, nurse, etc.) on current events. People in Chapoto do not feel empowered, partly because of the historical experience of indirect rule, the inaccurate perception of lack of resources in their area and the whimsical nature of political power at the center, during the pre-colonial, colonial and the post-colonial eras. Political authority is now required to set the ball rolling for such participatory programs as CAMPFIRE. The project and the idea of community participation and empowerment need a political blessing before they get off the ground, mainly, I feel, because they might be conceived of as being against the wishes of authority, that is, subversive. In Chapoto ward, the political blessing

---

8. Called 'protected villages' by the Rhodesian Forces who built them to prevent guerrillas from having contact with local people. They were referred to as 'concentration camps' by the nationalist forces.

has been a partial one and the ward seems to have been deliberately kept in the dark during 1989 and 1990, as far as possibilities for wildlife utilization are concerned. Representatives of the district administration and the district council cite the inactivity, the lack of motivation and the lack of capacity in the ward for the problems of development. The local people blame the council for hoarding their funds and keeping them purposely in the dark. In a sense, both are right, there is a history of thwarted development in the ward and local micro-political rivalries have played an important part in this (see below). On the other hand, these rivalries exist in the context of the broader political economy of Zimbabwe and the particular historical experiences that have led to the present system of district government.

Local attitudes towards the issue of wildlife utilization (and to my presence in the ward) changed after I brought the wildlife committee from Kanyurira ward, where household revenues from wildlife had been distributed, to address people in Chapoto. They attended a *doro* (beer-) drinking session the day before addressing a ward meeting and therefore had both a formal and an informal venue for the exchange of ideas. They reported on the various aspects of CAMPFIRE in their area and answered questions from members of the Chapoto community. In general, the community was keen to see the benefits of CAMPFIRE, but still felt powerless as to how to proceed. Some were still not convinced about the benefits of the program and the possible issue of fencing off a communal resource area for wildlife in the ward illustrated that there were a number of different ideas about how this should be done.

In May 1990 I was given minutes of meetings held with the district council which claimed that they had paid Z$53,000 out of Z$168,600 accruing from Zambezi Hunters' operation (the local safari operation) for building Chapoto school. I gave these papers to my research assistant, recommending that they be given to the councillor, secretary of the wildlife committee, and other members of the community to discuss since I had heard that these issues had not been discussed. Members of the community were not satisfied with the district council accounting. They claimed that they had not been consulted on what should be done with the wildlife revenues, despite the presence of the councillor at district wildlife committee meetings.[9] Furthermore, they were not

---

9. In all the time that I lived in the field the councillor did not formally address the ward on these issues.

convinced that the money had been spent on the school. However, at a district wildlife committee meeting that I attended shortly afterwards, these burning questions were not raised by representatives from Chapoto. At the same meeting the presiding natural resources officer read out the figures indicating the allocation of revenues for each ward, but warned us not to include these figures in the minutes of the meeting. Later I enquired why there was so much secrecy associated with this and was told that it would be difficult to work in the area if one was seen to be acting against the council. Such fears really get in the way of debate on these subjects, and without debate, meaningful and beneficial decision-making is difficult. This is not to say that the negotiations within the ward committees were not inherently political. They were beneficial in that they conscientized people about their rights and the potential of their resources. However, at the end of the day, these committees do not have the legal right to control resources and to decide how to use them, since they do not have appropriate authority status. They must defer to the paternal hand of authority at district level.

In my opinion, the CAMPFIRE program should empower the local communities by providing the possibility for appropriate authority status to be earned by ward wildlife management committees. This could be possible once the committees have proved that they are capable of fulfilling certain basic conditions, which might include that: committees are representative and have primary authority (rather than rhetorical assertions of authority) over use of wildlife in the area; they are strictly accountable to the smallest wildlife management unit in their area (i.e. the household/cluster); they are capable of making decisions over revenues in consultation with all members of the ward who they represent; and they are willing and capable to work with government and NGO's to achieve their goals. Amongst other things, this could lead to an openness of debate which is currently lacking.

As well as there being a need to devolve appropriate authority status on the ward, there is a need to take local people's current wildlife management practices into account and to make committeeing accountable to the households/clusters which are intimately involved with wildlife resources. In order to fulfil the criteria outlined above concerning the accountability of the wildlife committee, it should be required that every household in the community has the opportunity to vote for the committee of their choice and that when important decisions concerning the distribution and expenditure of funds from wildlife revenue are made, it should be mandatory that the committee give each household an opportunity to decide what they want to do with these revenues. To date, these decisions have not been brought to the household, but instead have been decided at district level or at wildlife committee level. As mentioned, this should be one of the conditions on which appropriate authority status can be earned. The wildlife committee, therefore, has an important educational and brokerage role to play. Since deciding what each household would like to do with its portion of revenue accruing from wildlife is a large task, I suggest that the wildlife committee should receive a stipend for its services to the community, which can be deducted from wildlife revenue. This would encourage active participation. Once the wildlife committee becomes empowered, I believe in the long term one may see that the role of indigenous belief systems (or modifications of them) discussed above, will buttress their authority and there may also be a revamping of indigenous controls on access to resources.

It should be added that there was very poor communication between the district council and the local people at the time that this research began. This was particularly because there had been a rapid turnover in the position of councillor for the ward. Four previous councillors had had difficulty in carrying out the duties entailed in this position. One person was declared resigned after not attending four meetings. Another tended to ignore the wishes of people and fell out of favor. Yet another came into conflict with the chief over the siting of the new school, while another councillor had lost favor with the community for being too strong willed and for acting unilaterally in reporting names of illegally resident Mozambicans. The existing councillor is a very young man who is still building up experience in local politics. There was, therefore, no continuity of knowledge or interests, which is vital for the development of CAMPFIRE in its initial stages.

Micro-political Rivalries and Thwarted 'Development': CAMPFIRE and the Grinding Mill

The CAMPFIRE document claims that, 'it is vital to the program, wherever it is applied, that the community forming a natural resource co-operative should be a cohesive community with common objectives' (Martin 1986: 33). Chapoto ward clearly does not fulfil this criterion and it might be worth rethinking this phrase in the document, as the type of community sought after may not exist. If the intention of this statement is to emphasize relative cohesiveness, it may be important to underline this. Even in Kanyurira ward, which is relatively homogeneous and cohesive in comparison to Chapoto, women were very upset that male household heads and widows were given the Z$200 award from wildlife revenues.

In Chapoto ward, there are four main currents of conflicting interest. First, there is the conflict between the chiefly authority structures and the formal political structures. Chiefly authority has lately been given increased importance in the eyes of the Zimbabwean government.[10] The newer more democratic processes concerning VIDCOs and WADCOs were instituted after a 1984 government directive (see Chapter 1 for a description of local government structures). Secondly, there is the conflict of interest between the Mvura and VaChiKunda populations. Thirdly, there are conflicts of interest between residential clusters competing for natural resources, particularly *dimba* and *munda* cultivation plots. Lastly, there are intergroup conflicts, rivalries or conflicting interests such as that between the Faith Apostolic Mission Church and those who attend the spirit possessions within the *Dendemaro* (see below).

The rivalry between chiefly (neo-traditional) power and the power conferred on the system of ward and village development committees, is a strong one. However, there are equally strong divisive forces in the community which have militated against development in the past and are likely to do so again in the future. A case-study of the World Vision grinding mill, one of the few assets in the community, illustrates this point aptly.

A previous ward councillor, now the secretary of the wildlife committee, was demoted from his position for having unilaterally given the names of people who had originated from Mozambique, and who had settled in Zimbabwe, to the immigration authorities. This same councillor had also reported the activities of the Faith Apostolic Mission Church, who were aiming to hand out food and clothing to the Mvura, as training a dissident army. This allegation, according to church goers, was based on the fact that khaki (a color used by the military) was often the color of the clothing given them. An additional reason for suspicion on the part of the authorities of such missionary activities near border areas, was

---

10. The judicial power of chiefs was increased in 1990.

the alleged involvement of right-wing evangelist churches from America in support of the MNR movement. By making this report to the district administration, he was successful in banning the church from the area for two years and the church missionaries from America were subject to investigation by the Central Intelligence Organization (CIO). As a result of this, animosity was built up between him and a local leader of the church, who blamed him for thwarting the plans for building an Apostolic Faith Mission Church in the ward. When this councillor became aware that certain materials given by the state for building a school were likely to be reacquired if they were not used, he suggested that the materials be used in building a World Vision funded grinding mill. He suggested that when the materials due to arrive for the mill appeared, they could be given back in replacement of those to be used on the school. He consulted the school committee on this issue and they agreed that it was a good idea. So, he went ahead and personally built the grinding mill using a small quantity of bricks and cement owned by the state. His rival in the Faith Apostolic Mission Church, who was also a member of the school committee, took this opportunity to report him directly to the police for theft of state property. The police arrested him and he stood trial. He was fined Z$200. Meanwhile, the grinding mill, which was otherwise financed by World Vision, has been an enormous asset to the community, mainly helping the women who would otherwise have to grind the grains by hand. This is by no means an isolated incident and reliable informants have explained to me that they do not want to be seen to be actively involved in 'development'. They claim that this will result in the community 'hating them',[11] and all their efforts will only result in their being punished or driven out of the community, as happened in the case of a previous councillor who came into conflict with the chief over the siting of the school.

Another feature that tends to thwart local plans for development is the attitude of many of the individuals serving on the many committees. Frequently, the same individuals are voted into many committees and as a result they have less time to work in their fields and they see little or no benefits arising out of serving on the various committees. As one particularly popular committee man said, 'I have to walk to the meeting and then back home.

---

11. People are also careful not to broadcast their good fortune, as this might attract jealousy and witchcraft accusations.

That takes two hours. Frequently the meeting takes the whole morning. Before I come I have to wash my clothes, but I am not given soap to do it. All we do is vote, vote, vote, but nothing ever changes.' People like this are frequently over-extended and have little incentive to put a lot of effort into something when they have seldom seen the fruits of labors in the past. Rivalries that thwart development reinforce and exacerbate these attitudes.

A related problem is the fact that the population of Chapoto ward are subject to the whims of authorities and powers elsewhere, usually on the escarpment. These authorities, in early 1989, decreed that the entire population of the ward would be placed in a consolidated village within three days. This was a government policy, arising out of concern over the security from the MNR bandit activity which had extended in recent years to within Zimbabwe's borders. As the ward was in a border area where attacks had taken place in neighboring Zumbo, it was suggested that the population should be placed in such villages for their own protection. Though the move never materialized, planning ahead for CAMPFIRE, under such conditions, is not easy.

The foregoing chapter has moved us from the practical arrangements associated with crop-protection to the committeeing processes associated with CAMPFIRE. The focus has been the mechanisms through which people cope with wildlife at the local level. The next chapter deals with these same issues from a different perspective. It attempts to describe and analyze the vested interests in wildlife and illustrates the competing claims which exist in the resource. CAMPFIRE claims to be dealing with common property management. The next two chapters scrutinize this assumption.

CHAPTER 6

Gardeners of Elephants: Competing Bundles of Rights to Wildlife

In Chapter 4 the broader political dynamics of wildlife resource use were outlined. In that chapter it was shown how global (e.g. CITES debates), national (policy towards natural resources), district and local claims as to how the resource should be used interact with each other. In this chapter we elaborate on the various vested interests, jurisdictions and rights in the resource, as they are manifested at the ward level.

Spirit mediums, a chief, safari operators, clients, subsistence hunters, local people, clusters of households, DNPWLM personnel, the district council, wildlife committees, poachers, policemen and a Faith Apostolic Mission Church missionary have all claimed rights of control, access or ownership of wildlife in the ward. To date, these ambiguous rights have largely been competing and conflicting and I argue that in this sense wildlife is not currently managed under a communal property regime (see Chapter 1). Furthermore, these competing claims and rights make it difficult to establish proprietorship of the resource at the local level, through a common property management regime.

This section deals with the question of bundles of rights of use and control, by focusing on illustrative case-study material. I refer the reader to Chapter 1 for details of the typologies of property rights identified by analysts. The argument I present below is essentially that instead of concentrating on the typologies of property rights and property rights regimes our focus should be on the complex bundles of conflicting and competing rights associated with the cultural and political dynamics of resource use. In my opinion it is necessary to acknowledge the ambiguity of the various bundles of rights to wildlife, by identifying the diversity of state, community, private sector and other interests in the resource. Any successful management regime will need to incorporate or clarify these multiple jurisdictions.

The first set of rights I would like to consider is that associated with the royal ancestral spirits and particularly that of Kanyemba, the owner of the land, and that of his spirit medium through whom he communicates. I start off by describing an incident that is symbolic of the clash between the values, interpretations and controls associated with wildlife by the state apparatus, tourists and big game hunters, and the values, controls and interpretations associated with wildlife in terms of ancestral beliefs and local dynamics. This concerns the death of the spirit medium of Chihumbe (brother of Kanyemba) at the horns of the treasured hunters' prize, allegedly the most challenging African animal to hunt, (see Plate 12) the buffalo[1]. I continue by explaining the degree of control that the spirit is said to exert over wildlife in contradistinction to the control exerted by other authorities, such as the district council, DNPWLM and the safari operator. Also included is an illustration of the controls exerted over illegal hunting by the spirit. The complex bundles of rights associated with specific elephant kills and other events, such as the poaching of buffalo by a senior police officer, are used as illustrations to make these more general points about competing rights.

Three weeks before the researcher entered the field, the long-standing spirit medium for the area, Mr. Tauro, who was possessed by the spirit of Chihumbe, was gored by a buffalo whilst in his field on the western side of the Mwanzamtanda river. Mr. Tauro had been warned by the spirit who possessed him not to move his house to the western side of the river, where wildlife is more abundant, and not to continue his illegal hunting activities. It was said that the spirit wanted him to engage in agriculture and to obey the law, and he had once before been gashed on the arm by a buffalo as a warning from the spirit not to hunt. According to a reliable informant, he had not wanted to live on the western side of the river but his wife wanted to live there. This conflict of aspirations between the spirit and the spirit medium led the spirit of Chihumbe to warn Tauro that 'we will see what will happen'. It was after this proclamation had been made by the spirit that Tauro was gored and after a gruelling trip to Harare hospital, where he was unsuccessfully treated, finally died from his wounds. In this sense, the spirit facilitated the death of the spirit medium through the vehicle of a buffalo.

The night before Mr. Tauro was attacked, a buffalo was feeding

1. The local safari operator specifically offers buffalo safaris.

from his maize crop. His wife threw stones at the buffalo and the buffalo went away. The next night the wife heard movement and the sound of chewing outside the *chikumbi* (grass enclosure). Again she threw stones, but this time the recalcitrant buffalo was in a mood to return the aggression. The wife shouted to her husband to awake and to clear out of the area, but as he was allegedly drunk he awoke groggily and noisily and was gored at the entrance of the *chikumbi*, whilst his wife escaped unharmed. As a result, Mr. Tauro was taken to the clinic,[2] situated about eight kilometers away. Apparently, part of his intestines were outside of his skin. I was informed that Mr. Grobler, Faith Apostolic Mission Church missionary in the ward at the time, laid hands on the spirit medium and prayed for him.

A theme emerging from the research is the competing forms of spirit possession which in the community coincide with other vested interests and which are reflected in the various committees. This has been elaborated elsewhere.[3] The present spirit medium for the area is a young woman who has recently arrived from Mozambique with her children. She is newly possessed with the spirit of Kanyemba and was diagnosed as such by a spirit medium in Mozambique, after having allegedly suffered a long period of mental illness. The role of spirit medium of Kanyemba had been vacant for many years and I believe that the possession reflects aspects of local politics. As outlined in Chapter 2, the chief is a direct descendant of Chihumbe (see section on contesting the chieftainship and the historical construction of the chieftainship pp. 61–5), while the house of Kanyemba has never provided a chief, though they believe that his descendants should rightfully be chief. The chief's power has waned in recent years with the coming of independence and he is very old. I suspect that the possession of the woman by Kanyemba is a reflection of these political realities and it places the descendants of Kanyemba in a good position to claim the next chieftainship for themselves.

---

2. The clinic is situated away from all habitation. When available, an ambulance from Mushumbi Pools, taking at least 10 hours, will get a patient to the nearest hospital in Mvura.

3. See section on thwarted development and the grinding mill for an elaboration of this (pp. 150–3). The Faith Apostolic Mission Church possession claims to be that of the Holy Spirit and this church condemns the spirit possession in the *Dendemaro* as demonic.

The Spirit Medium as Appropriate Authority For Wildlife

The chairman of the wildlife committee is the paternal great grandson of Kanyemba and it is he who presides over the spirit possession taking place in the *Dendemaro*, a shrine where the herbs, walking sticks, axes of the various *svikiros* (mediums) are kept (see Chapter 2 for information regarding the contestability of the chieftainship pp. 61–5). It is here where the spirit is consulted on a wide range of matters, including personal problems, good and bad luck, sickness, and moving a homestead. The spirit also deals with a number of issues to do with natural resource management, pest problems, crop-raiding animals, problem animal control, hunting, etc. At the end of 1989, a thanksgiving celebration was held in Bauwa, the closest Mozambican town to Kanyemba, situated opposite Zumbo on the southern bank of the headwaters of Lake Caborra Bassa. Various spirit mediums were present, including Bepe, who is closely related to the three brothers, Kanyemba, Chihumbe and Nyanderu. The ChiKunda of Bauwa are closely related to the ChiKunda of Kanyemba, though they live on either side of an arbitrary colonial boundary. The celebration was a thanksgiving to Kanyemba for having fulfilled promises related to the control of pests (locusts, birds (e.g., queleas) and rats and in controlling crop-raiding and problem animals, notably baboons.

Whilst attending the *Dendemaro* when the spirit was in possession of the medium, I asked the spirit questions concerning the control of pests and crop-raiding animals. In relation to pests it is clear that there are two main competing mechanisms for their control or eradication. Individuals may use one or both of these and there is no apparent conflict in using both methods. Cotton is seriously threatened by a number of inveterate pests including aphids and bole worms. Commercial pesticides are liberally applied for these pests, using a hand pump strapped to the back of an individual. Usually the individual does not wear protective clothing and often does not even wear shoes. However, these pests that scourge the cotton crop are also brought to the *Dendemaro* for treatment. A sample of the live pests are brought in glass or plastic containers and are ritually treated with herbs (roots and tubers from a variety of plants). The *svikiro* (medium) may ask the *vanyai* (messenger of the spirit) to obtain certain herbs that are not in stock in the *Dendemaro*. The medium herself (see Plate 13) may go out into the contiguous forest area. It appears that the contiguous forest area is protected for this and other reasons, and the siting of the *Dendemaro* is frequently in a grove of old trees. This area and its surrounding vegetation is considered sacred and only the spirit and his messengers are permitted to tamper with it. The pests are treated with various herbs. The messengers of the spirit frantically select different bundles and bags of herbs with which to treat the various worms, pests, etc. The spirit mediums, simultaneously, select particular herbs from the bundles and bags and curtly give commands to the messengers to pass on these bundles. After this, the spirit of Kanyemba selects individuals to run to an unspecified cross-roads and to distribute the various pests there. These designated messengers were informed that if they should look back at the *Dendemaro* whilst on their way to the cross-roads, this would invalidate the treatment of the pests.

The symbolism of the ritual treatment of the pests and their distribution at the cross-roads, is a powerful expression or manifestation of the power of the spirit who can dispense with all the pests. The purging of the pests may fail if the community has neglected the spirit's wishes or has not obeyed the rules laid down by the spirit. It may also fail if the individuals involved in the collection and later distribution of the pests have not done this in accordance with the instructions of the spirit. If the purging fails, this will not be seen as a failure on the part of the spirit, but rather as a problem of neglection of the laws of the spirit by the community.

As regards problem-animal control, crop-raiding by animals, and the extraordinary behaviour of animals, spiritual controls emanating from the ancestral spirits appear to be situational and contextual. There is much variation in interpretation as to the extent to which the spirit controls various animal species. Contradictory information was gathered, including claims that the spirit controlled all animals. If the spirit overtly claimed control of the larger species, such as elephant and buffalo, it could find itself in conflict with government agencies and the law of Zimbabwe which claims that all animals are under the protection and control of the Minister of Environment and Tourism and the appropriate authorities of wildlife management. Furthermore, by making sweeping claims, the spirit could be proved not to control these animals.

The question of 'who controls the animals' was asked of the spirit medium whilst possessed. Before the medium herself (i.e. the spirit) could answer, the great grandson of Kanyemba interjected that the spirit could control certain crop-raiding animals, such as warthog and bush buck, but the larger animals, notably buffalo and elephant, were not controllable by the spirit. This response may have been influenced by the above-stated issues. Other responses to this question indicate that the spirit does control, or can control, these large animals, as well as the smaller animals. Both previous and present hunters and safari operator personnel are reported as having consulted the spirit medium prior to a successful kill. A portion of the meat was thereafter appropriately given to the spirit medium and the chief in thanksgiving. Local illegal hunters are also reported as having consulted the spirit medium for herbs to enable successful hunting and protection whilst in the forest. An important piece of evidence is that local illegal hunters have been sanctioned by the spirit, after not reporting and/or thanking the spirit for hunting successes or for not sharing parts of the carcass designated for the spirit.

The local community is, however, split as regards their professed belief in the offices of the spirit medium. The most significant split is between the Faith Apostolic Mission Church and those who believe in the spirit medium. The Catholic church stands in between, as it does not condemn the belief in such spirits and leaves it up to the individual conscience to decide whether attendance at the *Dendemaro* is evil or not. Probably, as the local parish priest pointed out to me, it is more evil to watch 'Dallas' than to attend the sessions at the *Dendemaro*.

The conversion of people to the Faith Apostolic Mission Church is a very recent phenomenon. As a result of this conversion, some individuals go through a tortuous grappling with their conscience over issues such as the church's prohibition on the use of herbs when their children are sick, the prohibition on drinking beer, smoking *mbanje* (marijuana) and tobacco. The church also prohibits the use of herbs for hunting, and for prevention of pests and crop-raiding animals. Families are often religiously and theologically split in half and this adds to the dilemma. Almost all of the Mvura who joined the church, when hand-outs of food and clothing were given out, were not willing to accept these rules as use of herbs was such a powerful feature of their way of life. Despite the fact that a significant number of people have maintained belief in the church, it is fair to say that the spirits of the land have a considerable influence over their lives. First, this is because such individuals spend a lot of time and energy condemning belief in the spirit, and secondly, despite (perhaps because of) these condemnations, there is evidence to suggest that a residual cultural empathy with the belief lingers. Incidence of members of the church secretly consulting spirit mediums and the use of herbs do occur.

Essentially, then, the institution of the spirit medium is a powerful cultural phenomenon. The Faith Apostolic Mission Church has not managed to separate the cultural components from the theological. As a result, members of the church continue to have residual empathy with the belief. As Schoffeleers (1979) has pointed out, the spirits of the land are the guardians of the land. Kanyemba is referred to as the owner of the land. Through him requests for rain are sent up the ladder of history to the original owners of the land (notably Chimombe, see Chapter 2). The spirit is the protector of the people, but may also punish people by withdrawing this protection. The spirit is also the protector of the land, and in general insures that all creatures, both fauna and flora, as well as inanimate features such as geology and water courses, are in equilibrium. However, if sinful humans do not attend to the spirit, or obey the commands of the spirit, all kinds of imbalances can occur in nature. Lions may wage war on the people (this occurred in the 1940s in Chapoto ward), the rains may not fall, honey may not be found in the forest, wild animals usually in abundance may disappear, or the people may be plagued by crop-raiding animals. It is, therefore, extremely important that the spirit be attended to and the correct forms observed. It is also obvious that from many people's points of view, the appropriate authority for wildlife at the local level is the spirit medium.

Problem Animal Control by the Spirit

In Zimbabwe, since wildlife has been officially owned by the state, PAC is historically taken to refer to the activities of the DMPWLM in culling animals, which are reported as being a threat to life and property. However, as has been elaborated above, there are cultural mechanisms which also deal with this problem. When discussing PAC, hunting control, and crop-raiding it is important to realize that there is a general distinction between charmed spirit animals (*tumwa*) and forest animals (*mhuka*). In general, these categories are established from 'common sense' and by reference to the expert advice of the spirit medium in possession. Biological animals are forest animals, that is the physical manifestations of the order of nature unless proved otherwise. Animals are proved to be spirits if they exhibit qualities that set them apart from the normal run of the mill animals one is likely to encounter. These animals belong to the order of culture and deserve specific explanation and often ritual treatment.

The best way to discuss this is by reference to specific examples. Animals that do not behave in the manner that their species is taken to behave[4] include: aggressive guineafowl, baboons that scratch themselves like dogs and, elephants that inveterately raid granaries and come too close to human habitation. These are all animals controlled by spirits, and their behavior can be explained in terms of cultural entities and forces.

In general, the procedure in dealing with these culturally problematic animals is to consult the spirit. The explanations offered for the above anomalies, for instance, are as follows: the guineafowl and baboons were sent by the spirit to people who had not obeyed the decree that Friday should be observed as *chisi* (a day of rest). The elephant was inhabited by a troubled spirit. After ritual porridge made out of grain and herbs had been placed at the crossroads, it no longer depleted people's granaries. As is well known, particular species of animal do have particular cultural significance. Lions (*mhondoro* – the royal ancestral spirit) and hyenas (*ngozi* – witch) are cases in point. In both cases, people can be possessed by these spirits. Lions can be royal ancestors who simultaneously speak through mediums, whilst hyenas can possess and control humans with a non-human hyena spirit of witchcraft. Lions that bear particular markings are said to be the physical manifestation of the *mhondoro* (Kanyemba is said to have spots like a leopard), as are those that act in a particular unaggressive or aggressive manner or who leave uneaten kill near human habitation, or that have other unlikely interactions with human beings. In one instance, a lion was said to have taken the blanket off a man while he was sleeping. In another case, lions were said to have eaten a man's maize crop. Cases like this are referred to the spirit medium. In the previous case, the lion had been sent by another *mhondoro* (royal ancestor) from a neighbouring area to establish if the use of witchcraft or the use of herbs was a factor in the dispute between

---

4. This is an interpretation which has some leeway. It is established through consultation with the spirit and is influenced by general consensus. Informal groups of people often discuss the happenings involving 'unusual' animal behavior. Church-goers who do not attend the sessions at the *Dendemaro* do challenge their colleagues on the nature of the 'unusual', claiming, of course, that such happenings are perfectly 'usual'.

two individuals. Both hyenas and crocodiles can potentially be sent by one's enemies, as the agents of witchcraft and malevolence.

Perceptions of animal control are, therefore, tied up with existing beliefs and practices. At the beginning of 1990, the spirit of Kanyemba decreed that the community should not work on Friday as this was the day on which the spirit medium for Chihumbe died. Many people in the community, notably the Apostolic Faith Mission Church-goers, did not obey this command. As a result, strange occurrences involving baboons and guineafowl were reported in the community. Guineafowl, which usually run away from human beings, were reported as having hounded and attacked church-goers working on Friday. A baboon was said to have sat down in front of a church-goer and scratched itself with its hind legs, in the same fashion as a dog. Other baboons were said to have approached people's fields with more aggression than usual. Some church-goers were not particularly impressed by these happenings, but the anomalies seem to have captured the minds of many others in the community. Faith Apostolic Mission Church-goers argued that it was absurd to have both Friday and Sunday as days of rest. They also argued that it would be reasonable to have one holiday a year in commemoration of Chihumbe, but to have one per week was like having Christmas once a week. This would interfere with their productivity.

The attempt to introduce observance of *chisi* has to-date effectively failed. This serves as an example of the limitation of control by the spirit. However, it also indicates that the institution of spirit possession waxes and wanes in response to currents in the society. In this regard, the issue of who controls the animals is shown to be an ambiguous one, in that the spirit has not overtly claimed control of these animals (*de jure*), but has exhibited *de facto* control in the minds of many people. This point is worth underlining. I believe it is not so much that the spirit medium in possession should, under recent restrictive resource management techniques, be shown to be in control of animals, but rather that a potential means of controlling access to animals has hitherto been underestimated. As the government policy is to give more responsibility and benefits from wildlife resources to local people, I believe that the spirit medium will become more openly or overtly involved in making decisions about the resource and enforcing sanctions on access to animals.

In Partial Control of Animals and People: The Spirits of the Land and the Illegal Hunters

A very important informant in my research was a 73-year-old seasoned illegal hunter, with whom I came to have a good rapport. He told me stories about himself, and others. Some of these stories illustrate the kinds of controls that exist on illegal hunters and on animals.[5] He is the head of one of three VaChiKunda households who live on the western bank of the river. The following was narrated by the informant but is transcribed into the third person for readability.

On one occasion, five elephants visited him in his field and came near to his *chibaracaou* (temporary raised structure for drying maize), but did not attempt to eat anything. He was astounded, as elephants do not usually come close without eating the maize. Though concerned, he did not consult the spirit medium of Chihumbe (Kanyemba's brother). One day he was at the *Dendemaro* and Chihumbe asked him if he had not seen elephants coming to his field. Chihumbe told him to watch out, as this was a warning of things to come. Later, while he was using a field on the banks of the Mwanzamtanda, at a place called Marirambwa, at about five o'clock in the morning, his wife took a bucket to get some water and noticed fresh footprints of lions. His wife called him to come and see these footprints and he tracked them to where they had entered his maize field. At that time, while he was talking to his wife and tracing the spoor, the lions had encircled his field. On the way to the *ntsaka* in the middle of the field he heard the lions roaring. He immediately started worshipping the *vadzimu* (spirits), saying that he was the grandson of Chaufombo, Kanyemba, Chihumbe and Nyanderu. If he had done anything wrong they should tell Chihumbe and Chihumbe would tell him what payments he should make in retribution. By the time he reached his *ntsaka*, he saw a light-colored lion feeding on a maize stem and cobs. When this lion saw him it ran closer to him and started tearing up the soil near to him, venting its frustration. He continued worshipping Chihumbe and Kanyemba until the lion went away.

Later he went to consult the spirit of Chihumbe. He was told

---

5. He was arrested for snaring buffalo and claims to have been treated cruelly in gaol in Chinoyi, where he was incarcerated with thieves. He lives next to his bananas and is constantly worried by buffalo and elephant, which tear down his trees and eat his crops.

that these lions were on their way to Chiyambo (headman of the Mvura people, and his father-in-law). Chiyambo had been assigned work by Mbayiwa (a neighboring spirit who often relays messages on behalf of Chimombe, the rain spirit) to make him a crown, but he had delayed and this was the only way to remind him. As these lions came across him, they noticed that there was a daughter of Chiyambo there (his wife), so they wanted to attack that daughter. He was advised to go back and look after his field. He returned and after three days the lions came back around seven o'clock in the evening. They came very close to the *ntsaka* where he was and roared. After this he went back again to consult Chihumbe. He was given some medicine (herbs) and advised to set them on fire in his field. He was told that the smell of it would keep the lions away. Three days after returning, the lions came back again and started eating from the maize cobs and from the stems. The man went towards the lions with his spear (i.e. he threatened them). The lions ran away into the thick bush around his fields. He packed up the few belongings he had with him, abandoned his field and went back to his permanent home for good (about three kilometers' distant).

Later the DNPWLM staff came to check on the occurrences and noticed baboons, elephants and some spoor of lions in his fields. They promised that this would be reported to their headquarters. To this day nothing had been heard from them.

Both the elephants and the lions in this story were described as spiritually and culturally significant animals and have to be contrasted with the 'normal' elephants and lions of the forest which act in a predictable manner. The animals in the story exhibited anomalous behavior and this shows that they were not 'natural' animals at all, but manifestations of supernatural powers and forces, controlled and influenced by ancestral spirits. On encountering the lions, the first thing that entered the man's head was that he had somehow displeased the ancestors, because these lions were the physical manifestation of ancestral beings and they had come to visit him in his field, to sanction him.

Versions of this story, narrated by other members of the community, included crucial aspects which the man left out: notably, that he was a prodigious illegal hunter and had on occasion offended the ancestors by killing and/or threatening lion. The visit of the lions, it is said, was a consequence of his having disobeyed restrictions on hunting lion, and not, as he said, because he was a son-in-law to Mr. Chiyambo. It appears that the usual restriction on killing lion is overlooked provided the skin is given to the spirit medium, and the hunter promises that he has not kept any part of the lion, normally used as a potent medicine.[6]

Bundles of Herbs and the Right to Hunt

As has been pointed out, knowledge and use of herbs are considered to be extremely important in being a successful hunter. An important political and economic feature concerning the ideology of herbs is that not everyone is endowed with them. Renowned hunters are said to be successful, in fact, are said to be hunters, because they have access to herbs. Hunting and herbs are in this sense synonymous. One cannot be a good hunter unless one has access to herbs, therefore, good hunters must have taken herbs. In a similar way, success in terms of power or economics can also be explained in terms of herbs (e.g. Kanyemba himself is said to have taken herbs). As previously stated, herbs are procured in at least four ways. One can approach the spirit medium when possessed. One can approach a herbal specialist who may share knowledge with you if you have a close relationship or offer to do something in return. One can inherit knowledge of herbs by doing an apprenticeship with one's father or close patrilineal relative. Lastly, a family spirit or *sahwira* (bond friendship) may appear to you in a dream informing you where to find herbs and the logistics involved in successful hunting or snaring (i.e., where to find animals, what herbs to use, where to place snares, in which areas, etc.). In the last case, the herbal and other skills of the hunter ancestor can be transferred (inherited) in this manner.

The main point is that the magical qualities of herbs facilitate successful hunting, and gives hunters the courage and the skill to hunt. In this sense, the right to hunt is normatively governed or sanctioned by broader indigenous knowledge systems concerning the environment. If hunting is controlled in the sense that only selected people have access to herbs, then we are not talking about an open access commons, we are talking about access of the initiated few. These ideas need to be qualified by the fact that we are talking about normative rather than pragmatic concerns. On the pragmatic level of day-to-day expediency, individuals do not

---

6. Other explanations include the idea that the man abandoned his field and the maize in it because the yield was too great for him to move it himself.

need to obtain herbs before setting a snare. There is no direct or causal link between the ideological and normative idea that one has to have herbs to be a hunter and the actual practice of hunting.

A further qualifying comment is that cultural beliefs are in a state of change, and broader political and economic issues can profoundly effect such indigenous value systems. Where societies have been dispossessed of many of their rights to use land and natural resources, any values that may have existed in relationship to access to the land and its resources are obviously affected. It would be entirely inaccurate to reify or romanticize values that may have been far more effective in the past. However, if the rights of ward residents are actively included with the many rights and multiple jurisdictions (DNPWLM, district council, wildlife lobbies, politicians, safari and tourist operators) involved in controlling and using wildlife, I believe that there may be a resurgence of such values. Naturally, this would depend on how meaningfully such rights could be exercised in concert with the many other vested interests involved. This might include controlled off-take from the Chewore safari areas by both Mvura and VaChiKunda. As Feeny, Berkes, McCay and Acheson say,

> a diversity of societies in the past and the present have independently devised, maintained or adapted communal arrangements to manage common property resources. Their persistence is not an historical accident; these arrangements build on knowledge of the resource and cultural norms that have evolved and been tested over time. (1990: 31)

In Partial Control of Animals and People: The Rights of the Safari Operator and Client

Though the CAMPFIRE program includes this ward, during the years while this research was going on (1989–1991), no decisions concerning money or other benefits accruing from wildlife revenues had been broadly discussed within the ward. This is mainly because the district council had not taken sufficient steps actively to include the ward in this process, though it had received revenues which essentially belong to the ward. Part of the ambiguity of the situation lies in the fact that the local safari operator leases a hunting concession, unlike Kanyurira ward where the safari operator is employed by the district council. The safari operation is largely run as a business operation rather than as a component of a management program. The safari operator's personnel, though they had heard about the goals of CAMPFIRE, were not briefed to build co-operation between themselves and the local people.

In August 1990 the safari operator himself was extremely reluctant to have contact with the representatives from the ward if representatives from the district administration and council were not present. He felt that this would jeopardize his relationship with the district administration and council, and possibly 'risk his concession'. His reluctance to meet representatives of the ward was due to the fact that he had recently paid up his trophy fees and lease fees to the district council, but the ward had not been informed about this. By letting ward representatives know the amount of revenue that had been accumulated by council, he felt he was going behind the back of the local government and district council officials and thereby possibly jeopardizing his concession lease, which at that time had not yet been renewed. The implication of this is that safari operator and district council/local government have a set of vested interests which need to be hidden from the ward.

In Chapoto ward, instead of co-operation between safari operator and people, there has often been conflict. The safari operator's assistant, as a manager of the concession area, has been briefed to police the area for poaching activities. This has resulted in harassment and arrest of the local people, mainly the Mvura. As has been mentioned, harassment has included checking people's pots, smelling their plates for traces of meat, beatings, arrests and feigning arrest. In one case a young boy was arrested and hand-cuffed and had to walk to the safari operator's vehicle where he was released at twelve o'clock at night. He then had to make his way home, in the middle of the night when wild animal activity is most pronounced.

Ward residents thought that this situation was likely to change at the end of 1990 when the district council claimed that they would employ a safari operator as a component of the CAMPFIRE programme. However, contrary to the hopes of local people, who had been led to believe that it was because of the safari operator that they were not benefiting from CAMPFIRE, the safari operator's lease was renewed for another two years on slightly different terms.

Thus, the immediate control of animals in the concession remains in the hands of the safari operator by virtue of his concession lease with the district council. This bundle of rights includes those of the DNPWLM, the district council, the client, and the safari operator's personnel. Specific quotas of animals are established by DNPWLM based on current estimation of numbers. The safari operator has to defer to the appropriate authority for wildlife in the area, from whom he obtains his lease (the district council), but he is the main controller of animals on the ground.

In regard to the rights of the ward wildlife committee, it is interesting that a white missionary associated with the Faith Apostolic Mission Church, who regularly visited the ward, approached a member of the wildlife committee in June 1991 and asked if it would be possible for him to bring a church colleague from South Africa to hunt under the CAMPFIRE program. The committee member, a son of the chief, was newly elected and did not fully understand the mechanisms by which the program would work. He, understandably, thought that local participation in wildlife utilization meant that the local committee had authority to give permits to outsiders interested in safari hunting, that is, he thought the ward would set up its own safari business. The missionary organized for his colleague to fly up from Pretoria, and brought him and his weapons down to the ward to hunt an elephant. Upon arrival, they learnt that the local committee did not have the authority to permit the man to kill an elephant, though the missionary claimed this as his right in terms of the agreement with the wildlife committee member and the expenses incurred in bringing his colleague up from South Africa. He also claimed that there were more clients which he could obtain for the ward, from the same source. It was suggested that the missionary should approach the safari operator, but he was reluctant to do this because he knew that the operator charged exorbitant fees. He believed that the committee would not charge such exorbitant fees. The missionary pointed out that since the local committee was not empowered to make such arrangements it showed that CAMPFIRE was a contradiction in terms; it showed that local people did not truly own their resources as professed by CAMPFIRE. The disappointed visitor did not shoot an elephant in Chapoto ward.

In my experience the safari operator's client (see Plate 14) claims ownership of the animal that he has shot, by virtue of paying as much as US$7,500 trophy fee for an elephant. The safari operator's assistant, in terms if this ownership, claims control of the skinning, removal of tusks, trunk, feet and ears, which are usually kept as trophies by the client. It lies within the discretion of the client what should be done with the meat of elephants, hippo, buffalo, etc., as it is often impossible to remove these from the kill before they rot. Often these are given to the local people. This is another source of conflict, as is clear from the case-study of the elephant kill narrated below.

The April 1990 elephant kill: Bundles of rights to distribution, ownership and control
On 4 April 1990, the trainee safari operator, working for the operator who holds the concession lease, returned to Mr. Mugonapanja's (literally 'you stay/sleep outside') home after a full day out with two clients in search of an elephant. He returned ahead of his clients, tired and sweating but in a good mood; they had killed an elephant. He winked at me that the clients were behind. The kill was approximately nine kilometers away, at the foot of the massif which forms the boundary with the Chewore safari area. After quenching his thirst, he sped off in his Toyota Land Cruiser to notify his local contacts about what would happen the next day. Whilst leaving, the clients, who had heard his motor, called out to him, but he continued on his way. Soon the clients arrived, one bearing an elephant's tail, like a fly swish in his hand.

They sat outside Mr. Mugonapanja's hut in deck chairs, two puffing Bavarians. The chief client, the one who had killed the elephant, emerged as a conservationist and claimed that something had to be done about poaching. He agreed that it was a good idea that his money should get back to the local people and he supported the ivory trade. He did not believe, however, that local people could manage resources themselves. Neither did he believe that a possible electric fence would be efficacious in separating agricultural areas from wildlife resource areas. Having engaged in safari ritual killing (he had shot 39 elephants in Zimbabwe over the last eight years in a number of areas), he knew that elephants would not be dissuaded from their intentions by an electric fence.

In the middle of the conversation, Mr. Mugonapanja politely joined the group, which included my research assistants and a couple of trackers. He greeted everyone by clapping hands and asking how they were. We were seated in the shade of his main hut. I said to the client, 'this is the owner of the house'. There was no response. Again I said, 'this is the owner of this house'. He looked in the direction of Mr. Mugonapanja, but he did not respond or greet him. Later, I discovered that the client owned an international construction business which employed 15,000 people in Germany alone.

I had arranged to meet the trainee safari operator the next day at the disused hunting camp on the banks of the Mwanzamtanda river, as he had offered me a lift to the kill in his land cruiser. Early in the morning, a party of trackers and skinners arrived from the safari camp at Kousangasanga in a Land Rover. When local people heard the vehicle they gathered at the old hunting camp. The safari operator's personnel scouted around for a place to cross the river, but were bogged down in sand and mud in the middle of the river. For nearly an hour they were engaged in attempting to get the vehicle across the river and up the steep sandy embankment on the other side. Local people were told to cut branches of trees to place under the wheels of the vehicle and the services of many local people were engaged in pushing the vehicle out. Without the help of the many local people, who had now gathered in the hope of procuring meat, the vehicle would not have been able to proceed. After crossing the river, the local people, some of whom had clambered on board the old Land Rover, had to disembark immediately as it was made clear to them that their responsibility was to make a road through the dense bush for the vehicle and not to travel on it. The vehicle drove through some Mvura fields, damaging some of the stunted maize and sorghum growing there.

I was told that usually no one is allowed to touch the elephant until the client had arrived, taken pictures, etc. However, by the time I arrived on foot (having decided it would not be politically correct for me to get a lift with the operator), local people, together with the safari skinners and trackers, were engaged in cutting off the ears, trunk, feet skin and tusks for the client. It was obvious that the local people had valuable expertise in expeditiously and efficiently carrying out these operations. This part of the exercise was conducted in a comparatively orderly and organized manner. It was explained to me afterwards that the locals are the real experts when it comes to skinning, as some of them have a life-time's experience at it.

Once the elephant had been skinned on the uppermost side, the safari personnel started to cut up pieces of the tender and sought-after meat from the jowls and cheeks of the elephant. At this point, I witnessed events which are central to my analysis of what happened later. Whilst the safari operator's assistant was busy putting large quantities of this tender meat in the Land Rover, Mr.

Penzura (a VaChiKunda) surreptitiously started cutting meat for himself, and threw it back to his wife who was sitting with the many other women about five meters from the carcass. She quickly put it in a sack. Men were all gathered around the carcass with knives at the ready, whilst the women sat further back from it. At first only a few others started cutting, and they were told by the safari workers to refrain. When they saw, however, that the best meat was being taken by the safari operator's personnel, about 10 men attacked the area around the head where the meat is said to be tender. Immediately the entire carcass was covered with at least a hundred men wielding knives and axes, tearing and cutting chunks of bloody flesh and throwing them back to women (usually younger women) who put them in bags. The entire corpse was encircled with people, at least five deep. It was almost impossible to get to the carcass and those who did not have access to it jostled those who did, in order to push them out of the way. Those who were not engaged in cutting, sensibly held their knives straight up in the air so as not inadvertently to stab someone. Whether inadvertently or not, people did get cut both in the throng and whilst cutting the meat.

At times the elephant, now a day old and bloated with bad air, would wheeze like a punctured hot air balloon, but the noxious stench from its innards did not distract the people from their tasks. Mr. Mugonapanja retired from the fray after being cut fairly badly on the hand. He pointed out his wound to others but they seemed more interested in getting meat. Blood and pieces of flesh were splattered on people's clothing, on their faces and in their hair. Blood was daubed all over their clothes. When most of the meat had been cut from the flank, people started to climb on to the carcass and I saw men with their trouser bottoms drenched in the contents of the elephant's stomach. Pieces of the innards which looked and smelt particularly offensive seemed to be sought after.

Whilst all this had been going on, the safari skinners had at times brandished branches to control the mob or to get access to pieces of the carcass that they were professionally concerned with (i.e. choice pieces of meat for themselves, recovering the bullets for the client, recovering skin, etc.). When the bullets were retrieved, they brandished branches and beat the crowd back so as to get access to the wound. Once most of the meat had been removed from the one side, they placed chains around the carcass and turned it over with the aid of the Land Rover. Skinning was carried out whilst safari personnel brandished branches to keep people back. The young bull elephant was not a large one. As Mr. Chipesi (the head of the wildlife committee) said, it was like Chidota, my research assistant, who he considered to be a young boy.

It was just after the innards had been reached on the one side that the client and hunter's apprentices arrived in the land cruiser. The clients were visibly amused, even enthralled at the sight of this orgy of flesh cutting. However, they wanted to take a picture of the carcass without any people on it. A hunter's apprentice appealed to the people to move away from the carcass, but they refused. The trainee operator wielded his large weapon over the crowd and fired two shots in the air. People momentarily fell back. He pointed his heavy calibre gun at the crowd, threatening them back, loaded, and fired again. People fell back, but almost as immediately proceeded with cutting. Finally, the safari personnel gave up these attempts to clear people and instead the client has pictures of masses of people wielding knives into his carcass. He seemed satisfied when I saw him retiring to the vehicle for refreshments.

After the gunshots Mr. C, a friend and neighbor who had spent time in goal for snaring a buffalo, said, 'was it good what he (the trainee operator) had done?' Others said that he should be reported to the police. The trainee had been fined for doing this before. After refreshments the clients and safari personnel stood and watched the butchering. They left the scene when most of the accessible meat had been taken and the bones were being cut up for the marrow.

The kill was situated in the south-west section of the ward, and I calculated that some people had walked as far as 16 kilometers to get there. Though the kill was situated within five kilometers of Mvura households, there were not as many Mvura in the fray as there were VaChiKunda. I noticed that a number of Mvura households did not take the kill particularly seriously. Mr. Chiyambo, the *sabhuku* (headman) for the Mvura, sent one of his young sons to get meat, whilst he and his brothers stayed at home. In general, the Mvura seemed to be restricted to the fringes of the carcass, and this became clear later when I saw how much meat they procured in comparison with the VaChiKunda cutters. Some VaChiKunda filled two to three sacks of meat, whilst Mvura acquaintances of mine who had spent the whole day trying to get to the carcass obtained only one piece of low-quality meat. In general, widows and women without husbands had no chance of procuring meat. The strategy amongst successful cutters was that a family would co-operate, the young or most aggressive men maintaining positions of access to meat on the carcass, throwing the chunks back to their women who would place then in sacks. Those who did not have this system (notably the Mvura), even if they were able to cut meat, would be unlikely to keep it, as any meat seen lying around would quickly be placed in somebody else's sack. Old people were also disadvantaged and few of them were successful in obtaining much meat, unless they had young sons or sons-in-law who could procure meat for them. Many old people and widows did not even bother to go to the carcass. Some of them claimed it was too far to walk, while others said that they expected their young male kin, if they had any, to get them a piece of meat. Even young boys did not attempt to enter the fray; the youngest boy that I saw attempting to get meat was in his mid-teens. Younger boys would be likely to get hurt.

The most successful cutters, in my judgement, were also the more politically significant members of the community. Notably, the VaChiKunda VIDCO chairmen, a previous councillor, and the owner of Black's store. In general, those with the higher social status obtained more meat. This effectively meant that most of the meat went to a small number of socially and politically significant VaChiKunda households.

It was with some of these more politically influential VaChiKunda speakers that I walked most of the way home with. This included Mr. Zhuwao, VIDCO chairman for Chansato, and Mr. Chimata, a burly elder; both are direct descendants of Kanyemba. All of them were carrying heavy loads of meat, and in many cases their wives and daughters had also gone ahead laden with meat. As Mr. Chimata is knowledgeable about local history, I asked him about the way meat was distributed by Kanyemba; was it conducted in the same manner as I had witnessed? The answer was a definite no.

Kanyemba himself was not concerned about meat, as he was more interested in the tusks. The flank of the elephant that fell on to the ground would be given to the chief and to the *mhondoro* since they were considered to be the owners of the land. This in turn would be distributed to kin and to neighboring headmen. Choice parts of the elephant, such as the trunk and other valuable items such as the skin, would usually be kept by Kanyemba. The rest of the meat was divided up amongst the people. It was cut up into portions by designated cutters and distributed to those present, portions being kept for headmen not present. This account was not borne out by investigations with other people and it may well be a glamorization of the distant past, based on more recent experiences. It was claimed that a previous hunter in the seventies (during the Rhodesian era), a Mr. Nichol, used to distribute meat to the chief, the *mhondoro* and designated cutters, who cut up the meat into equivalent bundles for all 'families' present at the kill. Other informants claimed that Kanyemba was not interested in the remaining meat, once the flank had been given to the chief.

Comment

'Families', relatives, neighbors and friends who share the proceeds of illegal hunting, share their resources as a secret. Individual hunters from these groups may team up, but this is also a secret. Individual hunters provide meat for their families and loyal relatives and friends in competition with those who are not considered loyal, who might report them to the authorities, or who might claim a portion of the meat. Thus, hunting is a secret activity and the resource is not common property, except as meat when it belongs clandestinely to people who share it within a closed circle. These individuals are, in legal terms, drawing on a resource that belongs to an outside agency and they are plundering the resource without concern as to its management. In cultural terms, they are acting appropriately as successful hunters. They may have inherited knowledge and herbs, in the form of dreams and visions, or learned through experience, as apprentices to their fathers and their grandfathers. Hunting is often an individual inherited phenomenon in the patrilineal line. Provided these hunters obey certain restrictions laid down by the spirit medium, and provided they keep the secret, they will be left alone to enjoy the fruits of their labor.

In the distant past it is alleged there were internal attempts to control hunting. The chief, for instance, is reported as having distributed guns to a few well-known hunters. They would go off on hunting expeditions into the Chewore safari area. After a kill a bundle of meat would be set aside for the owner of the gun and another bundle would be set aside for the hunter who killed the animal. Another bundle would be set aside for the carriers and laborers who attended the huntsmen; these were usually their young sons or other close relatives. The rest of the meat would be distributed among the remaining hunters.

Local hunting has emerged as an individual, competitive and secret activity, because there is and has been much ambiguity over ownership and control of the resource, in terms of conflicting bundles of rights and jurisdictions governing ownership and use. I believe that the foregoing discussion sheds light on the manner in which the kill was distributed in April 1990. Legally, the client, under the tutelage of the safari operator who in turn defers to the appropriate authority for wildlife (the district council), who in turn defers to the DNPWLM, under jurisdiction of the Minister of Environment and Tourism), owns (has a right of usufruct) the elephant at the time when it is shot. The spirits of the land enable the kill to take place and facilitate an abundance of wildlife in the area. The spirit has a significant but, at the present time, ambiguous control over large animals and illegal hunters in the area. This is largely ill-defined, because if overtly claimed it could well come into conflict with the government forms of control. The safari hunters' work is to obtain the skin, ears, tusks, etc. and they have a supervisory role over proceedings at the kill, but they really have no authority over ownership. Ironically, they do end up controlling the resource in this context. The local people, competing amongst themselves as hunters (over time) and as competitors for a limited resource (the carcass), try to obtain as much as they can for themselves, at the expense of others. This is in resource management terms what one might be tempted to call a tragedy of the commons. But is the carcass truly a common resource? A number of agencies are involved in the ownership and control of this resource. This sets up a tension of conflicting currents of ownership and control, at different stages of resource management:

1. When an elephant is wandering around stamping on people's fields in Chapoto, the agents in control are DNPWLM, the district council, and the safari operator, and, less obviously, the ancestral spirits of the land and the illegal hunters.
2. When the elephant is tracked, the agent in control is the safari operator, but he is unlikely to be successful if the spirits of the land have been offended.
3. When the elephant is shot, the owner/agent is the client, but, again, ultimately the spirits can drive away all the animals so that clients will not be successful.
4. When the carcass is given to local people, the owner/agent is local people under the supervision of safari personnel. Only

after meat has been cut is ownership established. However, if the spirits are ignored, people will not be able to obtain meat.

Local people were, in general, not happy with the way the resource was distributed. The reason they gave for not distributing th resource in a more equitable manner was because they were told that the carcass belonged to the client and they therefore had no authority over how it was distributed. They did not feel that it was appropriate for the wildlife committee to control distribution, as the elephant did not belong to the committee. However, members of the wildlife committee claimed that they would be able to control distribution if it was made clear that they were in control of distribution.

The head of the wildlife committee pointed out that they themselves had initiated the kill (in a sense they were controlling events) by reporting to the natural resource officers in Mushumbi Pools that there were crop-raiding elephants in the area. These officers had come down for a day and a night, but were not successful in apprehending an elephant. This lack of success was attributed by the chairman of the wildlife committee to the fact that the spirit of Kanyemba had not been consulted before these officers had been contacted. Only after consultation with Kanyemba was there a successful kill by the safari operator, who had been asked by the natural resource officers to kill an elephant in the area, to appease the local people. Mr. Chipesi (chairman of the wildlife committee) had asked the safari hunters if the *mudzimu* (spirit) would be given a portion of the meat. They replied that the *mudzimu* would not be given a share, because the resource had been bought by the client and he could do with it as he wished.

The alleged unsatisfactory distribution is, in my opinion, a result of the ambiguous nature of ownership and control of the carcass. More-successful mechanisms of distribution emerged when local people were told that they own the animal (see case-study of elephant kill at Mr. Phineas Charuma's home below), rather than to be in the ambiguous situation where they only have a right of access in competition with others, the pecking order being: client, safari operator, people, animals, birds, etc.

The August 1990 Elephant Kill at Mr. Phineas Charuma's Home: The Dynamics of DNPWLM PAC Activity in the Ward

A test case for some of the ideas above was provided by the case of the DNPWLM PAC elephant kill at Mr. Charuma's house. As this kill is also mentioned in Chapter 5, I will summarize some of the contextual elements which were not referred to in that chapter. One morning when woken by the sound of heavy caliber and automatic gunfire, I narrowly missed being shot at. Outside my tent, a bullet ricocheted through the dust and a wounded elephant lumbered towards my camp. Children ran towards the commotion and an unhealthy situation emerged where PAC officers (i.e. DNPWLM staff) were firing into inhabited areas and driving the heavily wounded elephant towards Mr. Charuma's huts and granary. It eventually thundered to the ground near his home. He appeared delighted at the prospect and the excitement. The hope of obtaining meat from the carcass outweighed any other considerations of safety for lives and property.

The elephant was a trophy bull and the reason it was killed was because a formal PAC complaint had been lodged with DNPWLM personnel about buffalo. The DNPWLM PAC unit at Mashumbi Pools came down and spent some time tracking buffalo, but although they saw them they were unable to get a good shot. Near dawn, they came across the spoor of a large elephant and tracked it until it was within sight. Members of the wildlife committee encouraged the PAC personnel to kill the animal. This was done, I was told, not because the elephant had damaged anything, but because these individuals realized that the sale of meat from PAC could earn money for the ward. Soon before this incident, meat from a PAC buffalo had been sold and approximately Z$400 had been receipted in a district council book. The trophy bull was worth Z$7,500 to the ward, if shot by a safari operator's client, but since no revenues had reached the ward from this source to date, this reckoning was not taken into account. Instead, the meat was sold largely outside the ward for a little over Z$1,000. The meat was sold for two dollars per kilogram. Few people in the ward could afford this, least of all those with a protein deficiency who needed it the most. The DNPWLM officers obliged the committee by transporting a large portion of the meat sold at Angwa Bridge and Mashumbi Pools. I have begun at the end of the story and need to backtrack in order to explain the distribution procedure more rigorously.

After the elephant fell to the ground, the secretary of the wildlife committee, who had escorted the PAC unit, handed over supervision of skinning and cutting of the animal to my research assistant, who had newly been elected to the wildlife committee. The DNPWLM official, who had killed the animal, went to report the incident to the police. My research assistant appointed those who had gathered to the various tasks of skinning, cutting off the feet and trunk and removing the tusks. Meat was cut up into medium-sized chunks and laid on leafy branches. In comparison to the April kill, everything was conducted in a very orderly and organized manner. In the course of cutting up the carcass, the vehicle used by the DNPWLM personnel arrived. The ward tractor and trailer, donated by World Vision, also arrived, bearing a number of people from as far as 20 kilometers away. Other members of the committee, including the chairman, joined in the activities. A scale was brought from the clinic to weigh the meat but unfortunately it did not work. The DNPWLM vehicle was loaded up with some of the best meat and it set off for Angwa Bridge and Mashumbi Pools. A member of the committee went along to ensure that the meat was sold in good faith. Next the ward tractor and trailer were loaded up with meat. Portions were set aside for both the chief and the spirit medium. My research assistant tried to explain that in fact the ward was loosing revenue by killing the elephant, but none of the other members of the committee agreed. Workers who had helped in cutting up the carcass were given portions of meat or intestines for their efforts.

By this time, the intestines having been reached, it was becoming difficult to cut up large portions effectively and the carcass was handed over to those who had been watching and waiting for this moment from the outset. As before, a free-for-all ensued, but since many people had accompanied the good meat loaded on the tractor which was to be sold in other places within the ward, there was not quite the same competition over the carcass as had occurred in April. However, bones were broken open for their marrow, and the next day nothing was left of the huge carcass except a few broken bones, flattened grass and soil drenched in the elephant's liquids.

All this work and community involvement was ostensibly for a Z$1,000 credit in a council receipt book which may or may not end up as part of a material benefit for some people in the ward.

The actual distribution of meat within the ward from the kill was rather sparse since a large portion of it was exported and many people could not afford to pay for it. Many individuals who participated in the butchery did not benefit significantly from the distribution of the meat. They were left with the idea that such revenues were to help finance community projects, but this was in the distant future and they would only believe it when they saw it happening.

I believe there is more at stake at a kill than this. The materialist issues are obviously very important, but there is also a symbolic value associated with the kill. A large portion of people's time in Chapoto ward is spent trying to prevent animals from destroying their hard work in the fields and gardens. People are constantly aware of the menace of wildlife, but are impotent to 'get their revenge' as they will be arrested for poaching. When the elephant fell to the ground, I saw a man who had been with the hunters jump on to the carcass with glee and stand there as conqueror. Aside from the hopes of attaining meat or other benefits, there is a sense of catharsis in the death, injury or suffering of crop-raiding animals. As one informant put it, 'it is a revenge for what they or their families have done to us'. On one occasion, prior to my entering the field, a DNPWLM officer darted a baboon with a sleeping drug. The baboon was later found drunken, but awake and dizzy by some young boys, one of whom poured paraffin over it and set it alight. The comment above was said in connection with this incident.[7]

In Partial Control of Animals and People: The Department of National Parks Game Scouts and the Anti-Poaching Unit

The Chewore safari area and the ward itself still has a limited number of black rhino. Local people have pointed out their spoor to me, within five kilometers of Mvura homesteads. The Zambezi Valley is one of the few places left in Africa where these animals still have a viable breeding population. Their numbers are rapidly dwindling and internationally organized poaching organizations are reportedly using Zambians to do the dirty work of killing the

---

7. Such occurrences have been regarded as unethical (Frazer Nash 1989). The incident does seem inhumane. Are animal activists now vocal because many nations have already wiped out most wildlife that posed a real or symbolic threat to human settlement, and therefore no longer have to live with both the material and ethical inconvenience attached to crop and livestock protection?

animal and tearing out its horn. The rhino protection campaign has turned into a sophisticated military operation.

Local people have been informed by DNPWLM game scouts that the boundary of their free movement is the foot of the mountains which form the boundary between the ward and the Chewore safari area. In fact, the actual boundary of the ward is the high points of these mountains. They have also been warned that the anti-poaching units are now shooting people on sight when they enter this area. People do, in fact, regularly make excursions into these forbidden areas, to collect *mpama* and other fruits and tubers on the western slopes of the hills, or to follow the course of the river up to some well-known fishing pools. At these pools the bark of a tree (*dupa*) is used to poison fish in the pools. The DNPWLM staff had records of Mvura arrested for this offence.

The DNPWLM staff in the area move through it on a regular basis with automatic weapons. They are mainly concerned with the 'poaching' menace. On one occasion, shortly before I entered the field, a game scout discovered a boat on the Chewore side of the Zambezi river. On hearing a shot he became suspicious and decided to investigate. He apprehended a senior police officer (assistant commissioner) who had been hunting buffalo in the Chewore. According to informants in Chapoto, the officer stripped the lapels from the scout and tried to intimidate him with his lofty position. The case has now been brought to court after a long delay, involving intimidation of DNPWLM staff. These reports have been verified by *Parade Magazine* (September 1990; 9), which have taken up this issue as a national scandal.

In addition to illustrating that the law enforcement agencies are a heterogeneous mix of interests and structures, this example serves to illustrate the point that these defenders of wildlife are not purely policing the area from the local people. On the contrary, the 'poachers' are often depicted as 'Zambians'. The senior authorities in charge of the war on poachers believe that there has been a lot of collaborative activity between alleged Zambian poachers and the local people in the ward. Kanyemba was described as a 'crooks' corner' and I was warned that I should be careful, as I did not know exactly who was involved.

To my knowledge, during the course of fieldwork, only on one occasion did an incident occur within the ward which may have involved foreign poachers. Two men, armed with automatic weapons and dressed in poor clothing, approached a neighbor and enquired for directions. They then proceeded across the border into Mozambique. The incident was reported to the police. 'Poachers' can be drawn from the ranks of a wide range of people. For instance, the illegal sale of rhino horn has been linked to the financing of the operations of the MNR. Zimbabweans from both inside and outside the wildlife producer areas have been apprehended. The law enforcement agencies (e.g. police, army, DNPWLM) are not above reproach. In such circumstances it is easy to identify scapegoats and it is difficult to maintain control or to establish the hierarchy of control when such competing jurisdictions are evident. Local people are aware of these competing jurisdictions. They sometimes refer to the 'owners of the wildlife' in a sarcastic way. For instance, when a field was trampled by elephants, the owner of the field might say 'why don't the owners (DNPWLM, safari operator and client) of these animals control them?'

Summary of Argument and Possible Alternatives

CAMPFIRE offers the possibility of creating alternative land-use strategies for Chapoto residents and developing more beneficial relationships with the safari operator and DNPWLM. The rationality of the CAMPFIRE program concerns people and wildlife. CAMPFIRE proponents argue that wildlife will become a more sustainable resource if local people receive both the benefits and the responsibility for it, thereby having an incentive to become proprietors for it. This will be good for people and good for wildlife, in that the marginal environment can be more effectively managed both to conserve the environment and to maintain off-take of wildlife.

Historically, the resource has been alienated from local people,[8] and today there are a number of competing vested interests in wildlife which are reflected in the competing and often conflicting claims to control, ownership and use of the resource. Furthermore, wildlife has complex dimensions as a resource. It is simultaneously: tourist resource, biological resource, safari hunting resource, game product resource, meat resource, and spiritual and ecological resource. The competing claims to ownership and control of these resources creates ambiguity. It is not clear who is responsible for the overall proprietorship of the resource. The best illustration of

---

8. As previously argued, the state has effectively reduced people's land-use strategies and not offered them alternative ones, as CAMPFIRE attempts to do.

this is the complex relationship between the district council (the present appropriate authority), the top (DNPWLM, local government and other government authorities, entrepreneurs in the wildlife industry), and the bottom (the producer wards).

As Murphree has pointed out, the Wildlife Act (1975) provides for appropriate authority status to be conferred on district councils, but they are not the 'producers or on the ground managers of wildlife' (Child and Peterson 1991: 2). This is an aspect which is emphasized in the material discussed above, as well as the subject-matter of the conclusion. Murphree argues that the formal combination of production, management, authority and benefit in regard to wildlife does not yet exist in the communal areas, in the same way that proprietorship is enjoyed by commercial wildlife ranchers.

In my view, the biggest obstacle to the establishment of propriertorship for the resource, at the local level, is that there is no legal provision for appropriate authority status to be conferred on producer communities. However, Murphree outlines that there are three possible ways in which to overcome this obstacle. One is to change the Act so that producer communities can acquire appropriate authority status. The next is for such communities to form natural resource co-operatives which would have authority over wildlife resources 'to determine the management and use of their resources' (ibid.). The last is for district councils with appropriate authority status to delegate that authority to producer communities whilst ensuring that their legal responsibilities are fulfilled.

In the case of Chapoto ward, all three alternatives could work in the short term. I would argue that the best long-term solution to the problem of having so many competing and conflicting jurisdictions in regard to wildlife, is to change the legislation and thereby give communities the possibility of attaining appropriate authority status themselves. Of course, this would involve a number of problems of its own. Which institution or institutions at the local level should be regarded as the authority? What skills (social, political, and ecological) and abilities should such an institution have? How could it be helped to attain these skills? To what extent is the program encapsulated at the district level? How could this be modified without disillusioning district and national level authorities on whose blessing the program may rely? These questions will be addressed in the conclusion.

One alternative suggested by Murphree is that of relying on the district council to delegate authority. In my opinion, this will not reduce the ambiguity over control and use of wildlife resources.

A clarification of rights is a prerequisite for a clearer sense of common property at the ward level. It is also important for the establishment of a management regime at this level. Relying on district council to delegate authority may in fact have the opposite effect, by adding to the existing ambiguities. Communities will always have to defer to the set of vested interests represented in the district council when making important decisions about wildlife which purportedly belongs to them.

In the conclusion to this study, it is also argued that the accommodation of the various vested interests, rights and jurisdictions involved in the use and control of wildlife at various levels (global, national, district, ward, village and household) is a crucial element for the success of CAMPFIRE. Yet, the goal of CAMPFIRE is to devolve decision-making, responsibility and benefits concerning wildlife to producer communities. Despite this goal, appropriate authority has been placed in the hands of district councils, which do not necessarily represent the interests of such producer communities. Perhaps the thinking behind this is that vested interests in wildlife have to develop at district level before they can develop at ward level. If this is the case, then the goals of the CAMPFIRE program may have to be modified along the lines suggested in the conclusion to this study.

The other alternative, mentioned above, suggested by Murphree (Child and Peterson 1991: 2–5), concerns the formation of a natural resource co-operative. As outlined in the CAMPFIRE document, this may be a major step in the process towards decentralization of control and benefits to the local level, because such co-operatives can be recognized by law. Furthermore, a great deal could be learnt by producer wards in the creation of such co-operatives. However, I emphasize, in the long term the possibility of being able to attain appropriate authority status should be an option, because without it such co-operatives may always be subjected to the political and economic currents at district and national levels (including local government and district administration). It may be argued that these currents need to be included if CAMPFIRE is to be a success, but such an accommodation of district and national interests should not pre-empt the locus of the program being firmly ensconced at the lowest accountable level.

For CAMPFIRE to achieve its goals, the ambiguity of the rights and vested interests in wildlife has to be clarified. The possibility of appropriate authority being earned by institutions at ward or village levels is a step towards such a clarification. Such a clarification may allow for common property institutions to develop at the local level. Without the hope or prospect of achieving appropriate authority, it is, in my opinion, unlikely that institutional capacities and vested interests at the ward level will strengthen over time and it may become increasingly necessary for CAMPFIRE to modify its goals. This is the subject-matter of the final chapter.

CHAPTER 7
Conclusion

In concluding this book I would like to draw the reader's attention back to my earlier discussion in Chapter 1 of common property theory and 'bundles of rights' (Maine 1884) to wildlife utilization. In that chapter it was pointed out that wildlife resource planners conceptual discourse in Southern Africa tends to emphasize the goal of enabling or creating sustainable community-based wildlife management regimes, through communal common property regimes (see definition Chapter 1 pp. 20–3). My research findings indicate that we are, in fact, discussing co-management or joint jurisdiction regimes (Lawry 1990; Berkes 1989: 38) in which global, state, private and communal bundles of rights are played out as portrayed in Chapters 4 and 6. Chapter 4 presents the broader vested interests in resources as an analytical framework for understanding the cultural and political dynamics of resource use at ward level (see Fig. 4.1). This chapter includes a discussion of historical factors such as the creation of safari areas, global factors such as the CITES debates, national policy, system of local government, competing land-use strategies, and shows how these and other factors are related to each other and to the changing ecological resource base. Chapter 6 is an account of the competing bundles of rights to wildlife, including claims of the ancestral spirits, illegal hunters, the wildlife committee, the safari operator, DNPWLM, district council and others. Both chapters indicate the complexity of wildlife resource use in Chapoto ward, because of these multiple jurisdictions.

In more general terms, CAMPFIRE aims to be a community-based wildlife utilization program, but it is also a state initiative and is likely to include considerable private and entrepreneurial vested interests at various levels (national, district, ward, village and household). Such vested interests at these levels will continue to exert rights of access and exclusion to the resource, despite the

CONCLUSION

hoped for devolution of control to the local level. Though this may appear obvious, it also has important theoretical and practical implications, both in terms of the goals of the program, and in the way we think about common property.

The cultural and political dynamics of wildlife resource use in Chapoto ward let us draw the following conclusions.

1. That there is both internal (intra-ward) and external (extra-ward) differentiation of vested interests in the resource, as well as multiple modes of use, ownership, access to or control of the resource through ward, district, national, and international channels (see Fig,. 4.1, and Chapters 4 and 6).

Internal differentiation of vested interests is illustrated by the ethnic and economic differences between the Mvura and VaChi-Kunda populations in relation to ecological factors; the different stances adopted by the neo-traditional leadership (and its contending houses) as opposed to the system of VIDCOs and WADCOs (see Chapter 2); and the differences between those who attend to the ancestral spirits and those who publicly reject the spirits (see Chapter 6). Internal differentiation is also the subject-matter of Chapter 3, which deals with the socio-cultural dimensions of the competition between agriculture, foraging and wildlife utilization. This chapter also deals with household clusters which are actively engaged in the management of wildlife (e.g. crop protection, hunting), both individually and collectively, but there is also competition between household clusters for scarce resources. Chapter 5, which is an account of the various practical, institutional and cultural mechanisms for dealing with wildlife, also underscores the diversity of internal and external mechanisms for dealing with the resource. On the one hand, we have the mechanisms of wildlife management used by individual family clusters, and then we have the formal mechanisms used by the DNPWLM, the safari operator and the committeeing process associated with the district council. Cultural belief systems add to the diverse mechanisms available for controlling and using wildlife. Both the internal and the external differentation of vested interests foster a situation where there are multiple, differentially weighted modes of access, control and use of the wildlife resource (see Figure 4.1 and the discussion of competing bundles of rights in Chapter 6).

2. Furthermore, there is currently an ambiguity of rights of access, ownership and use, which is especially manifested at the ward level. This is illustrated throughout the book. One example is the

manner in which a hunting safari elephant kill took place (see Chapter 6). This illustration indicated that different agencies (safari operator, client, ancestral spirits, illegal hunters, DNPWLM, wildlife committee, district council) exert control, and have access to use of the resource at different times. Another example might be in regard to the Mvura and their culturally appropriate, but legally unacceptable, use of the Chewore safari area (see Chapter 3). Conflict also exists among VaChiKunda and other agriculturalists dealing with the ambiguous interface between crop-protection and illegal hunting (see Chapter 5). Such ambiguity is the result of the multiplex internal and external vested interests.

In these ambiguous circumstances, it may not be possible, or desirable, to confine the promotion of common property solely to a community-based management regime. Instead, through CAMPFIRE, a multi-tiered common property regime may be in the making, with a synergy of rights of access and exclusion existing between state, community and the private sector.

3. The Chapoto ward material also tells us that identifying a 'community'-based management regime is problematic. The material indicates that it is even more problematic to identify a regime which has the characteristics identified by Bromley for successful common property regimes (see Chapter 1) and the 'cohesive community' qualities sought by the CAMPFIRE document (Martin 1986:33). It is problematic because of social and economic differentiation and the diversity of cleavages and interests within the ward, as well as because of the exertion of rights of access by state mechanisms (e.g. DNPWLM, local government), private sector interests (e.g. safari operator) and the historical legacy of dispossession of people and protectionism of wildlife in the surrounding safari areas.

4. The material also tells us that, despite the tension between the state and the divided community, there are potentials in existing local political and cultural institutions (household cluster, VIDCO, WADCO, wildlife committee, chief and spirit medium) in setting down 'the rules as to who has access to the commons' at the ward level (Lawry 1990: 406). In Lawry's view this is a minimum definition of common property in contrast to common property arrangements required for intensive regulation of the resource. At present in Chapoto ward there is insufficient incentive to move beyond this minimum definition, because collective action is thwar-

ted by both intra-ward factors and extra-ward factors. The economic benefits have not been realized despite the ongoing disruptions and deprivations (e.g. curtailing foraging and hunting, crop-raiding, dealing with anti-poaching units) caused by state protection of the resource. However, there are possibilities for the potential of local institutions to participate more fully in the multi-tiered property system which currently exists.

5. A key issue in enabling this participation would be the provision for a clarification of the current ambiguity of rights of access and exclusion between the DNPWLM, district authorities, the ward and the safari operator (or other entrepreneurs). This, I believe, could be done by bringing about the possibility for the ward to attain appropriate authority status in the long term, provided it was able to meet certain criteria. Such criteria might include:
(a) accountability to households/clusters (this will be discussed below);
(b) competence in fulfilling obligations to state institutions, such as not exceeding DNPWLM quotas and keeping adequate records;
(c) 'co-operation with NGO and state institutions in co-management training; and
(d) the achievement of the required institutional capacity (supported by state and NGO assistance) to meet the various challenges.

6. The Chapoto ward material indicates that there is a need for a modified analysis of common property.

The Need for a Modified Analysis of Common Property

Despite the interesting and new angles which current analysis of common property presents in understanding resource use, a weakness in the debates is that they tend to focus on typology rather than process. Common property is in itself part of a typology of property relations, which as Macpherson points out (1978:1) are properly analyzed as political relations between people *vis-à-vis* their rights to things. For example, when we are talking about crop protection or Mvura foraging, various bundles of rights in wildlife such as the safari operator's, the DNPWLM's, the spirit's, the illegal hunter's, the wildlife committee's, the chief's and local government's all become evident. Such claims may be typologized as falling into various overlapping categories of property regime, such as private, state, communal or open access. Macpherson's conception of property suggests that the many facets and dimensions of property are intricately intertwined with the social process, and therefore, dynamic. This study indicates that there is a need to focus on the dynamic political relations of the social process when talking about common property and sustainable use of resources. Unlike many typologies, which may be reifications or ideal static abstractions, the social process is fluid – a veritable moving target. Over-generalization is always a danger in both the creation and the explanatory power of typologies. Though typologies can be important heuristic devices, the dangers of pigeon-holing are well known, especially to those anthropologists and other social scientists who question the role of positivism in their disciplines.

The material in this book depicts relatively complex differentiation in regard to resource access and use, and therefore highlights the danger of over-generalization. For example, there is a danger among common property theorists in over-simplifying rights of exclusion and inclusion, in terms of a binary system constituting an either/or proposition. A feature of this book is that there is considerable ambiguity associated with resource use. In this situation, it may be more helpful to analyze common property in terms of degrees of inclusion and degrees of exclusion of the various subsets of resource users (Murphree: personal communication). This notion of accommodating various degrees of ownership and access to resources is essentially what is meant by bundles of rights of use. This process of variated degrees of resource use does not merely take place at the local level. Various rights are accommodated at all levels of social organization (global, national, district, ward and household). A description of the cultural and political dynamics of resource use is one way to trace these rights in resources.

Since bundles of rights are accommodated at all levels of social organization, it is therefore not sufficient to focus analysis of common property only at the community level. State, global and private rights and interests in the resource have to be recognized, as they play an ongoing and key role in how the resource is used and perceived at ward level. As Redclift (1987) indicates, local level initiatives towards sustainable development need to be cognizant of the argument that remote rural communities may be systematically being marginalized by the larger political and economic dispensation.[1] This reinforces the view that communal property regimes do not exist in a vacuum. They are situated within larger property regimes which include global, state and district rights and yet, simultaneously, they are institutions dealing with the rights of smaller configurations, such as clusters, households and individuals.

There are two analytical strands which need to be incorporated in understanding common property and, more generally, sustainability. The first refers to the micro-level systems approach, such as Marks' (1984) account of a lineage-based wildlife management regime amongst the Valley Bisa. The second refers to the macro-level political and economic dispensation within which such community-based regimes exist. Many scholars argue that the term 'common property' should be restricted to situations where there are 'communal arrangements for the exclusion of non-owners and for the allocation among co-owners' (Berkes 1989:37). This argument tends to play down the macro-level analytical stand. However, Berkes also argues that limited access, commonly owned resources (see Chapter 1) are associated with three property rights regimes (1989:38). He says resources may be managed under the auspices of a local-level arrangement or institution (communal property) or solely by the government (state property), but he also says that joint jurisdiction (co-management) is an increasingly significant development in the contemporary world, in which local-level traditional controls alone are in many cases insufficient. Japanese fishing rights (Ruddle, ibid.) and the Maine Lobster industry (Acheson ibid.) are examples of the success of co-management strategies.

Both Berkes and Macpherson (see Chapter 1) indicate that common property regimes ensure that participating individuals will not be excluded from the benefits associated with a resource. In terms of my experience of Chapoto ward, such a regime does not as yet exist because many of the assumed beneficiaries (e.g. the Mvura and others), are not benefiting or participating. By talking

---

1. As Redclift has pointed out, international processes may be systematically marginalizing local communities, such as Chapoto ward (see section on sustainability) and therefore one might argue that outcomes are determined globally not locally. However, a strength of CAMPFIRE is that it is operating on international (CITES debates, funding), national (ministerial blessings and policy), district (appropriate authority), and local levels (wildlife committees). I have stressed the importance of the local and district level dynamics above national and international dynamics, only for heuristic purposes, and realize the tension that exists between these various levels, as outlined in Fig. 4.1.

about co-management rather than community-based management, our analysis can more conscientiously bring into focus the dynamics of the social process at various levels. It can more readily incorporate ambiguous bundles of rights and the two tensioned strands of analysis mentioned above.

Some Important Components of a Multi-Tiered, Co-Management Property Regime

Lawry conceives of co-management as an arrangement which addressed both the weaknesses of state and community control of resources. However, as this study points out, neither the state nor the community are monolithic. Both the state and the community are multi-dimensional and multi-faceted and they are both subject to dynamic social and political processes. The term co-management assumes a unity of purpose (Derman: personal communication) both vertically, in terms of levels (global, national, district, ward, household), and horizontally, within the the various levels (such as ethnic differentiation within the ward or diverse approaches by government departments such as the local government authorities and the DNPWLM). Such a unity of purpose may often not exist, but an aim of a co-management regime would be conscientiously to clarify or recognize ambiguous rights in order to facilitate co-operation within and between these multi-tiered levels. Co-management in this sense refers equally to the articulation and the clarification of rights to resources in both the vertical and horizontal planes associated with social and institutional organization. The main actors need not be the rigid conceptions of state and the community, but can be conceived in terms of the dynamic political process.

In Chapoto ward, where bundles of nested rights exist in the resource and use patterns are constrained by ward cultural and political dynamics as well as the broader political and economic dispensation, the components of a successful multi-tiered co-management property regime may well include:

(a) that the hidden hand of the state be exposed. Self conscious participation in and clarification of rights of access held by different state institutions (e.g. DNPWLM, local government) should be accountable to and articulated with other levels of organisation. Given the history of centralized control of wildlife, one can argue that state-vested interests in this resource is a given. The making of a successful common property regime requires state institutions to claim their rights, while more importantly accommodating other sets of rights. Where decentralization of control is devolving to lower institutional levels, vested interests developing from national to district level may preclude or work against vested interests developing at lower levels (Murphree's law, see Chapter 1). Where there is less ambiguity over rights of access and exclusion, this may empower the local community and encourage the development of community vested interests in and proprietorship of the resource (see Murombedzi 1992 who independently makes the same point about the need for clarification of wildlife resource use rights in Nyaminyami);

(b) a clarification of private rights in wildlife (safari operator rights, client's rights, household meat from legal kills, etc.) properly integrated with and accountable to the other sets of rights, for example, (a) and (c); and

(c) a clarification of community rights, in terms of the empowerment and accountability of cultural and political institutions at ward level and their articulation with other sets of rights. This could be facilitated, for example, by the possibility of conferment of appropriate authority at the ward level.[2] Such an earned conferment could be a part of the co-management package. As mentioned in the text, this would require a change of the law.

However, co-management does not preclude appropriate authority status being maintained at the district level, provided the articulation and clarification of rights does indeed take place. Institutional flexibility is, therefore, possible under co-management. The delegation and division of authority may appropriately mirror or modify the existing cultural and political structures/dynamics associated with resource use. Institutional development at ward and village levels should emerge situationally as a matter of con-

---

2. District council appropriate authority status does currently assume a form of co-management in the following ways. District council is accountable to the top (DNPWLM, the Ministry of Local Government) and the bottom (the various wards in the district). For CAMPFIRE to work, mutually beneficial arrangements have to be worked out laterally (between the wards in the district) and horizontally (with government departments concerned). One could argue that CAMPFIRE is a district-based co-management co-operative.

venience. The importance is not so much the identification of immutable authority structures, as the possibility of attaining successful out comes through co-operation within the existing political dynamics.

The dynamics of wildlife resource use in Chapoto ward (see Fig. 4.1) indicate that the making of common property is likely to demand a highly complex synergy of interests, both within the ward and outside it. This is the main reason why co-management, rather than strictly community-based management, may well become the modified emphasis of the program, especially in areas where 'cohesive communities with common goals' are difficult to identify (Martin 1986:33). It is clear from this study that local situations are often not homogeneous, static, bounded and integrated 'communities'. Instead, they may be characterized by differential access and competition over these resources. In the case of Chapoto ward, many people have been dispossessed of their land (e.g. in the neighboring safari areas) and the resources which it supported, in order to create areas for wildlife. In the past, vested interests in these resources developed at the national level, and now new legislation and initiatives such as CAMPFIRE allow vested interests to develop at the district and local levels. District interests are legally buttressed by the appropriate authority status, but ward level authority over wildlife is not legally sanctioned, in the sense that it falls under the district management regime. This further empowers the district authorities and representatives, but does not necessarily empower the smallest accountable units at the village or ward level, who are identified as the beneficiaries of the program. Hence, the practical recommendation that provision be made for appropriate authority status to be achieved by the ward, and that the wildlife committee be directly accountable to the households of Chapoto ward (discussed below).

The differentiation within the ward is compounded by the fact that the people do not all have common-felt needs or goals. For instance, Mvura have more faith in herbal specialists than in western medicine. Thus a western-style clinic built from revenues from wildlife would not be a good community project for those who are skeptical about western medicine (see discussion above on 'rationality'). If local people are largely excluded from the resource and any benefits derived from it, we cannot say that such resources are their common property. However, if an accountable and empowered institution dealing with wildlife matters existed at the ward level, this picture could change.

Identifying Appropriate Institutions for Managing Wildlife Resources

An important question asked by international scholars (Berkes 1989; McCay and Acheson 1987) is what type of institution is 'appropriate' for managing wildlife and other resources at the local level? The anthropological answer might be to say it is those institutions which are involved in the maintenance of political, ecological, economic and cultural affairs at the local level. In the context of Chapoto ward, there may be no straightforward answer to this question because a number of competing institutions and jurisdictions are engaged in this process. These include the official institutions (mainly committees), the neo-traditional institutions such as the chief and headmen, and cultural and religious institutions such as the spirit medium and churches. Lastly, there are relatively autonomous household heads, the leaders of extended families. All these interests need to be taken into account if an effective co-management institution is to be established. The CAMPFIRE document (Martin 1986) initially suggested that the appropriate institution for managing wildlife resources in Zimbabwe might be a locally based, legally empowered natural resource co-operative. According to Thomas (1991), the performance of such co-operatives has been uninspiring and their potential has been undermined by the fact that they are instrumentalized by the state for purposes of penetration and integration of the countryside. Given the multiple jurisdictions and numerous levels associated with the use and control of wildlife, co-operatives may lend themselves to a co-management property regime. If, however, appropriate institutions are to be effective, the idiosyncrasies of each situation have to be taken into account and prescribed formulae must give way to adaptive management. The establishment of co-operatives may indeed be the appropriate institutional framework in Chapoto ward, but these should probably evolve as a matter of convenience from existing management arrangements for CAMPFIRE.

In this regard, it is important to remember that wildlife 'management' at the local left is not simply a question of committeeing and the artificial administration and decision-making concerning revenue from safari operations. For most people it is to do with protecting fields, building wildlife-oriented granaries, huts, *dara*, fences and chicken coops. It is to do with gathering herbs, foraging for tubers and wild fruits, setting snares, praying to the ancestors, witchcraft accusations, and, of course, obtaining meat; all done largely for the benefit, maintenance and reproduction of oneself and one's immediate family.

To date, the material value of wildlife to the ordinary citizens of Chapoto ward is largely its meat value. Household economies require meat, yet when elephants are legally killed in the ward and the committee decides to sell the meat, large quantities of it are sold outside the ward and those who need meat the most cannot afford to buy it. The committee does not want to reduce the price of meat because this will reduce their revenues. Ironically, however, the idea that the elephant should be preserved for a professional hunter's client to kill, who would be prepared to pay seven or eight times its meat value, is not widely accepted and this could well be because the people of Chapoto are not convinced that they are receiving these revenues from the district council. In my opinion, unless they are strictly held to be accountable (see below), committees can often become highly ineffective, even in circles where the obstacles of illiteracy and lack of formal education do not exist.

What institution or institutions which is actively engaged in the management of natural resources on a daily basis could liaise with the wildlife committee? The direct management of resources is the domain of the family/extended family and/or clusters of families co-operating together. The family is the core labor unit for household production. Families jointly manage the available resources, making decisions about agriculture, foraging, the making of clay pots, hunting and other activities. Where brideservice is practiced, brothers-in-law become integrated into the economies of their in-laws' households. The male head of the family often consults his wife and other members on important decisions. Perhaps because there are no cattle in the area, the ethos that the man can do the ploughing and then retire from work is not marked in Chapoto ward. Men, women and children work hard all year round and work out mechanisms amongst themselves for sharing their production. Families, which are geographically centered in clusters of households, exploiting *dimba* and *munda* plots, are under the *de facto* leadership of both men and women heads, though women do not share the status of men in the society. I feel an improvement in the institutional management capacity at the ward level would come about if the ward wildlife committee would be responsible for direct and tangible benefits to families and not more diffusely to the 'ward' as a whole.

Tangible benefits might include a range of items (meat, household dividends, community projects, etc.). Given the generally low quantities of protein in the diets of people, the obvious benefit from wildlife for families is meat. This is in line with past practice and it is something that every family wants and needs, especially in drought-prone areas. The ward is just small enough to be able to work out mechanisms for the distribution of items such as meat to heads of families. Inequities and other problems will undoubtedly occur in such a system (men versus women, powerful families versus less powerful), but I believe that if the wildlife committee is made formally accountable to family heads who can legitimately expect tangible individual benefits from the wildlife resource, a number of ward-level institutional problems will have been ironed out. Primarily, this may go a long way to increase local participation in the co-management regime. Secondly, the wildlife committee will become accountable to the bottom (household heads) rather than to the top (district level authorities), because accountability to households will be stipulated as one of the conditions upon which appropriate authority could be earned. Thirdly, it will ensure a wide and more equitable distribution of resources. Fourthly, a rigorous consultation with household heads would, in my opinion, cut across the main axis of conflicting vested interests at the local level (outlined in Chapter 2). This would be a potential lever for the management of these conflicts and could lead to the establishment of a management regime which reflects all these interests and is not simply dominated by one of them.

As far as wildlife revenues from safari operations are concerned, it should be incumbent on the wildlife committee to solicit a formal vote from every permanently resident household head[3] as to what the person would like done with his or her share of the revenue. Initially, the household head might be presented with alternatives such as:

1. an equitable share of the revenue given as a household dividend;
2. a community project that will be financed by wildlife revenues,

---

3. One could argue that votes should be solicited from all legal adults. I would suggest that this could occur after people in the ward became familiar with the process suggested above. First, because this would be an educational process and secondly, because at the present time many women and Mvura legal adults in the ward are extremely marginal to the current political processes in the ward.

for example, the building of a clinic or school (to be specified by household head); and
3. other ideas to be specified by household heads.

It should be part of the constitution of wildlife committees that they have to solicit votes from all permanent resident household heads before the money can be allocated, rather than to consult a gathering at a ward meeting. If options are mutually exclusive, such as 1 and 2 above may be, then the option which the majority of household heads voted for could be selected. Alternatively, those who vote for household dividends, rather than community projects, could be asked to pay contributions towards such projects when they decide to use them.

The committee should be paid a generous stipend for the services which it provides to the people,[4] and if members do not carry out their duties, they should be replaced by others, without delay. The ideas above are neither new (Kanyurira has awarded household dividends), nor set in stone. The idea that the wildlife committee should be accountable to the people is part of the CAMPFIRE program, but the mechanisms by which it can become accountable are not spelt out. By involving household heads in a formal ballot about what should be done with revenues (rather than a show of hands at a sometimes sparsely attended ward meeting) and by making the wildlife committee answerable to them will simultaneously educate people about potential alternatives to the status quo, while at the same time increasing participation. These activities and participation at the local level will make it more difficult for vested interests in wildlife at the district level to ignore or steam-roller the claims in the resource at the ward level. As institutional capacity and participation increase, with inputs from both NGOs and government departments, the committee could be trained in preparation for the establishment of a co-operative and/or transfer of appropriate authority from the district level to ward level.

Though the CAMPFIRE document aims the program at communities which are relatively cohesive (Martin 1986: 33), in practice there may be very few such communities in existence, and Chapoto ward is certainly not one of them (see Chapter 2). If we

4. Though other committee work is not paid, a precedent for this had been set by World Vision local level project managers who do receive a stipend. Committee stipends should be set by local residents themselves so that committee members are accountable to their constituents.

accept the issue of conflict of vested interest as a given, which seems to be at the heart of the question, the next step is to work out mechanisms for managing this conflict at the various levels (household, village, ward, district, national and international). Being aware of the cultural and political dynamics at ward level is only a part of this broader picture.

References

Abel, N. and P. Blaikie (1986), 'Elephants, People, Parks and Development: The Case of the Luangwa Valley, Zambia', *Environmental Management*, 10/6: 735–51.
Anderson, I. (1987), *Communal Land Physical Resource Inventory – Guruve District*, Report No. A536 (Harare: Ministry of Agriculture; Chemistry and Soil Research Institute).
Anon (1975), *Parks and Wildlife Act* (Zimbabwe: Government Printers).
Arnold, Steven, (1989), 'Sustainable Development: A Solution to the Development Puzzle?' *Development*, 2/3: 21–5.
Atal, Y. (1984), 'Swidden Cultivation in Asia: The Need for a New Approach', *Nature and Resources*, 20/3: 19–26.
Bailey, F. G. (1969), *Stratagems and Spoils* (Oxford: Basil Blackwell).
Baldus, R. D. (1989), *Village Participation in Wildlife Management*, Selous Conservation Programme, Discussion Paper, No. 4 (typescript, 32 p.).
Barritt, David (1979), 'Africa's Amazing Two-Towed Ostrich People' *Scope* (6 July), pp. 6–9.
Barth, F. (1966), *Models of Social Organization* (London: Royal Anthropological Institute).
Beach, D. (1980), *The Shona and Zimbabwe: 900–1850* (Gweru: Mambo Press).
Beinart, W. (1984), 'Soil Erosion, Conservationism and Ideas About Development: A Southern African Exploration', *Journal of Southern African Studies*, 11/1: 52–83.
Bell, R. H. V. (1988), 'The Concept of Wildlife Management Areas: Experience in Zambia', in *Sustainable Wildlife Utilisation: The Role of Wildlife Management Areas* (Kalahari Conservation Society, Gaborone), pp. 18–21.
—— (1990), 'The Luangwa Integrated Resource Development Project', Luangwa Integrated Resource Development Project (typescript, 15 pp.).
Berkes, F. (ed.) (1989), *Common Property Resources – Ecology and Community-based Sustainable Development* (London: Belhaven Press).
Biebuyck, D. (ed.) (1963), *African Agrarian Systems* (London: International African Institute).
Brokenshaw, D., D. M. Warren and Oswald Werner (eds) (1981), *Indigenous Knowledge Systems and Development* (Washington, DC: University Press of America).
Bromley, D. and M. Cernea (1989), *The Management of Common Property Natural*

REFERENCES

Resources; Some Conceptual and Operational Fallacies, World Bank Discussion Paper, No. 57.

Brundtland, G. H. (1987) *Our Common Future: From One Earth to One World* (Oxford: Oxford University Press).

Buchan, A. J. (1989), *An Ecological Resource Survey of Chapoto Ward, Guruve District with Reference to the Use of Wildlife*, Harare: WWF Working Paper.

Bullock, C. (1950), *The Mashona and The Matabele* (Cape Town: Juta).

Capone, D. L. (1971), *Wildlife, Man and Competition for Land in Kenya: A Geographical Analysis* (E. Lansing: Michigan State University).

Caughly, G. (1976) 'The Elephant Problem: An Alternative Hypothesis', *East African Wildlife Journal*, 14: 265–83.

Chambers, R. (1986), *Sustainable Livelihoods*, Institute of Development Studies, University of Sussex (mimeo).

Child, B. (1985), *A Preliminary Investigation of Game Ranching in Zimbabwe* (Zimbabwe: Mimeograph Department DNPWM).

—— and Peterson J. (1991), *CAMPFIRE in Rural Development: The Beitbridge Experience*, Joint Working Series, 1/91: 51–86 (Harare: Branch of Terrestrial Ecology, Department of National Parks and Wild Life Management and Centre for Applied Social Sciences, University of Zimbabwe).

Child, G. (1970), 'Game Ranching', *Proceedings of the South African Society of Animal Production*, 9: 47–51.

—— (1984), 'Managing Wildlife for People in Zimbabwe', in J. A. McNelly and K. R. Miller, *National Parks, Conservation and Development – The Role of Protected Areas in Sustaining Society* (Washington, DC: Smithsonian Institution Press).

—— and W. K. Nduku (1986), 'The Concept of Wildlife Utilization – Wildlife and Human Welfare in Zimbabwe', Bamako, Mali: African Forestry Commission Working Party on Wildlife Management and National Parks – Eighth Session, 15–17 January. FAO Publication.

Ciriacy-Wantrup, S. V. and R. L. Bishop (1975), 'Common Property as a Concept in Natural Resource Policy', *Natural Resource Journal*, 15: 713–27.

Cooke, H. J. (1985), 'The Kalahari Today: A Case of Conflict Over Resource Use', *Geography Journal*, 151: 75–85.

Cox, S. J. B. (1985), 'No Tragedy on the Commons', *Environmental Ethics*, 7: 49–66.

Cumming, D. H. M. (1990), *Communal Land Development and Wildlife Utilisation: Potential and Options in Northern Namibia*, Multispecies Animal Production Systems Project, World Wide Fund For Nature, Project Paper, No. 14.

—— and R. D. Taylor (1989), *Identification of Wildlife Utilisation Pilot Projects* (Ministry of Commerce and Industry, Department of Wildlife and National Parks, Government of Botswana).

Cutshall, C. R. (1990), *Kanyemba/Chapoto Ward: A Socio-Economic Baseline Survey of Community Households* (University of Zimbabwe: Centre for Applied Social Sciences).

Dahlman (1980), *The Open Field System and Beyond* (Cambridge, UK: Cambridge University Press).

De Blij, H. J. and D. L. Capone (1969), 'Wildlife Conservation Areas in East Africa: An Application of Field Theory in Political Geography', *Southeastern Geographer*, 9/2: 94–107.

Deutsch, K. W. (1975), 'On the Interaction of Ecological and Political Systems: Some Potential Contributions of the Social Sciences to the Study of Man and His Environment', *Social Science Information*, 13/6: 5–15.

District Commissioners Delineation Report For Chapoto Ward (1965), Guruve District Administrator's Offices.

Douglas, J. H. (1975), 'Harvesting the Wild', *Science News*, 107: 259–261.

Douglas-Hamilton, I. (1992), *Battle for the Elephants* (New York: Doubleday).

Douglas-Hamilton, I. and Associates (1988), *Identification Study for the Conservation and Sustainable Use of the Natural Resources in the Kenyan Portion of the Mara-Serengeti Ecosystem*, Final Report: European Development Fund of EEC (typescript, 185 pp.).

'Earthday 2030' (1990), *World Watch*, 3/2: 12–21.

Feeny, D., F. Berkes, B. J. McCay and J. M. Acheson (1990), 'The Tragedy of the Commons: Twenty-Two Years Later', *Human Ecology*, 18/1: 1–19.

Forster, R. (1973), *Planning for Man and Nature in National Parks* (Switzerland: IUCN Publication. New Series No. 26).

Fortman, L. and J. W. Bruce (1988), *Whose Trees? – Proprietary Dimensions of Forestry* (Boulder, Colo.: Westview Press).

Frazer Nash, R. (1989), *The Rights of Nature: A History of Environmental Ethics* (Madison, Wis.: University of Wisconsin Press).

Freeman, M. M. R. (1989), 'Graphs and Gaffs: A Cautionary Tale in the Common Property Resources Debate', in F. Berkes (ed.), *Common Property Resources – Ecology and Community-based Sustainable Development* (London: Belhaven Press).

Freire, P. (1978), *Pedagogy in Process* (New York: Seabury Press).

Garbett, K. (1963), 'The Political System of a Central African Tribe with Particular Reference to the Role of Spirit Mediums', unpubl. Ph.D. thesis, University of Manchester.

Geertz, C. (1972), 'The Wet and the Dry: Traditional Irrigation in Bali and Morocco', *Human Ecology*, 1: 23–9.

Gelfand, M. (1974), 'A Two-Toed Man From the Doma People of the Zambezi Valley', *Rhodesian History*, 5: 93–5.

Giddens, A. (1979), *Central Problems in Social Theory* (London: Macmillan).

Gilbert, F. B. and D. G. Dodds (1987), *The Philosophy and Practice of Wildlife Management* (Malabar, Fla.: Krieger Publishing Co.).

Giles, J. L., A. Hammoudi and M. Mahdi (1986), 'Oukaimedene, Morocco: A High Mountain *Agdal*', *Proceedings of the Conference on Common Property Resource Management*, National Academy Press, Washington, DC, pp. 281–304.

Goodland, H. (1988), 'Implications of Sustainable Development. Ottawa: Paper presented at the Canadian Government Affairs Seminar,' World Commission on Environment and Development – Canada's Response, 17–19 October 1988.

Graham, A. D. (1973), *The Gardeners of Eden* (London: George Allen and Unwin).

Habermas, Jurgen (1984), *The Theory of Communicative Action*, vol. i, *Reason and the Rationalization of Society* (Boston: Beacon Press).

Hames, R. (1987), 'Game Conservation or Efficient Hunting?' in B. J. McCay and J. M. Acheson (eds.), *The Question of the Commons – The Culture and Ecology of Communal Resources* (Tuscon, Ariz.: University of Arizona Press).

REFERENCES

Hardin, G. (1968), 'The Tragedy of the Commons', *Science*, 162: 1234–48.
—— (1986), 'Cultural Carrying Capacity: A Biological Approach to Human Problems', *Bio-Science*, 36: 599–606.
Harris, M. (1968), *The Rise of Anthropological Theory: A History of Theories of Culture* (Thomas Y. Crowell: New York).
Hart, T. B. and J. A. Hart (1986), 'The Ecological Basis of Hunter-Gatherer Subsistence in African Rain Forests – The Mbuti of Eastern Zaire', *Human Ecology*, 14/1: 29–55.
Hatch, E. (1973), 'The Growth of Economic, Subsistence, and Ecological Studies in American Athropology', *Journal of Anthropological Research*, 29: 221–43.
Hughes, R. S. (n.d.) *Notes on the Chewore History* (Harare: Department of National Parks and Wildlife Management. Duplicates).
Isaacman, Allen E. (1976), *The Tradition of Resistance in Mozambique: Anti-Colonial Activity in the Zambezi Valley 1850–1921* (London: Heinneman).
ITC, IUCN, Ministry of Lands, Natural Resources and Tourism of Tanzania (1988), *Wildlife Utilisation in Tanzania*.
Kandawire, J. A. K. (1981), 'The Conservation of Wildlife Versus the Use of Natural Resources: Report of a Sociological Study of the Attitudes of People Towards Wildlife in the Area Around Mwabvi Game Reserve in Nsanje District', Seminar Paper of the University of Malawi, Department of Sociology, pp. 1–35.
Kassas, M. (1986), 'The Imperial Lion – Human Dimensions of Wildlife Management in Central Africa – S. A. Marks', *Economic Geography*, 62/1: 89–90.
Kuper, A. (1988), *The Invention of Primitive Society* (London: James Currey).
Lan, D. (1985), *Guns and Rain – Guerillas and Spirit Mediums in Zimbabwe* (London: James Currey).
Lancaster, C. S. (1974), 'Ethnic Identity, History and "Tribe" in the Middle Zambezi Valley', *American Ethnologist*, 1: 707–30.
Lawry, S. (1990), 'Tenure Policy Toward Common Property Natural Resources in Sub-Saharan Africa', *Natural Resource Journal*, 30: 403–22.
Leonard, H. J. (1989), *Environment and the Poor: Development Strategies for a Common Agenda* (Oxford: Transaction Books).
Lindsay, W. K. (1987), 'Integrating Parks and Pastoralists: Some Lessons From Amboseli', in L. Anderson and R. Grove, *Conservation in Africa: People, Policies and Practice* (Cambridge: Cambridge University Press), pp. 149–67.
McCarthy, Thomas (1978), *The Critical Theory of Jurgen Habermas* (Cambridge: Polity Press).
McCay, B. J., and J. M. Acheson (eds.) (1987), *The Question of the Commons: The Culture and Ecology of Communal Resources* (Tucson, Ariz.: University of Arizona Press).
MacDonald, I. A. W. (1987), 'State of the Art in the Science of Wildlife Management – A North-South Comparison', *South African Journal of Science*, 83/7: 397–9.
Macpherson, C. B. (1978), *Property: Mainstream and Critical Positions* (Toronto: University of Toronto Press).
Maine, H. (1884), *Ancient Law*, 10th edn. (New York: Henry Holt).
'Man in Ecosystems' (1982), *International Social Science Journal*, 34/3: 25–30.

Marks, S. (1976), *Large Mammals and a Brave People: Subsistence Hunters in Zambia* (Seattle, Wash.: University of Washington Press).
—— (1979), *An Integrated Social-Environmental Analysis of the Luangwa Valley in Zambia. Case Studies in Development* (Washington, DC: US Agency for International Development).
—— (1984), *The Imperial Lion: Human Dimensions of Wildlife Management in Central Africa* (Boulder, Colo.: Westview Press).
Martin, Peter (1970), 'Illustrated Life', *Rhodesia* (23 March), p. 31.
Martin, R. B. (1978), ' "Project Windfall", Salisbury', unpubl. report, Department of National Parks and Wild Life Management.
—— (1986), *The Communal Areas Management Program for Indigenous Resources* (Zimbabwe: Department of National Parks and Wildlife Management).
Masona, T. (1987), 'Colonial Game Policy: A Study of the Origin and Administration of Game Policy in Southern Rhodesia 1890–1945', unpubl. MA thesis, University of Zimbabwe.
Matowanyika, J. (forthcoming), 'Common Property Issues of Natural Resource Management: Zimbabwean Case Studies' (exact title unkown), Ph.D. thesis, York University, Canada.
Matzke, G. (1971), 'African Wildlife vs People, Politics and Plans', *Proceedings of the Oklahoma Academy of Science*, 51: 120–6.
—— (1985), 'The Imperial Lion – Human Dimensions of Wildlife Management in Central Africa – S. A. Marks', *Professional Geographer*, 37/4: 512–13.
Mkean, M. A. (1986), 'Management of Traditional Common Lands (*Iraichi*) in Japan', *Proceedings of the Conference on Common Property Resource Management* (Washington, DC: National Academy Press).
Mombeshore, S. (1987), *Report on Chapoto Ward* (University of Zimbabwe: Centre for Applied Social Science).
Mtamayi (1959), 'A Visit to the VaDoma Massif', *NADA*, 36.
Muir, A. (1992), 'Evaluating the Impact of NGOs in Rural Poverty Alleviation: Zimbabwe Country Study', London: Overseas Development Institute, Working Paper, No. 52.
Murombedzi, J. C. (1992), *Decentralization or Recentralization? – Implementing CAMPFIRE in the Omay Communal Lands of the Nyaminyami District*, University of Zimbabwe: Centre for Applied Social Sciences, Working Paper.
Murphree, M. W. (1989), *Research on the Institutional Contexts of Wild Life Utilization in Communal Areas of Eastern and Southern Africa* (University of Zimbabwe: Centre for Applied Social Science).
—— (1990), *Decentralizing the Proprietorship of Wildlife Resources in Zimbabwe's Communal Lands* University of Zimbabwe: Centre for Applied Social Sciences, Working Paper.
—— (1991), *Communities as Institutions for Resource Management*, University of Zimbabwe: Centre for Applied Social Sciences, Working Paper.
Nhira, C. (1989), *A Socio-Economic Appraisal Study of the Chapoto Ward – Guruve District*, University of Zimbabwe: Centre for Applied Social Sciences, Working Paper.
Nicholas, G. (1969), 'It May Really Exist: The Two-Toed Tribe of the Zambezi', *Daily Colonist* (Victoria BC) (18 September), p. 24.

REFERENCES

Norgaard, R. (1985), *The Scarcity of Resource Economics*, Paper presented to the American Economics Association, New York.

Orlove, B. S. (1980), 'Ecological Anthropology', *Annual Review of Anthropology*, 9: 235–73.

Owen-Smith, R. N. (1983), *Management of Large Mammals in African Conservation Areas* (Pretoria: Haum).

Parker, I. S. C. (1978), 'Elephants a Valuable Resource?', in M. L. Nchunga (ed.), *Wildlife Management and Utilization*, Proceedings of the Fifth Regional Wildlife Conference for Eastern and Central Africa Gaberone, Botswana, 3–7 July. Botswana: Department of Wildlife and National Parks, pp. 275–86.

Parker, I. S. C. (1983), 'Rainfall, Geology, Elephants and Man', *Mimeograph Proceedings of a Conference in South Africa*, pp. 137–70.

—— (1984), 'Rainfall, Geology, Elephants and Men', in P. Mundy (ed.), *Proceedings of the Tenth Anniversary Symposium: Endangered Wildlife Trust*, Pretoria.

'Parks Win War Against Rhino Poachers' (1990), *The Herald* (14 September), p. 4.

Pearce, D. (1989), 'An Economic Perspective on Sustainable Development', *Development*, 2/3: 17–20.

Peterson, J. (1991), *CAMPFIRE: A Zimbabwean Approach to Sustainable Development and Community Empowerment through Wildlife Utilization*, University of Zimbabwe: Centre For Applied Social Science, Working Paper.

Pilgram, T. and D. Western (1986), 'Managing African Elephants for Ivory Production Through Ivory Trade Regulations', *Journal of Applied Ecology*, 23/2: 515–29.

'Putting Poachers Out of Business' (1986), *Africa*, 178: 48–9.

Rappaport, R. A. (1984), *Pigs for the Ancestors*, rev. edn. (New Haven, Conn.: Yale University Press).

Redclift, M. R. (1987), *Sustainable Development: Exploring The Contradictions* (London: Methuen and Co. Ltd.).

Sahlins, M. (1968), 'Notes on the Original Affluent Society', in R. Lee and I. DeVore (eds.), *Man The Hunter* (Chicago, Ill.: Aldine), pp. 85–9.

Schoffeleers, J. M. (ed.) (1979), *Guardians of the Land* (Gweru: Mambo Press).

Scott, E. P. (1985), 'The Imperial Lion – Human Dimensions of Wildlife Management in Central Africa – S. A. Marks', *Geographical Review*, 75/1: 105–7.

Selous, F. C. (1881), *A Hunter's Wanderings in Africa* (London: Bently).

'Senior Police Officer Might Face Poaching Charges' (1990), *Parade* (September), p. 9.

Skelton, J. and M. Matanganyidza (1978), 'Amylolytic Activity in a Rhodesian Legume', *Trans. Rhod. Scient. Association*, 59/2 (6–11 July).

Sommerlatte, M. (1988), *A Wildlife Management Plan for the Communal Areas Surrounding the Selous Game Reserve*, Dar es Salaam: Paper prepared for the Selous Conservation Programme (typescript).

Steward, J. H. (1948), *The Concept and Method of Cultural Ecology*, International Encyclopedia of the Social Sciences.

Taylor, R. and R. B. Martin (1983), 'Wildlife Conservation in a Regional Land-Use Context: The Sebungwe Region of Zimbabwe;, in R. N. Owen-Smith (ed.), *Management of Large Mammals in African Conservation Areas* (Pretoria: Naum Educational Publishers).

Thomas, S. J. (1991), *The Legacy of Dualism and Decision-Making: The Prospects for Local Institutional Development in CAMPFIRE*, University of Zimbabwe: Centre for Applied Social Sciences, Working Paper.

Thompson, M. (1986), *The Cultural Construction of Nature and the Natural Destruction of Culture*, University of Maryland: Center for Philosophy and Public Policy, Working Paper, 8.

Trail of the Vanishing Rhino (1985), *Africa*, 171: 52–3.

Trench, C. T. (1967), *The Poacher and the Squire* (London: Longmans).

Vayda, A. P. (1986), *Actions and Consequences as Consequences of Explanation in Human Ecology*, Bar Harbor, Maine: Paper Presented at the Second International Conference of the Society for Human Ecology.

—— and B. Mackay (1977), 'New Directions in Ecology and Ecological Anthropology', *Annual Review of Anthropology*, 4: 293–306.

Von Richter, W. (1978), 'Wildlife Utilization and Management as a Form of Land Use in Botswana', *Saeugetierkd Mitt*, 26/4: 241–9.

Weeden, R. B. (1986), 'The Imperial Lion – Human Dimensions of Wildlife Management in Africa – S. A. Marks', *Wildlife*, 20/1: 110–12.

Western, D. (1982), 'Amboseli National Park: Enlisting Landowners to Conserve Migratory Wildlife', *Ambio* 11: 302–8.

—— and J. Thresher (1973), *Development Plans for Amboseli: Mainly Wildlife Viewing Activity in the Eco-System* (Nairobi: World Bank).

White, J. D. (1971), 'History and Customs of the Urungwe District', *NADA*, 10/11: 70.

World Resources Institute (1991), *World Resources 1990–1991* (New York: Basic Books).

World Watch (1990), 'How Much is Enough: Living within Earthly Limits', 3/6: 12–19.

Zimbabwe Wildlife (1990), 17 (March).

Index

agriculture 73–9, 92–9
ambiguity of rights of access to wildlife 182
ancestral spirits 11, 52–65, 156–66
anthropology, theory 9–12
anti-poaching activities 119, 180–2
appropriate authority 30, 33, 37, 48

Berkes, F. 20–3
brideservice 9, 66–71, 103–5
bundles of rights 12, 17, 22, 186; to wildlife 155–85

Centre for Applied Social Sciences (CASS) xiii, 42
Chewore Safari Area 45, 58
chief 24, 26, 58–65
Chimombe 55, 69
ChiShona 45
co-management 21, 24–9, 186–99; multi-tiered 192–9
common property theory 1, 3, 186–99; property rights 12–17; tragedy of the commons 17–19; typologies 20–3; wildlife utilization in Africa 23–9
Communal Areas Management for Indigenous Resources (CAMPFIRE) 1, 3, 42, 127, 143–54; description of 29–39
conflicting interests at ward level 151–4
control of wild animals 129–54, 158–85
conservation through sustainable use 29–39
cotton growing 96–9
crop protection 9; from wildlife 75, 76
cultural conceptions of natural resources 140–3

cultural ecology 9–12, 19

development 26–8; sustainable 4–8
district council 30–2, 36–7, 148–50
district wildlife committee 32, 34, 36
drought relief distribution 120–2
dry season cultivation (*dimba*) 75–7

ecology, wildlife ecologists 9, 12
elephant kill 136–8, 170–80
empowerment 148–51
ethnicity 52–8
extended observation 40

Faith Apostolic Mission Church 114, 160
fishing 22, 43, 109–11
food for work 101–3
foraging 39, 79–90, 101–10
forest walks 122–8
fruits 44, 83–7

Game Scouts 43, 180–2
global factors 111–15

herbs 140–1
honey collection 101
household decision-making 101–3
hunting 20, 28, 39, 43, 44, 72, 73, 105–8, 133–7, 141, 145, 164, 170–80; Valley Bisa 10
hunting concession area 34, 46

International Convention on Trade in Endangered Species (CITES) 36–7, 113–15

Kanyemba 47, 53, 58–65

207

INDEX

Kenya 26, 27
KoreKore (population group), history 52–8

Lan, D. 53–7
land tenure 71, 72
Lawry, S. 23, 24
lions 164–5
local government 31, 32, 116–17, 120–1, 148

marriage, arrangements of 8, 66–71
meat, benefits from wildlife 38; *also see* hunting
methodology 6, 9, 40–7
mixed grain strategies 95
multiple jurisdictions concerning wildlife 1, 17, 21, 23, 111–19, 186–9
Mutapa State 54–7
Mvura (Doma, VaDema population group) 101–5; agriculture 79–90; foraging 73–80; history 51, 52–8

Namibia 28
national policy 116
natural resources: institutional arrangements 29–39; rights 1, 26; theory 19, 24–5
natural resources cooperative 184
Nyamapfeka 54–6

open access 19, 21–3

poaching 39, 104, 129–30, 138, 119, 180–2
political history 52–65
political and economic relations 111–28
population 66–8
predators and domestic animal loss 105
private sector interests *see* safari operations

Problem Animal Control (PAC) 136–7; by ancestral spirit 161–6
Project Windfall 33

rain 50, 55–6, 103
rationality 2, 7, 9
Redclift, M.R. 4, 6–7
rhinoceros 126

safari areas 48
safari operations 39, 41; operators 20, 44, 119, 167–77; revenues from 30, 144
Selous Conservation Area 27
snares 134–5
spirit medium 158–67, 58–9
stream bank cultivation 43
sustainability 4–7, 39

Trypanosomiasis (sleeping sickness) 50; tsetse fly 49–51
tubers 83–7

VaChikunda (population group): agriculture 73–9; history 52–65
Village Development Committee (VIDCO) 31, 32, 36, 40, 45, 70, 113

Ward Development Committee (WADCO) 31, 32, 40, 45, 113
wildlife committee 36, 130, 143
wildlife management 10, 51, 52, 143–8, 186–99; anthropological aspects of 9–12; belief systems 139–43, 158–67; cultural aspects 129–43, 158–67; institutions 143, 195–9; programs 24–39; revenue 144–51; *also see* district council, safari operations, wildlife committee
World Wide Fund For Nature (WWF) xiii
worms (edible) 127

Zambia 10, 25, 26